Assessing Radical Education

Innovations in Education

Series Editor: Colin Fletcher (Senior Lecturer in the School of Policy Studies, Cranfield Institute of Technology).

There have been periods of major innovation in public education. What do the achievements amount to and what are the prospects for progress now? There are issues in each slice of the education sector. How have the issues come about?

Each author analyses their own sphere, argues from experience and communicates clearly. Here are books that speak both with and for the teaching profession; books that can be shared with all those involved in the future of education.

Three quotations have helped to shape the series:

The whole process – false starts, frustrations, adaptions, the successive recasting of intentions, the detours and conflicts – needs to be comprehended. Only then can we understand what has been achieved and learn from experience.

Marris and Rein

In this time of considerable educational change and challenge the need for teachers to write has never been greater.

Hargreaves

A wise innovator should prepare packages of programmes and procedures which . . . could be put into effect quickly in periods of recovery and reorganisation following a disaster.

Hirsh

Current titles in the series

Pat Ainley: *From School to YTS*
Garth Allen, John Bastiani, Ian Martin and Kelvyn Richards: *Community Education*
Bernard Barker: *Rescuing the Comprehensive Experience*
Julia Gilkes: *Developing Nursery Education*
Knud Jensen and Stephen Walker: *Towards Democratic Schooling*
Gerri Kirkwood and Colin Kirkwood: *Living Adult Education*
Herbert Kohl: *36 Children*
Julia Stanley: *Marks on the Memory*
Jan Stewart: *The Making of the Primary School*
David Terry: *The Tertiary College*
Paul Widlake: *Reducing Educational Disadvantage*
Nigel Wright: *Assessing Radical Education*

Assessing Radical Education

A Critical Review of the
Radical Movement in English
Schooling, 1960–1980

Nigel Wright

Open University Press
Milton Keynes · Philadelphia

Open University Press
12 Cofferidge Close
Stony Stratford
Milton Keynes MK11 1BY

and

1900 Frost Road, Suite 101
Bristol, PA 19007, USA

First Published 1989

LB
1027.3
W75
1989

British Library Cataloguing in Publication Data
Wright, Nigel
  Assessing radical education: a critical review of
  the radical movement in English schooling, 1960–1980.
  (Innovations in education)
  1. Education. Innovation. Assessment
  I. Title II. Series
  379.1′54

  ISBN 0-335-09228-4
  ISBN 0-335-09227-6 (paper)

Library of Congress Cataloging-in-Publication Data
Wright, Nigel
  Assessing radical education: a critical review of the radical
  movement in English schooling, 1960–80 / by Nigel Wright.
    p. cm.—(Innovations in education)
  Bibliography: p.
  Includes index.
  ISBN 0-335-09228-4   ISBN 0-335-09227-6 (pbk.)
  1. Educational innovations—England—Evaluation. 2. Radicalism.
  3. Education—History. I. Title. II. Series.
LB1027.3.W75 1989
370′.942—dc20   89-34693 CIP

Typeset by Inforum Typesetting, Portsmouth
Printed in Great Britain by Bookcraft (Bath) Limited

Contents

Series editor's introduction

The 1960s have been dug up and hyped so often that almost all age groups are rightly resistant to any more narcissistic glorification. But Nigel Wright is forthright. He shows that good ideas did not lead to success. He has the courage to say that radical education failed despite the huge surge of human energy which occurred. He assesses radicalism in education, its sources, its struggle and its lack of substantial sustained achievement.

Radical education is one of what Foucault calls 'the long tides of history'. Its guiding moon is learning: by children, by adults or, better still, together. There are fierce criticisms brought ashore by radical education, yet it fetches up profound problems of its own. Nigel Wright carries the reader in both directions, too: the assessment by and of radical education. To do so he has revisited the late 1960s and early 1970s when so much was 'going on'.

A Chinese proverb says 'it is better to light one candle than forever to curse the darkness'. The thoroughness of this book makes it cast much more light than a single candle. It is researched through documents, interviews and participation. It is constructed with cool judgement. For those it does not remind it will reveal – and for either there will be the feeling of coming into contact with courage. Here is a writer whose opinions you can trust. He has thought *through* what has so far only been thought *about*. Here, too, is controlled prose. It does not get excited or bored – there is always clear argument, clear evidence or clear expression of opinion.

Wright makes understanding radicalism manageable, he gives quotations and examples of real quality and then appraises with an unblinking honesty. Such, then, is the scope and style and skill of this resource book. Open it anywhere and it is literate, perceptive and honest. Read from cover to cover and the case unfolds from what radicalism is to who the radicals were and what its dilemmas are.

The dilemmas he describes within radicalism remain. But they still convey more hope than does being machine-minders in a military state. Wright spells out what an understanding of learning requires and shows the mix of dilemmas which all teachers have to think through for themselves. Teaching will never be easy because of them.

This book succeeds as a cultural history of radical education in the 1960s and 1970s, as a review of radicalism and its realizations, and as a challenge to teachers of today and tomorrow to consider their own values.

Education has inherent problems. If they are repressed they still bob up again before too long. Wright recognizes that a new dependency culture has developed – a dependency on superiors who set targets, in the language of marketing, and who reward those who express beliefs as distinct from enact achievements. Is he naive in persisting with the view that teachers care, that they realize the politics of their work and their school, that they struggle with how to stop abuses and start activities which have a vision of future well-being for all?

I cannot accept that all trainee teachers are cynical, or that all practising teachers have become robots rushing about with pieces of paper. Neither can Nigel Wright. His book is a major contribution; it kindles what Henry Giroux calls 'civic courage and critical spirit'. His last chapter on radical education in the 1990s shows what has to be thought and done. His assessment of the recent past leads to a clear argument for an imminent future.

Colin Fletcher

Introduction

My chief reason for starting to write this book was a personal one. Having been involved in the radical movement in education in the 1960s and 1970s, I wanted to re-evaluate my own experience and my own ideas about education. I started teaching in 1968 and, over the next 15 years, participated in several radical groups – primarily the Schools Action Union, Rank & File, *Radical Education* and White Lion Street Free School. It was during my four years at White Lion that I became convinced that a re-evaluation was necessary. I still felt strongly sympathetic to the radical movement, but was becoming convinced that some radical thinking was mistaken. White Lion was an inspired attempt to put radical ideas into practice, but I'm sorry to say it did not work.

My original plan was to undertake a wholesale review of radical theories of education, I soon realized that this was a vast undertaking, far beyond my capabilities. I was obliged to limit myself to three areas of study: first, a review of the groups and publications of the radical movement; second, the selection of a single topic – learning – for analysis; and third, a critical examination of the experience of White Lion Street Free School. The first two of these areas are the subject of this book. The third is published elsewhere.[1]

The first seven chapters are mainly descriptive: their purpose is to document the radical movement. To my knowledge this hasn't been done elsewhere and there is a danger of much being forgotten.[2] Chapter 1 describes the background to the radical movement: its genesis in the 1960s and the currents of thought which contributed to it. Chapter 2 looks at the radicals themselves and their characteristics. Chapter 3 discusses two radical teachers' ventures: the magazine *Libertarian Teacher* (which later changed its name to *Libertarian Education* and then *Lib Ed*); and the Rank & File group. *Libertarian*

Teacher was the first magazine in the field and is the only one which, still existing today (as *Lib Ed*), spans the whole period. Rank & File was by far the largest radical teachers' grouping.

Chapter 4 examines the other radical teachers' journals of the 1970s – *Blackbored, Teaching London Kids, Hard Cheese, Radical Education, Teachers Action, Teachers Against Racism, Right to Learn,* and *Socialist Teacher* – and one or two other teachers' groups.

Chapter 5 is about the school students' movement and its three main organizations, the Free Schools Campaign, the Schools Action Union, and the National Union of School Students. Chapter 6 deals with the children's rights movement and a number of smaller groupings which participated in the radical movement. And Chapter 7 looks at the 15 free schools which were established in Britain in the 1970s.

The final four chapters of the book are of a different character: they are concerned with ideas. The question of learning seems to me to be at the centre of radical concerns about education. That radicals have not always recognized this merely reinforces my decision to focus on it. If the thesis of Chapters 8 and 9 may be summarized in one phrase, it is that learning is a social phenomenon. In my view, radicals have erred in one of two ways. Either they have ignored the question of learning, as if it was no more a matter which *radicals* need to bother about than, say, the functioning of the gall bladder. Or they have taken it seriously, but viewed it in purely individual terms. At the end of Chapter 9 I show how each of these errors can lead to dubious prescriptions for schooling.

Chapter 10 examines a series of questions pondered by radicals throughtout the 1960s and 1970s. Is it more resourcing we want for schooling, or is it a drasticaaly different use of existing resources? Is it only working-class children who suffer from schooling as it is? Can radical reforms be achieved without a revoluntionary transformation of society? What is the relationship between politics and education? And between society and education? Should we work 'within the system' or outside it? How far can children be let to direct their own learning? What *do* children *want*? Should we call for the abolition of schools? How far should we be 'idealistic' and how far should we be 'reaistic'? What are the competing claims of reasons and emotion?

Let me say at the outset that no brilliant answers will be found in the pages of this book. All I can do is clarify the agenda for discussion. My proposal will be, for some, a tedious one: we must do more work. And particularly, more work is needed at the level of theory. I was one of those who joined together in 1974 to establish *Radical Education*: we were motivated by the belief that there was no socialist theory of education, and that there needed to be one. Although great strides have been made since then, I still believe that the decisive breakthrough has yet to be made. By decisive breakthrough, I mean a set of theoretical insights which will make it quite clear what socialists need to do about education, in the same way as Marx showed nineteenth-century socialists what they needed to do about the economy.

And so in Chapter 11 I try to outline the kind of work radicals need to be doing. At the time of writing (1989) it might seem a most unpropitious moment to be making such suggestions. But consider this account of the 1960s and 1970s:

> An outpouring of tracts and pamphlets between 1960 and 1976 voiced discontent with prevailing educational conditions and put forward proposals for reform . . . Throughout this controversial literature the same proposals and denunciations recur, and often they are only parts of more ambitious schemes for the reformation of society as a whole . . . In some respects these two decades were propitious for large-scale educational advance. The ancient forces of conservatism were temporarily driven underground and new ideas of democracy and equality flourished in an atmosphere of free discussion and debate . . . [3]

In fact, I've cheated with the dates. The period this passage refers to is actualy 1640 to 1660. I've quoted it because it is a reminder of the periodicity of educational developments. There are good decades for radicals and there are bad decades for radicals. My belief is that the 1990s will present new opportunities for radicals in education and my hope is that this book will help radicals prepare themselves to take advantage of those opportunities.

This book is about education as it applies to schools. I have not dealt with further and higher education. Of course, there was a wave of radicalism in further and higher education in the 1960s and 1970s, but that is beyond my scope. And this book is primarily about the radical movement in England. Scotland, Wales, Ireland, and elsewhere, need their own treatment. Radicals in England have been appallingly insular; we know so little about radical developments in education just a few miles away across the Channel and the North Sea. Regrettable as that is, I cannot do anything about it here.

A few words about the spirit in which this book is written. In places I will be sharply critical of radical groups and radical ideas. I do not make these criticisms with a feeling of superiority; on the whole I am criticizing ideas which I myself held, and actions which I supported, until I had the time to do the thinking about them which this book represents. It is, really, a book of self-criticism.

Many people have helped me in my research for this book and by reading drafts, but I would particularly like to thank the Open University for allowing me a reasearch grant for three years, and my supervisors there, Peter Woods and Donald McKinnon. Thanks, too, to Ron and 'N' Brand, Phil Collins, Roger Diski, Liza Dresner, Michael Duane, Rhiannon Evans, Peter Ford, Pat Holland, Trisha Jaffe, John Ord, Patricia Potts, Susie Powlesland and Alison Truefitt. I am grateful to Colin Fletcher, whose editorial task was not so much pruning as deforestation: what might have been traumatic for me was made very easy. And very special thanks to Teri Connolly who has supported me throughout the project and whose love and encouragement have been indispensable. And, lastly, to Joey Connolly-Wright for bringing a new joy to my life these past two years and enabling me to think about education in a spirit of optimism when, sometimes, despair seemed more appropriate. My son Joey has constantly reminded me of what surely will always be the starting point for educational radicals: children are miraculous.

CHAPTER 1

The background

If, in the early 1970s, you had gone into an alternative bookshop – Compendium in London, say, or Grass Roots in Manchester – you would have found on display more than 20 radical magazines about education, and perhaps 25 or 30 radical pamphlets. At the end of the 1980s those two bookshops stocked just two radical magazines on education and no pamphlets at all.

This book is about the movement which, in the 1960s and 1970s, generated those radical publications. The radical movement in education was, of course, only a part of a much broader radical movement which flowered in the late 1960s and early 1970s. There were campaigning radical groups of philosophers, historians, psychologists, scientists and sociologists; there were radicals in the health service, in architecture, in computers, in the media, in child care, in social work; there were radical economists, radical anthropologists, radical photographers, radical statisticians, radical lawyers and radical criminologists. And there were many radical groups of women, of homosexuals, and of black people.[1] In fact there were very few spheres of established society that did not find themselves under attack from vociferous groups of left-wing critics.

Linking up these specialist groupings were information agencies like Agitprop, Release, Rising Free and the People's News Service. There was a vigorous alternative press: *IT (International Times)*, *Oz*, *Ink*, *Black Dwarf*, *Red Mole*, *Friendz* and *Idiot International*, as well as the papers of the numerous left-wing sects. Particularly diligent in discussing educational questions were the anarchist weekly *Freedom* and monthly *Anarchy*, the pacifist weekly *Peace News* and the radical Christian *Catonsville Roadrunner*.

All these radicals shared a contempt for what they saw as the complacency of the 1950s. They shared a long list of criticisms of our society: inequality and class divisions; poverty in the midst of plenty; poor housing; urban decay and regional decline; the evils of 'consumerism' – waste, advertising, a culture increasingly monopolized by commercial interests; the decline of community and the growing privatization of life; pollution and the destruction of the environment; growing militarism – nuclear weapons and wars in, for example, Vietnam, Guatemala, Algeria; injustice – for example in Northern Ireland; the secrecy and dissimulation of governments; the exploitation of the Third World; racism; authoritarianism at all levels of society; sexual repression and hypocrisy; the alienation of youth; the excessive powers of the Civil Service, the police and the large corporations; the consolidation of centralized power in the corporate state; the denial of working-class values and culture; rampant technology; the cult of the expert; male domination in every sphere of public and private life; and the inability of established political institutions to tackle these problems.

To talk of '1960s radicalism' is misleading if we forget that the rebellion against the things just listed was under way in the 1950s. In 1956, for example, the collaboration of Britain, France and Israel in the invasion of Suez brought forth massive protests. At the same moment the supposed antithesis of imperialism – Soviet socialism – was exposed in all its ugliness in Poland and Hungary. Thousands of political radicals who had found their 'natural' expression in the British Communist Party left it, and the 'New Left' was born. The 'ban the bomb' movement got under way, beginning that fusion of politics and 'the culture of protest' which was to prove such a potent mixture in the following decade. Nineteen fifty-six also saw a seminal development in British arts – John Osborne's *Look Back in Anger* opened at London's Royal Court Theatre, and the 'angry young man' (the angry young woman was yet to receive recognition) was launched into society. Angry young men had already been seen on American cinema screens, notably Marlon Brando in Laslo Benedek's *The Wild Ones* ('much banned because there was no retribution'[2]) and James Dean in Nicholas Ray's *Rebel Without A Cause*. In 1956 these films were showing in Britain, as was another American film which was of even greater significance in the formation of the 1960s: Fred Sears's *Rock Around the Clock*, whose stars Little Richard, Bill Haley and others had audiences dancing in the cinema aisles and sometimes, in several countries, rioting in the streets. At a more esoteric level, 1956 was the year in which Raymond Williams wrote his important book, *Culture and Society*.

And the 1960s opened with significant events. The failed prosecution of D.H. Lawrence's *Lady Chatterly's Lover* opened the door to a wave of free expression. The Committee of 100 – the archetypal protest organization – was formed, and the Labour Party Conference voted for unilateral nuclear disarmament. Meanwhile, cinemas were packed out for Karel Reisz's film of Alan Sillitoe's *Saturday Night and Sunday Morning* which established three features of 1960s radicalism – contempt for authority, acknowledgement of the reality of working-class life, and a new attitude to sex. In America liberals who were soon to become radicals were euphoric at the election of John Kennedy to the presidency. Paul Goodman's influential *Growing Up Absurd* was published in America. In education, a new and firmer strain of progressivism was established with the founding of the journal *Forum*, and a school which was to become a radical *cause célèbre* opened – Risinghill in North London.

For the radical movement in education, 1966 seems to have been a key year: it saw the first of the radical magazines, *Libertarian Teacher* (see Chapter 3). In 1966 the 'student revolt' reached England (from America) and the London School of Economics faced its first student 'sit-in' (one of the leaders was an American). In the same year the Radical Students' Alliance – eventually to spawn the Schools' Action Union – was formed, as was the Vietnam Solidarity Campaign which mobilized enormous protests against the Vietnam war. The Cultural Revolution in China aroused much interest in Britain, the hippy newspaper *IT* was launched in London, and the Beatles' LP *Revolver* came out, considered by some to mark a major turning point in popular music.[3]

Between 1966 and 1968 something important happened: radicals and dissidents began to believe their own rhetoric. They began to believe that it might really be possible to change the world, rather than just protesting about it. The ideas which had been developing over the previous decade quite rapidly took on organizational and strategic forms. Nineteen sixty-eight is often mentioned as the key year, politically, with the Soviet invasion of Czechoslovakia[4] and near revolution on the streets of Paris. But the radical momentum had been building up long before that. If politics is 'the art of the possible', the events of May 1968 in Paris seemed to confirm that it was possible to mount a challenge to the corporate state. But May 1968 was to the radical movement what the Plowden Report (of 1967) was to progressive education – not the start of something new but confirmation that something new was well under way.

Contributing currents

Educational radicalism combines various currents of ideas which had years, decades, or sometimes centuries, of history behind them. I will consider ten such currents, in order of origin.

The English radical tradition

Several historians have shown how the radical tradition in English education[5] belongs to a broader tradition of radicalism which dates back to the English Revolution and before.[6]

The stage was set for the 1960s radicalism by four books – Richard Hoggart's *The Uses of Literacy* (1957), Raymond Williams's *Culture and Society* (1959) and *The Long Revolution* (1961), and Brian Jackson and Dennis Marsden's *Education and the Working Class* (1962). All of these writers belong squarely to the English radical tradition.[7]

In his introduction to *The Radical Tradition in Education in Britain*[8] Brian Simon identifies five characteristics of that tradition as it developed in the nineteenth century: first, an emphasis on the formative power of education; second, an emphasis on science and scientific education as the road to truth; third, an insistence that the totality of social influences, including those of political institutions, are and must be educative; fourth, emphasis on a secular education based on rationalism, and emphasis on development of a secular morality; fifth, an emphasis on the role that knowledge and education could play in social change.

The first of these has remained the subject of intense educational debate throughout this century. It is at the basis of the debates about intelligence, selection and comprehensive schooling. Belief in the formative power of education is now widespread and while the radicals of the 1960s and 1970s accepted it, the belief itself was no longer a radical one.

The question of science and scientific education as the road to truth became freshly controversial in the 1960s. As Liam Hudson put it:

> Science is no longer accepted uncritically as the expression of Progress, as the cutting edge of our civilisation's fight with ignorance. Its pursuit is seen as dangerous, even lethal – and its devotees are suspected, not entirely unfairly, of substituting one system of superstition for another.[9]

The atomic bomb, the destruction of the environment, nuclear power, 'high-technology' medicine – to give just four examples – revealed a face of science which was unacceptable to radicals. Some turned (though not, I think, many in education) to mysticism; others launched an attack on the spurious objectivity (as they saw it) of science[10] or urged a reassertion of subjectivity. For such reasons, an emphasis on science was not a characteristic of the radical movement of the 1960s and 1970s. In fact, this question of the attitude to science was one of the things which divided 'radicals' from 'progressives' in this period. Progressives, in general, retained a faith in science and, particularly, a confidence that progressive educational ideas could be shown to be *right* by objective, scientifically based, educational research.

Simon's third point – the insistence that the totality of social influences must be educative[11] – was stressed at the beginning of the 1960s by Raymond Williams in England and Paul Goodman in the USA,[12] and became a central tenet of the radicals. By 1971 it reached an illogical conclusion, and was turned on its head, when the deschoolers declared that 'all over the world the school has an anti-educational effect on society'.

Like his first, Simon's fourth point – the emphasis on a secular education based on rationalism – no longer seemed particularly radical, although it does remain an issue in British education.[13] The fifth characteristic of the older radical tradition – the emphasis on the role that knowledge and education could play in social change – was, defined broadly, integral to the post-war progressive consensus. However, it was rehabilitated in the early 1970s from three distinct sources. One was the renewed interest of historians in the working-class self-education movements of the nineteenth and early twentieth centuries.[14] The second was the conception of education as social action, which I will discuss in Chapters 7 and 9. And the third was the revolutionary educational programme of Paolo Freire.[15]

Thus certain lines of thought from the older radical tradition did re-emerge in the 1960s, while others did not. It may be that the older tradition was somewhat overwhelmed by the variety of other influences which I am about to describe. A distinctive feature of English radicalism – its commitment to a 'common culture' – was all but lost in the iconoclasm of the late 1960s, to the chagrin of some.[16]

It would be a mistake to equate the radical tradition with social-ism, not only because it pre-dates socialism, but also because that would be to ignore the strong current of radical liberalism ex-emplified in the 1960s by the Young Liberals, who were active in the radical education movement.

The working-class movement[17]

In the early 1960s several books appeared which disclosed the important part which education had played in the early development of the working-class movement.[18] The fact of the appearance of these books at that time is significant, because it reflected a heightened awareness of the relationship between class and education. This was also occupying the attention of sociologists of education at that time, who produced abundant evidence that schooling discriminated between children of different class backgrounds.[19]

Since the 1830s there has been a fundamental division of opinion within the working-class movement. In the words of G.D.H. Cole:

> Either education is a by-product of class, and each class must build up its own educational philosophy and practice to suit the needs of the class struggle – that is, as long as class divisions persist – or, alternatively, education rests on fundamental values which transcend class differences (though not uninfluenced by them), and stands for a social heritage which is to be developed and transmitted to coming generations rather than uprooted and replaced . . . In Great Britain, where Marxism as a social philosophy has never struck deep roots, the Socialist tradition is mainly on the side of the second view.[20]

Ken Jones[21] has argued that the first view – that education must be organized for use as a weapon in the class struggle – was decisively defeated in the 1920s. Certainly in the post-war period the official Labour movement (the Labour Party and the trade unions) has adhered to the second view.

Both views can be found in the radical movement of the 1960s, although, with the revival of Marxism in 1968, the first view enjoyed a new popularity. Theories which had sought to explain working-class educational failure in terms of some inherent deficit in working-class children (low intelligence, cultural deprivation, etc.) or in terms of organizational barriers to 'equality of opportunity' (bipartite schooling, streaming) were ousted by new theories which viewed schooling as a concrete mechanism for keeping the working class 'in its place'. Radicals took up the new theories, often proclaiming that they were the only ones who recognized the true interests of working-class people.

Radicals were divided between those who held that the chief evil of schooling was its discrimination against working-class children, and those who felt that schooling damaged all children regardless of their class origin. The latter view was more common in America, the former in Britain; with few exceptions, the groups of the radical movement which I will be describing located themselves consciously within the working-class movement. This was, at once, a source of strength and a source of weakness. The strength came from the fixed reference points within which ideas could be expressed, a framework which provided a sense of being part of a continuing historical process – a sense of being part of something bigger. This was an advantage which British radicals had over their American counterparts. But the weakness lay, as I shall argue, in the romantic illusions which in the end prevented radicals from finding a realizable way forward – the illusion, for example, that the working class would flock to the radical banner as soon as it was raised.

Many radical teachers held that teachers were themselves workers and as such should play an active part in the trade union movement. This was, for example, the orientation of the Rank & File group. But whether teachers really were working-class remained an unresolved debate: one view was that the ambiguous class position of teachers meant that to be *with* the working class, or not, was a matter of personal choice.[22] This was perhaps a choice more easily made by teachers who had themselves come from a working-class background.

Marxism

When Cole wrote (in 1952) that 'Marxism as a social philosophy has never struck deep roots' in Britain, he could not have foreseen the revival of Marxism with the founding, just a few years later, of the *New Left Review*, and its explosion into student politics (and thence elsewhere) in 1968.

Until 1968 the Marxist analysis of education was peculiarly sterile, keeping usually to the well-worn paths and often finding itself in broad agreement with the liberal educational establishment. But 1968 unleashed a new wave of critical examination of schooling by people who used Marxist techniques of analysis. At first much of the writing was simplistic or incoherent: the problem was that Marxism is a sophisticated and difficult theoretical field. Since it wasn't taught as a full-time course in any British college or university, there were few people with an adequate grasp of Marxist theory, and few of those were interested in schooling. The field was wide open to all those who had read a few chapters of Marx to start elaborating a 'Marxist' analysis of education. This they did in large numbers. Even when academics started to apply Marxist concepts to the sociological analysis of education in the 1970s, their grasp of sociological theory was rarely matched by their grasp of Marxian theory (or vice versa). Ironically, it was the United States (where the Marxist tradition is weak) which produced the first book which attempted a full-blown new Marxist analysis of schooling.[23]

Nevertheless, certain Marxist ideas exercised a powerful influence on the radical movement of the late 1960s and 1970s. In particular, Marxism provided the structure for a radical *class* analysis of schooling.

Anarchism

Modern anarchism has a history dating back 150 years, but it has never had the mass following in Britain which it attained in southern Europe in the 60 years before the Spanish Civil War. Nevertheless, it has been a tenacious tradition in Britain, kept alive by the paper *Freedom* which in 1986 celebrated its centenary year. The monthly journal *Anarchy*, edited by Colin Ward, played an important role from 1961 onwards in promoting the kind of radical ideas which were to arouse wider interest some years later. It was anarchists who established the first radical educational journal, *Libertarian Teacher*. And anarchists were closely involved in the first school students' union (see Chapter 5).

Although much of the thinking of the radical movement had connections with anarchist thought, the part played in the radical movement by avowed anarchists was a limited one. They were divided on important issues – whether or not to involve themselves in state schooling and, after 1970, whether to support deschooling. They eschewed the organizational skills of socialists and were therefore never able to establish a clear anarchist presence in either the actions or the debates of the movement. But Malatesta's notion of 'the propaganda of the deed' was embodied in all the radical movements of the 1960s – for example in the Schools Action Union's invasion of Dulwich College in 1969 (see page 63).

It was Colin Ward who in 1965 first introduced the idea of deschooling.[24] When talking of anarchism and education one thinks of Herbert Read (especially perhaps his *Education through Art*) but, as we shall see, his brand of genteel anarchism did not find favour with the younger radicals of the 1960s.[25] The most important anarchist contribution to the radical educational literature was Keith Paton's *The Great Brain Robbery*.

Progressive education

The modern progressive movement in education – a world-wide phenomenon – dates from the 'New Education' of the 1890s[26] although its roots go further back, to Rousseau, Pestalozzi and Froebel. The movement has had two discernible strands in Britain: the independent progressive schools, on the one hand, and the progressive movement within the maintained sector, on the other.

Although there were considerable differences between them, the independent progressive schools had a sense of belonging to a single movement.[27] All were fee-paying schools (except for some of those which specialized in taking problem children) and therefore provided only for the children of wealthy parents. These schools 'carried the flag' of progressivism right up until the Second World War. A specific contribution of this tradition to the radical movement was that their form was partially adopted by the free schools (see Chapter 7). Significantly, no independent progressive schools (with the exception of Epping House) were established between 1940 and 1965. After 1940 the second strand of progressivism had taken over.

The course of progressivism within the state sector is more difficult to chart because, apart from schools which have attracted special attention – such as Sompting Village School, Prestolee Village School, St George's in the East, Braehead and Risinghill[28] – the development was gradual, influencing many schools in varying degree. The Plowden Report estimated that one-third of primary schools could, in 1967, be called 'progressive'.[29] The development of progressivism in secondary schools was less certain.

There were links between the two strands of progressivism, notably in the New Education Fellowship and its journal, *New Era*. However, there was also tension between the two strands, centring on the issues of elitism and privilege. This tension was explored at a colloquy at Dartington in 1965:

> A colloquy? Rather a confrontation! For what began as an intended meeting of minds between two groups each considering themselves to be educational progressives ended in an irreconcilability of attitudes that was distressing, perplexing and ominous.[30]

From 1960 the banner of progressivism within the state sector was carried by *Forum* magazine, and many of the ideas it championed were taken up by the radical movement at the end of the decade. *Forum*, however, did not jump on the radical bandwagon, remaining aloof from what it might have termed the 'ultra-leftism' or 'anarchism' of the radicals. Progressivism had established a base camp (itself too high for many people) from which the radicals set out to scale new heights (or plumb new depths, in the view of some). If the progressive movement had not existed, there would have been no radical movement in the 1960s.

W.A.C. Stewart[31] summarized the recurrent emphases of progressivism as: the outdoor and rural life; art, music and crafts; mental health, honesty and frankness; informality in relationships and clothing; against punishment; liberal individualism; freedom rather than restraint; responsiveness and spontaneity; emotions as well as intellect; the unconscious mind; reaction against the experience of war; the school as a community; diluted, if any, religion. These are themes which recur throughout the 1960s and 1970s.

In concluding this section, we should note the continuing influence of John Dewey and also the part played by humanist and rationalist organizations in England, such as C.E.M. Joad's Progressive League, the National Secular Society, and the British Humanist Association.

Existentialism

Existentialism was a less important influence on the radical movement, but it was clearly there in the writings of Paul Goodman, George Dennison and Paolo Freire, in the political philosophy of Herbert Marcuse – 'guru' of the 1960s student revolt – and in its seminal influence on humanistic psychology. Existentialism is also related to the philosophical school of phenomenology, in which sociologists of education found renewed interest in the 1970s and which influenced journals like *Hard Cheese*. The existentialist concepts of 'authenticity' and 'commitment' can often be found in radical writings of this period.

Third World liberation

A consciousness of what the imperial powers and industrial economies had done, and were still doing, to Third World countries loomed large in the minds of radicals and constituted one of the major (and one of the more morally credible) motivations of their radicalism. Protest against the Vietnam war brought millions of young people in North America, Australasia and Europe into radical political activity. We might remember, too, the ubiquitous poster of Che Guevara. And there was great interest in China: followers of Mao Zedong were an appreciable element in the radical movement, especially in the Schools Action Union. Frantz Fanon influenced certain radical writers, and both Paolo Freire and Ivan Illich had the concerns of the Third World at the centre of their educational arguments.

Nor should we overlook the relationship between Third World liberation movements and the struggle against racism in the cos-

mopolitan countries. The Black Power movement was a strong
influence on radical politics in America, where activists like Eldridge
Cleaver, Stokeley Carmichael, George Jackson, Angela Davis and
Malcolm X were cult figures for white as well as black radicals; they
were often quoted in the radical education literature.[32] In Britain it
took the radical movement much longer to adopt the struggle
against racism as a central concern.

Finally, we might note that the term 'cultural imperialism', coined
to describe the process by which oppressed peoples have their
culture and interests marginalized, was taken up by radical educationists to refer to an analogous process operating on children and
young people.[33]

Humanistic psychology

A quite different, but no less powerful, current was the humanistic
psychology movement which developed in America in the 1960s
and then crossed the Atlantic. Therapeutic psychologies had had an
influence on earlier generations of radicals: psychoanalysis, for
example, on Homer Lane, Susan Isaacs and A.S. Neill; or the 'life
adjustment' movement of the 1940s and 1950s. And the writings of
Wilhelm Reich enjoyed a renewed popularity in the 1960s.

But humanistic psychology marked a distinctive departure from
these older traditions.[34] Its most prominent protagonists in America
were Abraham Maslow, Erich Fromm and Carl Rogers, all of
whom had a good deal to say about education.[35] Fromm had written
an introduction to A.S. Neill's *Summerhill: A Radical Approach to
Education* (on the insistence of Neill's American publisher: Neill was
not happy about Fromm) which was published in England in 1962.
But the real impact of humanistic psychology in Britain came with
its adoption by the women's movement, on the one hand, and the
attack on orthodox psychotherapies led by Ronald Laing, on the
other. Humanistic psychology drew attention to the importance of
the emotions and of personal relationships, and emphasized client-
led therapy (analogous to 'child–centred' learning). It influenced the
radical education movement by suggesting new organizational
forms and more intimate emotional relationships between the people involved. Its influence was also evident in the children's rights
movement,[36] and on the Resources Programme for Change in
Teaching (see Chapter 4) which included 'encounter group' methods
in its meetings: they urged that teachers needed to *know themselves* if
they were to be truly radical.

But humanistic psychology was more significant in this period in

America than in Britain. Gestalt therapy was a strong influence on both Paul Goodman and George Dennison, and a seminal journal, *Issues in Radical Therapy*, was widely read. (It reached Britain in only small numbers but a few of its articles were reprinted and sparked off important discussions within the radical movement.)

Humanistic psychology was anathema to the left-wing sects involved in the radical movement. They perceived, accurately, that it was an exclusively middle-class phenomenon and concluded (not logically) that it had no relevance for the working-class struggle. But its implications for pupil–teacher relationships were recognized[37] and its ideas about the conditions of learning were taken up by the free schools.

The counter culture

I use the term 'counter culture' as a generic term for the unprece-dented goings-on that no one failed to notice in the 1960s, ranging from rock and roll, hippies, flower power, LSD and marijuana, protest songs, brown rice, the sexual revolution, and 'the under-ground' to *Oh, Calcutta!*, *Easy Rider* and Arts Labs.[38] It created a climate which was favourable to a radical movement in education: a climate of iconoclasm, of daring to challenge taboos and orthodoxy, of permissiveness, of cultural renewal, of fun for its own sake, of 'doing it'.

It is worth making the distinction (although there are obvious interconnections) between the radical counter culture, on the one hand, and the commercial fashion boom dubbed 'the swinging sixties' on the other. As has often been remarked, the 1960s saw a sharp increase in the spending power of youth and there were rich pickings to be had (notably in the record industry and the clothing trade). What characterized the *radical* counter culture was that it was all run on a shoestring amidst the conspicuous opulence of the 'swinging sixties'.

Among the currents which combined to form the counter culture, four are relevant here. The first is expressionism, which entered radical educational thought both through the writing of Paul Good-man (Goodman had been involved in founding the Living Theatre which, in the 1960s, epitomized expressionism in drama) and through its well-known influence on the teaching of art, drama and English.

Second, and related to this, is a radical individualism which, in Raphael Samuel's words, 'made personal identity and individual self-assertion the highest good'.[39] Such individualism was compatible with some elements of the radical movement – such as libertarianism and free schools – but came into sharp conflict with others – particularly Marxism and the working-class movement.

Third, there was the interest in mysticism and other non-rational modes of experience; this influence may be perceived in, among other things, the fashion for 'gurus' and the commitment of most radicals to non-violence, especially in their dealings with children.[40] The books of Carlos Castaneda found their way on to some College of Education reading lists, bringing forth an indignant response from Rhodes Boyson, who muddled up Castaneda's Don Juan with the European legendary rake of the same name. The 1960s was not the first time that Eastern religions had made an impact on progressive educators: Edmond Holmes, author of the 1911 classic *What Is and What Might Be*, had been strongly influenced in that direction.

Fourth, we must mention English Romanticism (although it might have been subsumed in the English radical tradition), exemplified by the widespread interest in William Blake, William Wordsworth and William Morris. One of the chief charges made against William Tyndale teacher Brian Hadow was that he had written a verse of Blake on the blackboard (Rhodes Boyson didn't know it was Blake; he thought it was Chairman Mao). Several radicals have told me that Wordsworth's 'Prelude' was a key influence. Historically, what the Romantics gave to education was their repudiation of the idea of the 'natural depravity' of the child, replacing this ancient tenet with a positive optimism about the potentialities of children.[41]

The counter culture won the allegiance of only a minority even of the generation most affected by it – those who were teenagers in the 1950s and 1960s. Few of those involved in radical education were wholehearted aficionados of the counter culture, although none could help being influenced by it. The radical movement in education was, simply, more *serious* than the counter culture tended to be. It had to be, because looking after children inevitably imposes a serious discipline on adults. Some hippies did work as teachers in schools, but were more often driven out by the children than sacked for non-conformity. The counter culture's interest in education was exemplified by the notorious *Schoolkids Oz*,[42] whose editors were prosecuted in 1971 on the charge of 'conspiring to debauch and corrupt the morals of children and young persons within the realm and to arouse and implant in their minds lustful and perverted desires'. *Oz* combined high anarchism with a prurient interest in teenage sexuality which commended itself to few radical activists: Neill called it 'sick'.[43] A distinction must be made between the radical support for the sexual emancipation of the young[44] and *Oz*'s 'Jail Bait of the Month' pin-ups.

Having said that, it is unlikely that the radical movement in education would have emerged so clearly had it not been for the social and cultural upheaval of the 1960s which the counter culture represented.

The American influence

It would be impossible to leave this account of the contributing currents without referring to the enormous American influence on the radical movement. This influence ranges from books (most of the Penguin 'Education Specials' came from America) and films[45] to the changing social customs of the 1960s, of which the increasing use of first names rather than surnames is a good example. Several radicals have mentioned the formative influence of American science fiction. I have often been struck, too, by the persistence of an anthropological perspective in American thinking about education[46] which had its impact in Britain.

The influence, it should be noted, was not entirely one-way. American radical thinking was strongly swayed by (somewhat idealized) descriptions of what was happening in English primary schools in the 1960s.[47] But in general the cross-Atlantic breeze was westerly, and brought us such archetypal phenomena as student rebellion, the 'alternative society' and free schools.

That completes my survey of the currents contributing to the radical movement in education. It will be clear that these currents are by no means easily compatible. Their diversity goes a long way to explaining why the radical movement in education was wracked by internal disagreements and factional squabbles. The sort of things they disagreed about are dealt with in Chapter 10. In the next chapter I will look at some of the characteristics of the radicals.

CHAPTER 2

Identifying the radicals

Defining 'radical'

What I mean by a radical is one who wants change that involves going to the root of the matter, as opposed to one who wants no change at all, or one who wants superficial change. That is all, and that is precisely what I mean by a radical.[1]

Robin Barrow's definition leaves open two vital questions: how *much* change is required for it not to be 'superficial'; and just what *are* the roots of the matter? Two people may agree that schooling is suffering a deep malaise but have quite different ideas of the root causes. And one's radical proposals for change may seem quite superficial to the other. Each of the currents described in the last chapter has its own ideas of the root of the problem: for Marxists, for example, it is the capitalist mode of production; for anarchists it is all forms of government.

While some words may be susceptible to timeless and universal definition (such as 'aluminium' or 'three'), others take on specific meanings for particular groups of people at particular moments in time. Raymond Williams has reviewed the confusing variety of senses in which the word 'radical' may be used, both favourable and pejorative.[2] 'Radical' belongs with a cluster of words – 'reformist', 'revolutionary', 'liberal', 'extreme', 'progressive', 'socialist', 'libertarian', 'left-wing', 'communist', 'innovative', 'dogmatic', 'moderate', 'conservative', 'continuity', 'consensus' – to which it may be related whether by association or opposition.

During the 1960s the word underwent subtle changes of valuation year by year and from place to place. In America it often meant a particularly vigorous form of liberalism; in Britain, however, it was usually used in opposition to 'liberal'. Between 1966 and 1968 an organization called the Radical Students' Alliance embraced Young

Liberals, British Communists and International Socialists. But in 1968 'revolutionary' became the fashionable word among left-wing students (who disbanded the Radical Students' Alliance and set up the Revolutionary Socialist Students' Federation[3]), and the word 'radical' was used, for a few years, to refer to the non-Marxist Left.

I will define the word 'radical', for the purposes of this book, by explaining what I use it to refer *to*. I am referring to radicals on the political Left and, specifically, to the groups and publications which are listed in the next five chapters and to the writings which are listed in the bibliography. Whether they succeeded in 'getting to the roots of the problem' remains an open question.

In the course of this book I sometimes make a distinction between 'radical' and 'progressive'. There are many progressive educational publications and organizations (such as *Forum, New Era, Education Today and Tomorrow*, the Programme for Reform in Secondary Education (PRISE), the Socialist Education Association, the Confederation for the Advancement of State Education (CASE), the Campaign for Comprehensive Education) which I have not included within the radical movement. But I do not think that a sharp distinction may be made between 'progressive' and 'radical' – the words describe different stretches of the same continuum and there is considerable overlap. It will be more useful to refer to points of difference as and when they arise in the discussion.

What kind of people were radicals?

The majority of people involved in the radical movement in education were young – under, say, 30 years of age. But it would be wrong to think of the radical movement as a 'youth rebellion' or as an example of 'inter-generational' conflict (although there were elements of that), not only because radicalism has a long tradition, but also because there were plenty of older people involved. If the audiences in the packed halls were predominantly young, the speakers were often from older generations – A.S. Neill, R.F. Mackenzie or Michael Duane in Britain, John Holt and Paul Goodman in America. Most of the influential books were written by older people, and older people were conspicuously active in many of the organizations of the movement.

Radical activists had, typically, been through grammar school (or even public school) and higher education. There was irony, often pointed out at the time, in the fact that it was those who had 'done well' by the conventional system who were now attacking it.

The movement was very largely one of students and teachers, or people who had 'dropped out' from these roles but still maintained links with them. It was possible to find a number of professionals such as architects, journalists, academics, psychologists, therapists, or social workers, active in the movement, but not many. There was very little appreciable participation by parents *qua* parents. There were organizations of parents, notably the Confederation for the Advancement of State Education (CASE), the Parents' National Education Union (PNEU) and, later on, Education Otherwise. CASE was progressive, certainly, but hardly radical; PNEU, a long-standing organization, had by this time become insignificant; and Education Otherwise was concerned solely with helping parents who wanted to educate their children at home.

Despite its advocacy of the cause of the working class, the radical movement was not a working-class movement. Even those particip-ants who had come from working-class backgrounds were, by virtue of their grammar school and higher education, and their current occupational status, distanced from the class. The organiza-tions of the labour movement – trade unions, the Labour Party and the Communist Party (the only other left-wing party with an appreciable working-class following) – were not sympathetic to the radical movement.[4]

Ethnically, the radical movement was almost exclusively white; although there was a handful of Asian and Afro-Caribbean activists, it cut no ice with black people in general.

The dramatic rise of feminism in the 1960s and 1970s was perhaps the most successful and enduring radical development of the period. Yet its relationship with the radical education movement was not a strong one. Women were active in the radical organizations (num-bers of men and women on the editorial boards of radical journals being in most cases roughly equal). But feminists had to fight their quarter within the radical movement just as much as outside it, and it was not until the 1970s were well under way that distinct feminist perspectives made any impact on radical educational thought, or on the structure of groups or on publishing. Few of the radical books and pamphlets about education in this period were written by women: Leila Berg, Mog Ball and Linda Gilchrist (both co-authors with men), Nell Keddie (as an editor), Nan Berger, Alison Truefitt and Chanie Rosenberg were exceptional.[5] The fact that the history of progressive education is studded with distinguished women – Mary Wollstonecraft (who tore into Rousseau's sexism in her *Vindication of the Rights of Women*), Maria Montessori, Dorothy Revell, Susan Isaacs, Ethel Mannin, Beatrice Ensor, Dora Russell, Sylvia Ashton-Warner, Dorothy Gardner, Alice Woods, Rachel and Margaret

Macmillan are examples – did not, for some reason, give women a 'head start' in radical education in the 1960s. By the end of the 1970s, of course, there was an established and growing feminist literature on education and this may now be considered to be at the core of radical analyses of education.[6]

Characteristics of the radicals

I want now to describe some characteristics of the radicals of the 1960s and 1970s. I do not suggest that only radicals have these characteristics; nor do I suggest that every radical had all of these characteristics. What I am saying is that, taken as a cluster, they allow us to identify radicalism as something distinct from, say, 'liberalism' or 'modernism'.

Challenging assumptions

The radicals were intent on looking behind appearances and questioning common assumptions: 'Genuine change . . . is not just a matter of modifying or even dismantling traditional structures; it is also a question of rejecting the dominant assumptions which underpin them, and evolving alternative definitions of what is possible.'[7]

Until the mid-1960s educational thinking in Britain was dominated by a consensus of assumptions, widely agreed and clearly articulated.[8] The radical attack on these assumptions was iconoclastic (indeed, with the arrival of deschooling in 1970 the iconoclasm was complete).

One technique for challenging assumptions is to *describe the ordinary*. This was the technique of 'kitchen sink drama' and 'social realism' in various art forms. The effect of this is to make us conscious of things we already 'knew' but weren't conscious of; once we are conscious of them we may begin to look critically at them. Ken Loach's film *Kes* (1969) was an example which made a considerable public impact; and the technique was used to some effect in the radical educational literature.[9]

In the early 1970s questioning taken-for-granted assumptions became part of the methodology of the 'new sociology of education',[10] posing, for example, some interesting questions about what is commonly understood by 'knowledge'.[11]

No stone was to be left unturned, no convention left unchallenged. But there is a danger for radicals in their desire to undermine accepted assumptions: communication can break down. Communication depends upon a host of shared assumptions: indeed, that is what makes language work. If too many assumptions are rejected, an unbridgeable gulf can be created between those who reject the assumptions and those who do not. This was brought home to many young radicals in a personal way: they found it hard to communicate with their families and it was common for radicals to have difficult relationships with their parents.

Oppositionism

Related to this questioning of assumptions was a stance of wholesale opposition to society which spurned any attempts to 'prop up the system'. Radicals did not see it as their role to participate constructively in society in order to make it work better. Thus Colin and Mog Ball announced at the start of their book, *Education for a Change*: 'This book is not about injections for survival, it is about administering a fatal dose.'[12]

The word 'underground' was sometimes applied to the counter culture of the 1960s (and it was sometimes used to describe the radical movement in education[13] although I do not think many participants welcomed the label). It alludes, of course, to the French resistance to the Nazis, and there was in the radical movement a sense of being 'outsiders' – both in politics and lifestyle – from mainstream society. It was a firm impression of mine at the time that the radical movement contained a high proportion of people who were, by background, Catholics, Quakers, Jews, Methodists or Irish – people who had, by upbringing, learnt to think of themselves as 'different' in some way. There is perhaps a connection here with the dissenting tradition.

Radicals were, in those days, not interested in participating in existing political institutions.[14] Few sought positions of power or responsibility, and those who did were vulnerable (as the experiences of Michael Duane and R.F. Mackenzie showed).[15] Radical teachers in schools walked a tight-rope between doing their best for the children and supporting the established powers. Although surprisingly few were sacked (England was tolerant in those days and, besides, there was a labour shortage), many more sacked themselves.

We can see here a distinction between radicals and progressives: progressives *did* seek positions of power. Their strategy was to increase the number of progressive schools by increasing the numbers of progressive headteachers; radical teachers, on the whole, did not want to be headteachers – rather they wanted to abolish the role of headteacher.

Let us leave the last words (for the time being) on oppositionism to
E.P. Thompson: 'The "oppositional" mentality of the British Left is
certainly a limiting outlook; but it has grown up simply because our
Left has had so bloody much to oppose.'[16]

Commitment and activism

The radicalism I am describing required moral commitment and the
translation of this into public action. It perceived as one of its chief
obstacles the apathy and quietism into which people were lulled by
contemporary society.[17] It complained of the increasing tendency for
people to respond to public social ills by finding private solutions.

Being an activist movement, it was dismissive of academics and
(rather more unfortunately, I shall argue) of 'mere theorizing'.
Actually, 'hyperactivist' might be a more appropriate description,
for the sheer pace at which many radicals pursued their causes was
extraordinary. They were in a hurry – hence the chant, so often
heard on demonstrations: 'What do we want?. . . When do we want
it? *Now!*'

Generalization

> It has become hard to talk seriously about schools any more, even
> with people who work on or in them, without finding soon that
> the subject of the talk has somehow moved out of the school
> building.[18]

An essential element of educational radicalism was that it insisted on
the relationship between education and the wider society. In Brian
Simon's words: 'The radical tradition in education is, then, that
tradition which sees educational change as a key aspect (or component) of radical social change.'[19]

When radicals pointed to a fault in schooling, they tried to show
how it related to a fault in society. A number of writers suggested
that this marked out radicals from progressives: 'Libertarian education has a consistent social and political reference which progressive
education typically lacks'[20] and 'progressives have made an incomplete analysis of the relationship between school and society'.[21]
The argument here is that the progressive critique was formulated
without any *necessary* reference to a critique of society. Its case was
justified on 'educational grounds', implying that these grounds were
independent of social and political considerations. For example,
progressives criticized streaming on the grounds that it hindered the

educational progress of some pupils.[22] Radicals, in contrast, regarded streaming as a manifestation within schools of a stratified and class-divided society.

If progressives sometimes seemed to lend their weight to the calls of 'keep politics out of education', radicals were quite clear that this was a nonsense since politics was already, and had always been, deeply involved in education: 'Not only must politics not be taken out of education – it can't be. Nor can education be taken out of politics: they are mutually inextricable and each is bound up with society.'[23] Of course, there was an element of strategy in the progressives' inclination to separate politics and education. The progressive movement drew support from across the political spectrum (it was Conservative Minister Edward Boyle who set up the Plowden Committee). To have placed emphasis on the political implications of progressivism might have splintered the movement.[24] For radicals, however, politics were of crucial importance, and they refused to put them to one side.

Structures

Radicals tried to aim their critiques at structures – at systems, at 'the system' – rather than at people or their attitudes. As Robin Barrow notes, the radicals' work 'is imbued with the characteristically Platonic idea that no-one willingly does wrong'.[25] The radicals of the 1960s therefore broke with the old idea that 'Education could make everyone good, wise and happy', as Robert Owen had put it.[26] It may be that this is another issue which divides radicals from progressives.

The radical emphasis on the importance of structural change is illustrated by their relative lack of interest in teacher training. The 1960s initiative SPERTT – the Society for the Promotion of Educational Reform through Teacher Training[27] – did not receive much radical support. Radicals did not consider that a new lot of teachers with fresh attitudes and approaches could make much impact, because what teachers ended up doing in schools was determined not by their individual consciousness but by the requirements, roles and constraints imposed on schools by the social structure.

Radicals were interested in structures in a rather more specific sense. They pointed out that many of the wrongs of schools could be detected not in the curriculum, nor in methods and practices, but in the organizational structure of the school.

Principle

As I shall be observing in later chapters, the radicals' firm commitment to their *principles* amounted to high moral rectitude. There was, for example, a dogged commitment to the doctrine that the end does not justify the means. This led them to decline the use of methods perceived as wrong in themselves, regardless of the desirable benefits they might produce. We have already seen an instance of this: the unwillingness of radical teachers to climb the school hierarchy (on the grounds that hierarchy is bad) even if, by doing so, they would have been in a better position to implement radical policies.

There was, too, an almost total refusal to compromise.[28] Many radicals felt that if they could not win a battle outright, it was better to lose than reach a compromise settlement. This was frequently illustrated by the Rank & File teachers' group's approach to pay claims: anything less than a complete victory was condemned as a 'sell-out' by the union leadership.

This firmness of principle was not just a moral stance. It was a conscious attempt to prevent radical initiatives from suffering the fate of gradual degeneration. Noting how previous utopian experiments had been corrupted and distorted, radicals wanted the *process of change* to reflect the ideals of the society which they eventually hoped to create. The fear was that if compromise and expediency were adopted as tactics on the way to the ideal world, then that ideal world would itself be fatally compromised.[29]

At its best, the radicals' commitment to principle showed a commendable determination not to be diverted from objectives. At its worst, it became a devotion to 'purity' which denied that any virtue could be made out of necessity and degenerated into an impotent negativeness.

Idealism

> in taking thought for the education of the young it is impossible to be too idealistic, and . . . the more 'commonsensical' and 'utilitarian' one's philosophy of education, the shallower and falser it will prove to be.[30]

It may be said that the fundamental premise of the radical tradition is a belief in the perfectibility of human society. What keeps radicals going is a vision of utopia. And indeed, much of the radical literature about education was concerned with how education could be in an ideal world.

This radical idealism (I use the word in the sense of a vision of how things ought to be, and not in the philosophical sense), when combined with the oppositionism and the firmness of principle which I have described, is sufficient to explain why radicals found it so hard to answer the question 'what do we do now?', even though *action* was what they wanted. Because what *could* be done in the immediate circumstances seemed so unsatisfactory (progress was minuscule, full of compromises, half-measures and 'tinkering') some radicals preferred to fantasize a catharsis of 'revolution', after which everything would come good all at once.

Strategy

Few radicals believed that the changes they sought could be achieved by reasoned argument alone. This was because such argument can only succeed if there is a firm ground of shared assumptions, and where there is a unity of social interest; only in such circumstances would there be the possibility of appealing to consensus. Radicals criticized the progressive strategy exemplified by the journal *Forum*: 'The *Forum* attitude seems to be that if you present your case soundly any "reasonable person" will agree with you.'[31]

Radicals expected their case to be opposed by those with a vested interest in the status quo, and their strategy, therefore, was to appeal to those who did not have any such interest. Their analysis generally led them to believe that this was the working class, which is why so much of the radical literature concerns itself with the schooling of working-class children. There were few signs, however, of a working-class response to the clarion call.

Radicals did not expect that significant changes would be implemented by the powers that be. They perceived the powers that be (and in the late 1960s this included Labour government at local and national level) to be part of the problem and not a means to its solution. It would therefore be inaccurate to describe the organizations of the radical movement as 'pressure groups': in general they were not lobbying for reforms. To be sure, they did state their 'demands' – see for instance the demands of the Schools Action Union in Chapter 5 – but such demands were made not so much in expectation of any response but rather as a means of publicly exposing the obduracy of the establishment.

Thus, for example, there were few radical submissions to official committees of enquiry like the Taylor, James or Bullock committees.[32] By contrast, there had been a good number of progressive submissions to the Plowden Committee. Instead, it was the tenet of

radicals that change would only come through popular mass action –
that is, by ordinary people taking action on a massive scale. The
appeal, therefore, was to the hearts and minds of ordinary people.

This is why the accusations sometimes levelled against radicals –
of secret conspiracy, of plans for subversion, of totalitarian aspirations[33] – were wide of the mark. Such methods were alien to the
radical strategy. Several radical organizations freely published their
membership lists, and almost all the radical journals printed the
names of their editorial boards. As MI5 doubtless discovered, it was
easy to get to the centre of each of the radical organizations and find
out what they were up to.

Irrefutability

A peculiar characteristic of radical ideas lies in their imperviousness
to refutation, either by argument or appeal to the evidence. There are
several elements of this irrefutability. First, much of the radical
argumentation is *prescriptive*: it is couched in terms of what *ought* to
be. For example, teacher–pupil relationships ought to be more
informal, schools ought to be open to the community at all times,
children ought to take to swimming like ducks to water. While one
can, if one wishes, disagree that things ought to be like this, it is very
hard to refute such prescriptions.

Second, the radical case is built upon axioms which are articles of
faith. The clearest example here is the belief in the fundamental
goodness of human nature and the allied belief in the perfectibility of
human society.

Third, much radical argumentation is based on uncertain or
shifting premises, and so it is always open to radicals who are in
danger of losing an argument to 'shift the goalposts' (this is related to
challenging assumptions). One technique for doing this is the use of
prescriptive definition, by which terms are defined so as to make the
argumentation self-evident. Indicators of this technique are the
qualifying of terms by 'real', 'true' or 'properly understood'– as in
'true learning is . . .' or 'real education means . . .', or 'socialism,
properly understood, stands for . . .'. The radical literature is rife
with such prescriptive definitions.[34]

Fourth, radicals were often unwilling to accept the conventional
rules of argument and conventional rules of what may be counted as
evidence. There were, for example, those who regarded the laws of
logic as an unnecessary imposition, and others who condemned any
recourse to empirical evidence as 'positivism' or 'empiricism'.

Fifth, it seems that many radical arguments were deployed not

primarily to support (or refute) a proposition, but to win people over
to the radical point of view. At times it appeared that the criterion of
truth being employed was not the weight of evidence, nor the
soundness of the reasoning, but the degree of response it could evoke
from the audience being addressed. A commonly used technique
here was to counter an argument by questioning the motives of the
person putting that argument. While it *is* legitimate to ask questions
about people's motivation, that is not *all* that needs to be done to
refute their arguments.

I do not think that the radical arguments are any worse in these
respects than most other talk about education. I have written
elsewhere about the inadequacies of the *Black Papers*,[35] and I think it
could easily be shown that 'middle-of-the-road' arguments fare no
better under scrutiny. What I do want to say is that it is not in the
interests of the radical case to use faulty argumentation. And that is
another theme of this book.

The size of the movement

In numerical terms, the radical movement was not a mass movement. I know of no way of assessing accurately how many people
were involved, but some figures give us an idea of the dimensions.
By far the largest membership organization was the National Union
of School Students (NUSS) which, in the mid-1970s, had a paper
membership of 15,000. This was some 5 per cent of the secondary
school population. It seems unlikely, however, that a majority of
these were active members with any consciousness of being part of a
radical movement. The next biggest membership organization was
the Rank & File teachers' group: its 1,200 supporters (at its peak)
formed about 0.3 per cent of teachers in maintained schools. Of the
radical journals, the NUSS's *Blot* achieved the largest circulation
with a figure of 10,000. *Children's Rights* also claimed a circulation of
10,000, but this may have been an overestimate. One issue of *Rank &
File* achieved a circulation of 9,000 copies; if we assume that all of
these were sold to teachers, this was over 2 per cent of teachers in
maintained schools.

Another quantifiable indicator is the sales of radical books. Some
publishers have been kind enough to provide me with figures,
although not, unfortunately, Penguin, who certainly topped the list
with books like Leila Berg's *Risinghill: Death of A Comprehensive
School*. Ivan Illich's *Deschooling Society* had, by 1985, sold a total of
81,000 copies in Britain, but more typical would be Chris Searle's
This New Season which sold just under 3,000, or R.F. Mackenzie's *A*

Question of Living which sold just over 3,000. A.S. Neill's *Summerhill: A Radical Approach to Education* sold close to 6,000. Gabriel Chanan and Linda Gilchrist's *What School is For* sold 8,300, and Samuel Bowles and Herbert Gintis's *Schooling in Capitalist America* over 13,000.

I do not think we can make very much of these figures, but, taken together, they are not inconsistent with an estimate of the radical movement as involving between 10,000 and 20,000 people, excluding those school students who were paper members of the NUSS. Whatever the figures, it is certain that we are talking about a very small percentage of teachers and school students, and an even smaller percentage of the population as a whole.

We are ready now to look at the radical movement in detail.

CHAPTER 3

Radical teachers: *Libertarian Teacher* and Rank & File

In this and the next chapter I will survey the teachers' groups and publications within the radical movement. Of the publications, I have chosen to give particular attention to *Libertarian Teacher*, the first in the field and (in its later forms as *Libertarian Education* and *Lib Ed*) the longest running; and, of the groups, to Rank & File, the largest.

Libertarian Teacher

Through the 1960s anarchist comment on questions of education was presented in articles in the monthly *Anarchy* and the weekly *Freedom*.[1] In 1966 two schoolteachers, Peter Ford and Alex Taylor, announced in *Freedom* the formation of a Libertarian Teachers' Association (LTA). Peter Ford recollects:

I had clear ideas about my own particular predicament and experience . . . the motivation to form an association came out of the predicament. Working in an institution in which I felt uncomfortable and critical, I extrapolated from my experience to think that there must be quite a lot of people feeling this way too. It was not tied to a theory about how things ought to be. But from an association, a linking up of those people, something might come – if no more than some sort of solidarity between them. The initial idea I had was an association of individuals – teachers or students – who were by their own assessment libertarians or anarchists, and it would be a kind of mutual aid association.[2]

To start with, the LTA simply circulated the names and addresses of kindred spirits; this was the first issue of what was to develop into the *Libertarian Teacher* journal. LTA had no officials, no formal membership, and no subscription rate: 'If you want to consider yourself to be a member of LTA then so you are!'[3]

The LTA held several day conferences, attended by 20 or 30 people.[4] These led, in 1968, to the following statement of 'Principles, Aims & Objectives':

Libertarian Teachers' Association

Principles, Aims & Objectives

It should be understood that the following is not an agreed statement of aims and principles endorsed by all members of the Association. It is unlikely that any such statement could truly represent the varied and changing opinions of such a diffuse group. Partly for this reason, the formulation of 'Aims and Principles' has not been seen as a matter of immediate priority. Nevertheless all individuals linked with the LTA must necessarily accept the word 'libertarian' as descriptive of their attitude to education and it is likely that most would support the general outlines of the statement below – but there is no question of membership hinging on the acceptance of it.

Principles, aims and objectives

(1) Education is to be understood as a continuing process in a healthy life. It is not necessarily enhanced by or inseparable from special people called 'teachers' or special places called 'schools'. True education may in fact be hampered by both. The Libertarian Teachers' Association is concerned with education in its widest sense and also with what is currently going on in institutions specifically designed to promote it – from nursery schools to universities.

(2) At both age-extremes attendance at educational institutions is voluntary, although some provisos should perhaps be placed around the word 'voluntary' in relation both to nursery school children and university students. In the light of the present general educational unrest and the unenthusiastic attitude of many children to the schools they are obliged to attend, the LTA questions the value of making school attendance compulsory, bearing in mind that children who are forced to attend a school that they dislike will be resistant to it and benefit little, whilst on the other hand there would be no need to apply compulsion to make

children attend schools that were attractive to them. A change from compulsory to voluntary attendance would mean a revolution in attitudes towards children and techniques of teaching which would affect all sectors of the educational system.

(3) The LTA is in general opposed to the involuntary separation of children either on the basis of sex-difference or alleged intelligence. We, therefore, support co-education and non-streaming in all schools.

(4) Schools, colleges and universities should properly be controlled by those most immediately concerned with them: pupils, parents and teachers; students and lecturers. There are various methods of doing this and a minority of existing educational establishments in this and other countries exemplify ways of moving in this direction. The LTA supports the growth of shared responsibility, pupil-participation, student power and workers' control in schools, colleges and universities. Whilst it may be helpful for practical organisational reasons to relieve busy teachers and lecturers of administrative work, the LTA opposes the traditional power-hierarchy that exists in most schools and colleges. If there is to be a headteacher or principal, his role should be functional and administrative rather than dictatorial.

(5) At this time the existing Unions seem to be obsessed either with largely spurious issues of professional status (for example: the attitude towards teachers auxiliaries and 'unqualified staff') or with salary scales and negotiations, to the exclusion of more fundamental issues. A Union which is structurally dominated by headteachers can hardly be expected to function well from a libertarian viewpoint. Therefore the LTA supports all attempts to democratise the existing Unions or to create a new Union which would be more capable of representing and defending the interests of all teachers.

(6) Whilst acknowledging the problems posed by over-large classes, often full of children conditioned to respond to force – the LTA is in principle opposed to corporal punishment and all other forms of institutionalised punishment. (This should not be understood to mean that adults should never be angry with children – or never show anger when they feel it.) Even though the effects of the carrot may not seem as insidious as those of the stick, artificial rewards (marks, house points, stars, etc.) do not aid freely motivated learning and are generally needed only because of the compulsory setting in which most teaching takes place.

(7) The current emphasis on competition in education – permeating the whole system but operative particularly through

streaming, house systems and examinations - is to be opposed. Examinations imply that knowledge is a kind of 'private property' to be withheld from others and to be used as a lever to gain superiority over them. The LTA supports the critical movement away from examinations and the emphasis on co-operation as an educational aid.

(8) The LTA campaigns for an immediate end to the public schools system, compulsory school uniform, religious indoctrination, and the prefectorial system.

(9) The LTA welcomes and gives support to all experiments inside or outside the official educational system which seem likely to extend the freedoms of those involved – both adults and children.

Practical proposals

We recognise that many of the above objectives can only be seen as long-term. Immediate action may seem only remotely related to their achievement. However, the libertarian tactic is essentially direct action in the here-and-now, embodying the ends as means in so far as this is possible. In the light of this, the following suggestions for action are made. These are addressed principally to teachers in schools but could be adapted to apply to lecturers in Training Colleges or Universities.

(i)   Try to realise the full implications of what in fact you are doing – or being made to do – at the present time.

(ii)   Introduce the voluntary principle at all possible points within the learning situation. Make clear the available options and try to extend them.

(iii)   The converse of this: with due circumspection, refrain from personally using coercion or punishments as far as your particular situation permits.

(iv)   Try to mobilise that residue of dissident opinion which exists in so many schools, to speak out against the use of corporal punishment, the enforcement of uniform, etc.

(v)   Regard with compassion the fact that children are to some extent conditioned to respond to fear and will frequently react with aggression or superficially irresponsible actions when fear is not present.

(vi)   Draw attention by all available means to the growing evidence against the effectiveness of authoritarian methods in education.

Postscript

All libertarians are concerned with wholesale change in the social structure. It is important to recognise that educational advances will not in themselves inevitably result either in more liberated individuals or a more liberated society. It is only necessary to look at the American educational system, which already contains many of the features that we are proposing above (absence of streaming, informality between teachers and pupils, no uniforms, etc.) to see that it is still an efficient method of preparing the majority of young American citizens to accept with docility a society which is arguably as barbarous as any on the face of the globe. There are many reasons to justify a liberalisation of educational methods – not least of which is an immediate increase in the chances of happiness for those who are having to undergo them – but it is still broadly true that education reflects rather than causes change in the social structure. It is thus essential that libertarian teachers should maintain contact and involvement with other areas of the libertarian movement. The various specific pressure groups which constitute this movement are ultimately interdependent and no advance towards freedom in any particular social field will be lasting unless matched and supported by similar pressures elsewhere.

(First published June 1968, revised April 1971.)

The deliberate structurelessness of the LTA arose from that strain of anarchism which is suspicious of all forms of organization (on the grounds that they inevitably lead to concentrations of power); it was also a feature of the counter culture, both in Britain and America.[5] It is doubtful whether LTA would ever have become more than a small mailing list which gave rise to small meetings[6] had it not been for the success of *Libertarian Teacher*.[7] The second issue was published in August 1966, a 16-page duplicated pamphlet which exchanged information between members. Two hundred and thirty copies were distributed. The third issue (July 1967) listed members, noted some schools of interest and reported on developments around the world. The main function was still as a notice-board. *Libertarian Teacher* was soon selling 1,000 copies. In Peter Ford's words, 'there was a response and quite a vigorous one. We were surprised. There was a lot of reaction to a little spark.' There were, it seemed, other people who shared Ford's predicament.

Although each issue contained one or two theoretical articles, such as Carl Rogers's 'Personal Thoughts on Teaching and Learning' in the third issue, and Colin Blundell's 'Notes Towards a Libertarian Philosophy of Education' in the fifth, the early issues consisted mainly of short pieces of interesting information. By the fifth issue the journal was able to report on the 1968 events in the French *lycées* and on the Free Schools Campaign in Britain (see Chapter 5). *Libertarian Teacher* had prefigured these events by two years, and this marks it out from the other groups and publications which arose in response to public events. *Libertarian Teacher* was an expression of 'spontaneous libertarianism':[8] there is no acknowledgement of the tradition until the ninth issue, six years after it was founded. Instead the influences were contemporary – Paul Goodman, John Holt, R.F. Mackenzie, Michael Duane, Jean-Paul Sartre, A.S. Neill, W. David Wills, Colin Ward and Anthony Weaver.

From the sixth issue of the journal (1970) editorial control began to be transferred to an anarchist group centred on Leicester's Black Flag bookshop, and by the ninth issue (1972) this changeover was complete. The change was marked by a new format, style and outlook, and with the tenth issue a new name – *Libertarian Education*. By this time the LTA had faded away – having had a 'membership' of 300 in 1969; from then on all the energy was put into producing the journal.

These changes were significant. In its early years *Libertarian Teacher* was produced by – and for – teachers who had a measure of confidence that they could do a worthwhile job in state schools. This had been the general tenor of articles in *Anarchy* and *Freedom* earlier in the decade: in fact, no clear distinction was drawn at that stage between libertarianism and progressivism. *Libertarian Teacher* owed more perhaps to the drawing-room strictures of Herbert Read than the revolutionaries who had fought against Tsarism in Russia. In general the targets – the things libertarians felt uncomfortable about in schools – were those of progressives: authoritarian teachers, corporal punishment, uniforms, streaming, the contempt which some teachers felt for the children. The 'schools of interest' listed in the early issue of the journal were, in the main, progressive schools. (The headteacher of one such wrote angrily to deny any association with libertarianism.)

After the ninth issue the new editors took a different stance. They had assimilated the outlook of the 1960s counter culture; they were sceptical of the possibilities of libertarians doing a 'straight' job like teaching. They did not patiently await gradual reforms in schools, but wanted to turn schools upside down. They were in the business of changing the world, not easing their own discomfort. The title of the journal was changed from *Libertarian Teacher* to *Libertarian Education*, a change not explicitly explained in the journal apart from the comment that 'the term "libertarian teacher" is a contradiction in terms/pretentious/exclusive'. The change reflected libertarian doubts about teaching which I will discuss further in Chapter 8. Curiously, John Holt was travelling in the opposite direction at this time, eschewing the word 'education' because it had been appropriated by the 'professional schoolmen', but insisting that the word 'teacher' must be retained because it refers to an ancient and honourable function.[9]

The changed title signified not only a rejection of the teacher's role, but also an appreciation that education goes on everywhere all the time: in other words the editors wished to emphasize the place of informal education as against formal schooling.

The first eight issues were produced on a stencil duplicator. From the ninth issue it was printed by offset litho. In common with other radical education publications (with the exception of *Teaching London Kids*) the graphic art of *Libertarian Education* was not of a high standard and tended to rely heavily on cartoons stolen from *The Beano*. *The Beano*'s characters – Dennis the Menace, Beryl the Peril and the Bash Street Kids – were (and still are) anarchistic in the tradition of the Good Soldier Schweik. The fun and games at Bash Street School, where the kids always get the last laugh and the teacher is a buffoon (but not entirely unrecognizable to teachers), were fruitful sources of inspiration.

From 1972 *Libertarian Education* came out fairly regularly – two or three times a year – and sold about 1,500 copies per issue. It needs to be remembered that all the radical journals we shall be discussing were produced by volunteers who had many other pressures on their time, and with negligible financial resources. A new issue could not be published until sales of the previous issue had paid the outstanding printer's bill. Significant donations of cash, from any source, were almost unknown. Until the Publications Distribution Cooperative was established in the mid-1970s, radical journals had no organized means of distribution and relied for sales on the individual efforts of supporters and requests for copies from people who had heard of it by word of mouth. A small number of radical bookshops could be relied upon to place firm orders, but like so many other radical enterprises, these tended to disappear overnight leaving unpaid debts. Against this background a sales figure of 1,500 was an appreciable achievement.

Libertarian Education entered a third phase from issue no. 21 (1977). There was a steady improvement in the format, production settled at a regular two issues per year, and the articles became rather more serious, with a growing acknowledgement of the historical tradition to which the journal belonged. The editors warmed to deschooling (whose chief protagonist, Ivan Illich, was by this time gaining a certain respectability) but didn't jump on that bandwagon: in Michael Smith's judgement:

> Illich's naivety about power marks him off from the anarchist movement. Anarchist analysis starts from the fact of power, and Illich's inability to imagine society in terms of power puts him on the fringe of serious anarchist thought.[10]

In this third phase the journal returned to some extent to the outlook of the first phase – dwelling on the preoccupations of libertarians who wanted to work in state schools, especially curriculum issues. With issue no. 25 the name changed again – to *Lib Ed* – on the grounds that 'Libertarian Education' was dull and cumbersome. *Lib Ed* ceased publication with issue no. 30 (in 1981), but it was resurrected in 1986 when *Lib Ed* (Second Series) was launched.

Any evaluation of a journal like *Libertarian Education* must begin with recognition of the sheer physical difficulty of producing it. Scarcely an issue passed without appeals from the editorial group for more money, more subscribers, more people to help with the tasks of production and distribution. Such appeals went, apparently, largely unheeded, but the journal kept on being produced. It was one of the few radical education magazines to be produced outside the London area (the others were the Scottish *This Magazine is About Schools*, the Brighton-based *Educat*, the Manchester-based *Women and Education*, Exeter's *Pied Paper* and a number of school students' magazines) and this had a bearing on the difficulty it had in finding helpers.

The journal played a significant role in the radical movement in six respects. First, it provided the first model of what a radical education magazine might look like. Second, it disseminated and popularized radical ideas – such as those of Holt, Goodman and Illich. Third, it generated a sense of there being a *movement*:

> Please let us start using *Libertarian Teacher* and each other's ideas and experience in such a way that each of us can feel that whatever we do that is radical is part of a *movement* for change in our schools, and that whether we 'succeed' or 'fail' the learning we gain is valuable.[11]

Fourth, it was a forum for the *cris-de-coeur* of young teachers who were distressed by the grim encounters of the classroom. Fifth, it was an information exchange which noted that other groups existed and described what they were doing, and reviewed books. And finally, it provided a sense of solidarity for libertarians – that feeling of not being alone which is essential for the social confidence, if not the mental health, of radicals:

> . . . many comrades gain strength from the knowledge that specific problems/difficulties are part of our common experience and are not necessarily caused by personal inadequacies as the school authorities try to convince us . . .[12]

With the benefit of hindsight, a major weakness of the journal was its failure to develop its ideas over the 14 years of its life. (Unfortunately the new series which started in 1986 seems to continue this weakness.) As the editorial in issue no. 10 (1973) noted: 'we have been appallingly backward in presenting and developing any real analysis of our attitudes'. After a dozen issues the journal ran out of anything new to say, and it read as if it was aimed at the person who had just discovered it for the first time. Determined not to be academic (a review of my own book *Progress in Education* in issue no. 24 was entitled simply 'Yawn') it also spurned the theoretical; but this is not to say that it advocated any practical strategy. Its account of schooling remained at the level of complaining about iniquities, and yet the libertarian tradition has provided potentially fruitful tools for offering an explanation that these specific phenomena are not mere accidents but can be seen as features consistent with the part schools are playing in society as a whole.

In their effort to be lively the editors invested the journal with an aura of frivolity (such as the *Beano* graphics) which, in the end, itself became boring. There was an element of recklessness in some of the causes the editors chose to espouse. Issues nos 16, 17 and 18 were much concerned with the case of a Nottinghamshire teacher, Manuel Moreno, who was twice dismissed from schoolteaching posts. Moreno, who liked to regale his classes with explicit descriptions of his own adolescent sexual exploits, was perhaps not the kind of champion which the older libertarian tradition would have chosen. It was left to an irate correspondent[13] to wonder aloud whether any parent would want their child to be compulsorily 'educated' by Moreno.

Questions of sexuality were frequently discussed in the journal in its second and third stages. There were 13 articles on childhood sexuality, paedophilia and homosexuality in 20 issues.[14] In contrast, there were only five articles about free schools – yet free schools were something the journal could valuably have documented, analysed and supported. There was, in general, a lack of coverage of matters which were 'in the news' at the time, and a consequent failure to offer a libertarian analysis of the issues of the day. For example, the journal did not respond to the deschooling debate until 1974, more than four years after Illich had launched the concept. And it carried no reference to the death in 1973 of A.S. Neill.

This is not to say that the journal did not, over the years, carry some fascinating articles. Taken as a whole, the journals stand as a valuable, if uneven, representation of radical ideas about education in this period. What comes through is sustained anguish about difficult questions: can an anarchist work in a state school? what is the role of a libertarian teacher? how can schools be reformed? should libertarians endorse deschooling? It is a shame that the journal did not develop an analysis to provide libertarian answers to these questions. No one else was going to do it.[15]

Rank & File

Rank & File was formed early in 1968 by a number of teachers who were members of, or close to, the International Socialism (IS) group.[16] While *Libertarian Education* was avowedly anarchist, Rank & File was – not avowedly – Trotskyist, and this accounts for the marked differences between the two. The small group which started Rank & File was not typical of the radical movement in one respect at least: most of its members were not young. In their forties or fifties, they were veteran Trotskyists or *émigrées* from the Communist Party. And yet they successfully appealed to young radical teachers in a way that no other group did. The founders of Rank & File started with the advantage of a great deal of political and organizational experience, and the group had a tight structure which was not matched by any other group in education.

The first issue of the group's journal *Rank & File* set out its aim:

> Rank & File is produced by left-wing teachers within the NUT, who believe that the Union could, and should, be the most important and effective factor in forcing change and progress, not only in the general sociological-educational field, but also – and most especially – in the struggle for better salaries and conditions for all teachers.[17]

The political strategy of IS was to intervene in the struggles of the labour movement in order to develop a revolutionary political consciousness among the working class. The primary intention of Rank & File, therefore, was to address teachers as trade unionists, and to develop trade union militancy in the teaching profession. This was, in fact, not difficult to do in 1968: teachers were feeling badly done by and within a year the NUT, sharply nudged by Rank & File, launched an 'Interim Award' campaign. Teachers all over the country came out on strike in the biggest action in the union's history.[18]

It is not within the scope of this study to discuss teacher trade unionism, nor Trotskyist political strategy. My concern here is with questions of education. The founders of Rank & File were interested in 'general sociological-educational' change and progress, but this was for them secondary to trade union issues. At the time of founding the group they did not envisage going far beyond the progressivism represented by *Forum* journal, and in common with the Communist Party they saw the NUT as an appropriate vehicle for this progressivism. But the young teachers who were attracted to Rank & File had other ideas:

> OK so we need to be militant, that I fully endorse . . . Why? To raise the standard of living of the already middle class teacher to a higher strata? What socialist ideas are these? What about the working class children in school, already alienated by the pre-dominance of middle class teachers and middle class standards and authoritarian heads . . . Why aren't the conditions of the children, the oppressed majority, our priority? Surely the top priority is not wages but to democratise the system – the running of the schools, limiting the head's power – these are true socialist ideals.[19]

and

> There is a contradiction in the teacher's position, since although he is engaged by the state machine to brainwash and mind children while their parents are at work, it is by education also that capitalism produces its own gravediggers. Education is needed for the efficient running of capitalist industry but man also demands from education some answers to the problems that beset him. Hence the student revolt.[20]

These young radicals found it hard to view the NUT as a force for educational progress. Of its nature the NUT had to take the public stance that teachers and schools were doing a fine job: how else could it justify pay claims? There could be no place within the NUT for the virulent attacks on teaching and schooling which radicals were by now voicing.

There was thus built into Rank & File a tension between trade unionism, on the one hand, and educational radicalism, on the other. It was a tension which was never resolved. Trade union militancy required that teachers should unite together in the common interest of winning better pay and conditions. But radical educational ideas tended to *divide* teachers rather than unite them. The most militant teachers (in trade union terms) were to be found in the National Association of Schoolmasters (NAS); and yet on educational questions the NAS was much less progressive than the NUT.

Rank & File was originally conceived as a quarterly journal, but within six months it was decided to make it into a membership venture, and a 'Supporters' Group' was established in September 1968. (In the same way as the Militant Tendency has 'supporters' rather than 'members', in order to stay within Labour Party rules, so Rank & File avoided breaking NUT rules by enrolling people as 'supporters' of the journal). Rank & File was one of the few radical groups to have a journal *and* an active membership oganization. It was an effective arrangement and it may seem surprising that other groups did not imitate it. Furthermore, Rank & File was unique in having the backing of two significant political groupings: IS and the International Marxist Group (IMG). (IS was the dominant partner and was always able to determine Rank & File's direction.) This backing was to prove valuable, not least in providing a ready-made distribution network for the journal and a steady stream of highly committed recruits to the Supporters' Group. But it was also the source of dissension which wracked Rank & File from time to time.

Rank & File built a sophisticated organizational structure which served its purposes well. There were annual policy-making conferences, a National Committee, an Executive Committee, an Editorial Board for the journal, and active local groups in many areas (by 1973 there were some 40 of these in England and Wales). As well as the journal, the Executive Committee published a regular *Internal Bulletin*, for supporters only, which carried internal debates and communicated to local groups the tactical decisions taken by the Executive Committee. Although it would perhaps be too much to call Rank & File a 'well-oiled machine', its organizational efficiency was unrivalled in the radical movement. Financially the group, depending on sales of the journal and occasional pamphlets, the subscriptions of supporters and collections at meetings, kept its head above water, helped by concessionary rates from the IS printworks. There was no need for 'Moscow gold' – not that Moscow had any sympathy for Trotskyists.[21]

As in other radical groups, there was a tendency for activists to take on an immense workload. In its peak years Rank & File had an apparatus of 30 to 40 local group convenors, 12 Executive Committee members, ten editorial board members, a business manager, a circulation manager and two national organizers, most of whom were putting in perhaps ten or fifteen hours a week on Rank & File work. This was on top of doing their work as teachers (and in my experience these people were, by and large, conscientious people who took their teaching work seriously), union activity and political commitments. For many the pace of life was frantic, placing a heavy stress on family and personal relationships. There was an intense *emotional* involvement in the work of Rank & File; while this helped to get the work done, the intense emotions tended to fire the internecine disputes which periodically broke out.

Rank & File was published regularly, five times a year, and sold on average about 4,000 copies per issue. By 1973 the number of supporters reached 1,200. The first 19 issues (until Spring 1972) reflected the primary concern with trade union issues, but there were regular articles advocating educational progressivism – against caning and religious instruction, for mixed-ability classes and comprehensive schools, against bias in textbooks, for the extension of nursery schooling and the raising of the school-leaving age. These articles related such educational issues to wider questions of class and the political structure of society. A regular feature was 'Casebook', which described the cases of teachers who had got the sack – often because they had come into conflict with their headteacher. These cases were viewed as trade union matters, and 'Casebook' usually demonstrated the reluctance of the NUT to support a member who had come into conflict with a headteacher.

Rank & File consistently supported school students' oganizations like the Schools Action Union, and this marked it out from mainstream progressives. Its journal carried regular articles, too, pointing to racist practice in schools. But with a few exceptions[22] any distinctly *radical* criticism of schooling was confined, in the first four years, to the letters column and the book reviews section. The major exception was its stand on democracy in schools.

In the fifth issue (April 1969) the group printed 'A Teachers' Charter' which was subsequently reprinted as a pamphlet. The central proposal of this charter was

> a shift of power from the minority, authoritarian position of the head and education authorities, to the full participation by the parents, staff, students and the community at large, in all decisions taken in an educational context.[23]

(Rank & File was not the first to make this proposal: the same thing had been proposed a year earlier by the Libertarian Teachers' Association.[24])

The ideas of *A Teachers' Charter* were extended and amplified in a longer pamphlet, *Democracy in Schools*, published in 1971. Originally Rank & File had conceived democracy in schools in terms of *workers' control*: at that time the annual conferences of the Institute for Workers' Control were major gatherings of the radical Left, and workers' control was very much on the agenda of the labour movement. But the democracy in schools policy had deeper educational implications, as the final words of *Democracy in Schools* hinted: 'the extension of democracy can release into education, in a great flood, the huge potential of ideas, abilities and energies that are now wasted in frustration, bitterness and cynicism'.[25]

There was a debate within the Rank & File group about how far the democratic control of schools should be extended to school students;[26] it was, in fact, a debate which brought out a fundamental division of opinion within the group.

Rank & File's strategy was to raise the issue of school democracy in the NUT. It was successful in doing this, and the 1971 conference of the union set up a working party on 'teacher participation'. But eventually Rank & File was outmanoeuvred within the union and the democracy in schools campaign was defeated at the 1972 union conference. Three years later, Rank & File did a U-turn and decided that it, too, was against democracy in schools because this would require teachers, as workers, to collaborate with capitalism. (A good example of the oppositionism I referred to in Chapter 1. The fear was that if schools were democratically controlled, then teachers would inevitably be drawn into implementing national and local government policies. Rank & File, after its U-turn, preferred the idea of classroom teachers being excluded from positions of control so that there would be no constraints on their attacks on those who were in control.)

The division of opinion to which I referred was between what I will term the 'quantitists', on the one hand, and the 'qualitists', on the other. Quantitists advocated 'more of the same': they held that educational problems could, by and large, be reduced to a shortage of resources – too few teachers, too large classes, inadequate buildings and equipment, insufficient books and materials, and limitations on access: the system was just not providing the means for working-class children to get the decent education which middle-class children received. Quantitists supported organizational changes – such as comprehensive schooling and mixed-ability teaching – which opened up opportunities for working-class children. The quantitist view fitted in well with the progressive role envisioned for the NUT: public campaigns for extra resources, and so on. The quantitists' criticism of the NUT was that its campaigning was insufficiently militant.

'Qualitists', on the other hand, subscribed to a fundamental critique of schooling. While they might welcome additional resourcing, they did not believe that this would in itself bring about the changes they desired. For them 'education' was profoundly problematic – they wanted a wholesale review of what it was for and how it should be done.

The debate within Rank & File had started with this question: 'how do we attract young teachers to Rank & File?' Quantitists believed that they would be attracted to Rank & File by trade union militancy: what bothered young teachers most was their poor pay and conditions. Qualitists believed that they would be attracted by educational radicalism: what bothered young teachers most were the frustrations of the classroom. In 1972 the qualitists who, like the writer of the letter quoted above (page 37), wanted to talk about children and education rather than salaries and resources gained a temporary ascendancy in Rank & File. The group organized a series of national education conferences which brought together many radical teachers for intense discussions of educational issues. Subsequently Rank & File groups around the country found that they could attract surprisingly large audiences of young teachers to hear speakers like Michael Duane and Chris Searle and discuss radical ideas about education. A measure of Rank & File's influence in this period was that its supporters successfully moved a series of radical resolutions at the 1972 Young Teachers' Conference of the NUT, suggesting that Rank & File possibly represented the views of a majority of young teachers active in the union at that time. The national executive of the union moved quickly and abolished the Young Teachers' Conference.

The issues of the journal numbered 20–25 (1972–3) reflected this new mood of educational radicalism. Issue no. 21 marked a merger with *Blackbored* (see Chapter 4) and carried articles on the Schools Action Union, the National Union of School Students, a transcript of an English lesson in a secondary modern school, a discussion of the language and class question, an article which attempted to relate the 'struggle in the union' to the radical movement in education, a discussion of violence in schools, and an analysis of the relationship between the state and schooling. This issue was quite different in content – and in graphic design – from earlier issues, reflecting the *Blackbored* input, and it sold 9,000 copies, a figure rarely approached by any radical education periodical before or since. It proved to be the high point for Rank & File.

In 1973 there was a change of policy within IS, and Rank & File stopped producing its journal. (The journal was resurrected later in the decade and continued publication into the 1980s; its stance was pure quantitism.) It produced instead an 'agitational paper' the purpose of which was to mobilize trade union militancy.[27] Although the new paper carried occasional articles on educational matters, its prioritizing of trade union issues and explicitly propagandist tone were incompatible with the exploratory, tentative character of the educational articles which had been published in issues nos 20–25. A political schism between the IS group and the IMG led to an increasingly tight control of Rank & File by its IS leadership. Although it continued to be an influence in the NUT, Rank & File's contribution to the radical education movement dwindled. Ultimately in 1977 the IMG and other Rank & File supporters who were not members of IS combined to launch a new group – the Socialist Teacher's Alliance – and a new journal, *Socialist Teacher*.

The contribution which Rank & File made to the radical education movement is not to be found in the pages of its journal (apart from issues nos 20–25). The politics of Rank & File's leadership conceived of the group as taking a 'vanguard' role:

> we also seek to lead teachers – lead them towards what we argue as being the only perspectives which can ensure that the rank and file achieves, and defines, its own best interests, and those of the working class as a whole.[28]

Those who feel that they are in possession of the only correct perspective do indeed carry a heavy burden. Leadership was understood to mean developing policies and then winning the support of the NUT membership for these.[29] It was always necessary to have a 'line' – the 'correct perspective'. Matters on which it was difficult to determine a firm line – matters which needed open-ended exploration – were pushed aside. There was no place within Rank & File for the kind of 'thinking aloud' which characterized the radical educationists.

A further difficulty arose from the strategy of working inside the NUT. In order to have a policy adopted by the NUT, whether at local or national level, it had to be framed in terms of a resolution which could be proposed at a meeting or conference. (Rank & File's obsession with framing resolutions earned the tag 'resolutionary socialism'.) But the ideas of radical education could not easily be squeezed into the form of a resolution, and the way of advancing the cause within the union seemed, therefore, to be blocked.

Rank & File was therefore left with a 'line' on education which was derived from the simplistic 'base and superstructure' model[30] which, although it supported the cause of progressivism, was not able to incorporate much of the radical critique which had been developing since Rank & File started. That socialists needed to attend to this critique had been urged by Ken Worpole, writing in *Rank & File* no. 14:

> There has been little co-ordinated work done in this country towards a socialist analysis of the education system . . . unless we get together to produce an overall critical theory of the system then the situation will remain, as now, one of isolated activity easily crushed, disillusionment amongst individual radicals in education and a general sense of powerlessness.[31]

However, Rank & File was not able to rise to this challenge, and it was left to *Hard Cheese* and *Radical Education* to take up the task of building a coherent socialist theory of education. This was a loss because at one time Rank & File had the attention of a large number of radical teachers and was in a position to promote a fruitful debate. There was a degree of 'auto-destruct' – characteristic of left-wing sects – in the way that it cut short this debate with the 1973 switch to the agitational paper.

Rank & File's importance lay in the fact that it was a focus for the concerns of young radical teachers. This, as I say, was not reflected in the journal but in the local group meetings where embattled individuals gathered and gave each other a sense of solidarity and common purpose. The three national education conferences which Rank & File organized gave further encouragement to radicals, because of the large attendances (about 400 people) and the fervour with which ideas were exchanged.

Militant Teacher

For the record, in the late 1960s and early 1970s the Militant Tendency produced a paper called *Militant Teacher* and organized a Militant Teachers Group. For a short period members of this group participated in Rank & File, but they were driven out by IS and IMG. The group showed even less interest in educational questions than Rank & File and gained little support. Militant supporters were also active in the Schools Action Union in its early stages but were eventually repelled from that organization as well.

In the next chapter I will look at the other radical teachers' groups which emerged in the 1970s.

CHAPTER 4

More radical teachers

Blackbored

Blackbored was a litho-printed magazine of which four issues were published in 1970 and 1971. Produced by a group of school teachers, College of Education lecturers and students, it was primarily aimed at College of Education students but it proved to be popular with young teachers because of its refreshing treatment of their problems. *Blackbored*'s main concern was with the undemocratic nature of teacher training courses, but it took a lively and radical stance on questions of schooling. Attractively written and interesting (if messy) to look at, it sold about 3,000 copies of each of its four issues and caught the mood of a significant element in Colleges of Education at that time. It avoided the 'workerist' jargon which perhaps made *Rank & File* unattractive to new readers: its success lay in its approachability, in the impression it gave to students and young teachers that it was written by people like them.

By 1972 *Blackbored* was finding it hard to get people to do the work of producing and distributing the magazine: students who had finished their courses left and were not replaced. The editors of *Blackbored* approached the Rank & File group and proposed a merger of the two journals. The outcome was the joint issue of *Blackbored* no. 5 and *Rank & File* no. 21 published in September 1972. It was the only issue in which the *Blackbored* identity and style were retained. Subsequently *Blackbored* disappeared inside *Rank & File*.

Pied Paper

Several issues of another short-lived magazine produced by student teachers, *Pied Paper*, were published in Exeter in 1975 and 1976. *Pied*

Paper was concerned particularly to build up a dialogue between student teachers around the country. The pressures on student teachers, and the fact that they move off when their courses end, made the production of such a magazine difficult to sustain.

Teaching London Kids

In the Autumn of 1972 the London branch of the National Association of Teachers of English held a series of conferences entitled 'Teaching London Kids'. The mood was one of radical optimism among English teachers that new possibilities were opening up for them in schools. A new magazine, *Teaching London Kids* (*TLK*), was launched to develop the ideas raised at the conferences. It stated its policy objectives in this way:

> *Teaching London Kids* is concerned with exploring among other things:
> – the practice and dilemmas of progressive/socialist teachers in state schools, especially as experienced by new teachers;
> – notions of 'progressive' teaching methods and their impact on the education of working class children;
> – the concentration of educational problems in London schools;
> – the ways in which the power structure of society affects the organisation and curriculum of schools;
> – the potential role of the school in the community and vice-versa;
> – the critical importance of language in teaching and learning;
> – above all, *Teaching London Kids* is concerned with presenting positive strategies for action.[1]

This was a fair description of what the magazine attempted to do in the following years, and it had the advantage over other radical journals of having clearly defined aims, tied concretely to the reality of practice. Its concern was to address the real problems of the classroom in a way which could be of value to teachers in the here and now.

This approach was predicated on the belief that it was possible to be a radical teacher in state schools, a belief explained by Gerald Grace in a later issue of *TLK*:

> in the crisis period in inner-city schools in the early 1970s, given a serious shortage of teachers in those schools, the possibility for such schools to keep smooth, impersonal, institutional functioning became fractured . . . in those schools, crucial spaces opened up that are not normally permitted to open up. These spaces were

available for both teachers and pupils to exploit. Enterprising teachers used these spaces to press all sorts of radical questions.[2]

TLK's determination to be practical was a sign of the times. The heady days of the 1960s had gone and radicals had realized that the revolution wasn't going to happen just yet. The Conservative Party was back in power and Margaret Thatcher was Secretary of State for Education. *TLK*'s new realism was a decisive break with those radicals 'frozen into a posture of non-involvement with the system for fear of inadvertently helping to prop it up'.[3]

As teachers of English, the founders of *TLK* owed something to the tradition of Leavis and Thompson (*Culture and the Environment*) and David Holbrook (*English for the Rejected*), but there was also a contemporary influence emanating from the English Department of the London Institute of Education, where innovative work was being done on several fronts.[4] *TLK*'s emphasis on *city* schooling was particularly significant, representing a break with earlier traditions in the same way as free schools broke with the independent progressive tradition in rejecting ruralism. There was an important, and explicit, presumption that the education of inner-city children was a qualitatively different matter from the education of suburban and rural children.[5] But the reference to 'London' in *TLK*'s name probably hindered teachers in other cities from appreciating *TLK*'s relevance to them.

TLK never quite managed to avoid giving the impression that it was written by English teachers for English teachers. Its emphasis was on questions of curriculum, and it rarely dealt with curriculum topics outside of the areas of English, social studies and history. *TLK*'s interest in the curriculum marked it out from other radical publications and groups, which during this period did not regard curriculum as a central issue. *TLK* stated its position on the curriculum in this way:

> As teachers we must begin to make sense of our roles in a conflict situation by rethinking the curriculum so that children can see and feel that knowledge and learning can represent the power to change and transform the world.[6]

But *TLK* was not exclusively concerned with curriculum. It overlapped with *Rank & File* (to which it was sympathetic) in considering it worthwhile to be active in the union, and in dealing with the practical issues of campaigning in schools over staff shortages, falling rolls, spending cuts, and so on.

In the quality of its writing and editing, and in its visual presentation, *TLK* was a considerable advance on other radical publications. Although still obviously an amateur production, its imaginative use of Letraset, plentiful use of good photographs, and the high quality of typesetting and printing (*TLK* was almost alone among radical publications in not making a beeline for the cheapest printer and insisting on the cheapest paper), made it look attractive. This helped to make it easier to sell than other magazines, and its third issue sold about 6,000 copies, a figure all the more impressive in that sales were largely confined to London. Subsequently sales settled down at around 4,000 copies per issue.

TLK's strength was that it tried to interpret the developing radical critique for practising teachers. It explored the implications for them of the debates about testing, intelligence, the politics of literacy, the limits of curricular reform, discipline, language, truancy, living history, racism and sexism. *TLK* offered ideas to teachers whose most immediate problem was 'what do I do Monday?'[7]

But this practical strength of *TLK* was, in the view of its critics,[8] also its weakness. In trying to be practical, it put to one side fundamental questions about the role of schooling in society, about strategy for changing schools, and about whether individual teachers, or groups of teachers, *can* offer their pupils a significantly different experience from that offered by conventional teachers. What its pages seemed to lack was a coherent overall theory or philosophy. The next three publications we shall be considering were all concerned with this problem of theory – in different ways.

Hard Cheese

Hard Cheese started out as an alternative, not to other radical publications, but to the established theoretical journals of education. It was started by Ted Bowden at London's Goldsmiths' College, who argued in the editorial of the first issue (January 1973) that these established journals were too exclusive in terms of readership, in terms of what kinds of people were allowed to write for them, in terms of the kinds of view which could be expressed in them, as well as in terms of cover price and circulation.

Influenced by the 'new sociology of education', *Hard Cheese* sought to break down the barriers between sociology, philosophy, psychology, history and politics. It rejected the orthodox model of academics as disinterested pursuers of truth who publish their findings regardless of whether they may be supportive of any particular cause, radical or conservative. The writers in *Hard Cheese* tended to declare their political commitments at the outset, and assumed that their readers would share these commitments. As the authors of *Unpopular Education* put it some years later:

> Like all students of social developments, we stand inside the social relations we describe, not outside them. We have consciously taken sides and have not held back from arguing political preferences. In particular, we have been influenced by a growing sense of the need for a more adequate socialist politics of education.[9]

While other radical publications had editorial boards or collectives, *Hard Cheese* was produced by just one person. (In every case those editorial boards were self-appointed, with the exception of that of *Rank & File*, which was, for the early issues, elected by supporters at open meetings, and later appointed by the elected Executive Committee.) This placed a heavy load on Bowden, and only four issues of the journal appeared over a period of three years, the final issue (numbered 4/5) being in November 1975.

The fact that *Hard Cheese* achieved a circulation of over 2,500 suggests that there was at that time a substantial interest in radical theory of education. But it made few concessions to its readers. Whereas other journals chose a 24-page A4 format and made an attempt to be visually interesting, *Hard Cheese* was A5 in size and ran to as many as 120 pages of densely-typed material. There was no artwork at all. There was no attempt, in terms of format or presentation, to break down the belief, common amongst teachers, that 'theory is boring'. Bowden was determined not to reject contributions on the basis of length or style – a fault he perceived in orthodox academic journals.

The approach of many, though not all, of the articles was ethnomethodological; that is, the writers treated educational questions by observing and reporting the perceptions and descriptions of ordinary people of these questions. Articles dealt with, for example, youth work, failure at school, truancy, how teachers perceive children, the raising of the school leaving age. Many of the articles, although theoretical, described the 'real world' of schools and young people: they were about youngsters who swear, truant, get bored, fight, get in trouble with the law, masturbate, and listen to pop music. Most *Hard Cheese* articles took the 'oppositional' stance described in Chapter 2. They were concerned to criticize orthodox theory, or offer a theoretical critique of orthodox practice. And yet, in contrast to *TLK*, there was little attempt to show how radical theory might inform radical practice, whether in ordinary schools or elsewhere. *Hard Cheese* never commented on current affairs, and it rarely acknowledged that it was part of a wider radical movement. It made no suggestions for taking the theoretical debate beyond the printing of unrelated articles. Bowden, in fact, took his editorial role to the limit of non-interventionism: he simply waited for anyone to send him articles, and when there were enough, printed an issue. As a result, there was a 17-month gap between the second and the third issues.

The pages of *Hard Cheese* represent some of the best attempts of radicals in this period to work out a soundly-based theory of education. The four issues included several articles of more than passing interest and, taken together, the series remains a valuable source for those interested in radical ideas about education. It is unlikely, however, that it helped break down that distrust of theorizing which is endemic among British teachers: 'Dr. Moss represented English empiricism at its most apoplectic. Any kind of intellectual elaboration seemed to him the mark of the devious, tragically over-brainy intellectual. He wanted to save us from it.'[10] Nor did it help convince the young teachers who were attracted, briefly, in large numbers to radicalism that theory can be exciting. If they had been put off theory by their college courses, they would have found the articles in *Hard Cheese* scarcely more appetizing, not only because of the presentation, but because of the impenetrable language and unrestrained (and unexplained) use of specialist jargon.[11]

Radical Education

Radical Education, first published in the autumn of 1974, was an explicit attempt to bridge the gap between theory and practice. It was the only radical journal whose editorial board included school-teachers and lecturers from further and higher education. The group formed in 1973 when a handful of polytechnic lecturers, who had started a Radical Education Group, met up with six people who had formerly been on the editorial board of *Rank & File*. Later the group was joined by a small number of university lecturers in education. In its preliminary broadsheet, the group stated:

> In the past decade or so, education has decisively entered the arena of political controversy. No longer is there anything more than a thinly veiled consensus on the aims of education or on its methods and content . . . *Radical Education* seeks to give voice to the revolt against the educational system of today, and assist in building a new structure for the education of future generations.[12]

The broadsheet listed the journal's aims as (a) providing a focus for the disillusion and frustration felt by increasing numbers of teachers, especially young teachers; (b) attempting to build a socialist critique of education; (c) helping to give a lead to the growing movement of rejection of current educational forms; (d) providing a forum for teachers and students who are critical of the present educational system; (e) confronting the day-to-day problems faced by teachers, and suggesting strategies, particularly collective ones, for dealing with these problems; and (f) serving as a notice-board for the numerous radical events and movements in Britain and overseas. In brief, its hope was to fulfil all the functions which *Libertarian Education*, *Rank & File*, *Teaching London Kids* and *Hard Cheese* nearly, but not quite, fulfilled.

The editorial of the first issue, echoing Ken Worpole three years earlier (see page 43), stressed the importance of theory:

> It is our contention that there is no socialist theory of education. Of course, socialists have ideas about education; but there is no coherent theory in the way that there is a socialist theory of the capitalist economy or a socialist theory of history . . . What then do we mean by a socialist theory of education? There are two parts to this. One is how education *ought* to be in a socialist society . . . The other part of the question – informed by the first, but different from it – is an analysis of the process of education as it is now.[13]

Thirteen issues of *Radical Education* were published between 1974 and 1979, the sales averaging between 3,000 and 4,000 per issue. Like other radical journals, it was handicapped by a shortage of people doing the work, a shortage of funds, and lack of an effective system of distribution. Given this, it did well to establish a sizeable readership for a journal with an avowed commitment to theoretical discussion. Compared with other journals, *Radical Education* got a good deal of feedback from its readers in terms of letters. Many of them were critical and suggest that the journal was having difficulty in locating a constituency, as these correspondents indicated:

> I bought *Radical Education* in the hope of finding people with sympathetic views to mine and stimulating articles about practical alternative approaches to education. I've been disappointed; all I've heard are left-wing intellectuals discussing 'education' and 'reform' and 'the development of a socialist strategy'. I expected to read articles by parents, children and other non-specialists, but your paper appears to be a limited one directed to a limited audience.[14]

and

> Your articles, I feel are being read by the converted. I do not
> believe that the supporter of a firm elitist 'education' system
> would be swayed by your magazine, in fact the opposite would
> probably occur. You may gain the support of a few 'don't knows'
> but on the whole what is happening is that your readers are taking
> the ideas and points that you are putting forward, kicking them
> around and obtaining their own interpretation of a socialist phi-
> losophy on education.[15]

The editorial board did not find it easy to steer its way through such
conflicting demands. In the editorial of issue no. 9 (Summer 1977) it
apologized to readers that earlier issues had had 'a rather philosophical character removed from any need to debate a concrete strategy'.
But the editorial of issue no. 13 (the last) said 'We need to develop a
Socialist Theory of Education . . .', repeating what had been said in
the first issue. It is hard to see how the task of developing a socialist
theory of education could be undertaken without the debate having
something of a 'philosophical character'.

In fact *Radical Education* had been launched at an inauspicious time.
Although 1974 had seen the return of the Labour Party to government, this was not to prove helpful to radicals in education. Reginald
Prentice, later to defect to the Conservative Party, was the Secretary
of State for Education. The world economic recession, sparked off
by the 1973 Yom Kippur war and the huge increase in oil prices,
forced the Labour government to adopt policies of economic strin-
gency. The question of 'fighting the cuts' in planned educational
expenditure became the central concern of left-wingers. This put
economic considerations at the top of the agenda at the moment
when *Radical Education* had hoped to move beyond the economistic
analyses of education which had characterized *Rank & File*. Thus the
editorial of issue no. 7 (Winter 1976) reported that 'The left is now
fighting to retain past achievements in the face of concerted ruling
class attacks'. But these 'past achievements' which the Left was now
'fighting to retain' were precisely what *Radical Education* had initially
set out to attack when it said '*Radical Education* seeks to give voice to
the revolt against the educational system of today'. The pressure to
produce 'concrete strategy' rather than 'philosophy' was thus a result
of circumstances which forced *Radical Education* into a stance of
reacting to immediate events.

Radical Education cannot be adjudged to have succeeded in its aim
of developing a socialist theory of education. It perhaps underesti-
mated the size of its task, and its format – it wanted lively, readable

articles of no more than 1,500 words in length – was not appropriate for the purpose. What it did achieve was to put theory on the agenda of the radical movement.

Teachers Action

Whereas *Radical Education* started out by saying that there was, as yet, no socialist theory of education, *Teachers Action*, which also first appeared in1974, declared that it had worked out a socialist theory. The problem of theory having been solved, what was needed now was *action*: hence the title of the new journal.

The origins of the *Teachers Action* analysis lay in the thinking of black militants associated with *Race Today*, prominent among whom were Darcus Howe, John La Rose and Farrukh Dhondy. Their analysis drew on Marxism but (unusually in Britain) not Leninism: in particular they rejected the notion of a 'vanguard party' and were critical of groups (such as Rank & File) which aspired to a leadership role. They put their faith, instead, in the self-initiating collective actions of the masses.

The Teachers Action Collective, all of whose members were teachers, set out its analysis in *Teachers and the Economy* in 1975. As the title of this pamphlet suggests, its view of education was strongly related to economic considerations. The theory it sets out may be summarized as follows. An analysis of schools must follow a Marxian analysis of industrial production. Teachers are workers, who sell their labour power to an employer (the state, acting on behalf of the capitalist class) who extracts surplus value from them. School students are also workers, but they are doubly exploited (like housewives) because they are unwaged. The most correct and first demand of school students should be a demand for a wage. (In the same way, *Race Today* proposed the demand for wages for house-work.) The teacher is a productive worker: 'The teacher produces a trained, skilled, disciplined labour force which is exchanged against capital not only to reproduce the value of that labour-power, but to produce surplus value'.[16]

The function of schooling in the capitalist economy is fourfold: to skill (i.e. train) the future labour force; to grade the future labour force; to discipline the future labour force; and the custodial role of looking after children while their parents go to work. Young teachers who enter schools full of ideas and ideals about education get a shock: they want to interest, excite, teach about life, but they find that this is not what happens in school. Instead, they find unwaged pupils who are, like other working-class people, struggling against exploitation at their place of work by refusing to learn, by acts of indiscipline and vandalism, and so on. The highest form of action is pupil revolt.

Like the deschoolers, *Teachers Action* insisted that a distinction be made between schooling and education. In its early issues, it was reluctant to discuss education at all, and was critical of journals like *Teaching London Kids* which encouraged the 'myth' that teachers are paid to improve the education of children. It was also critical of sociologists, sociology being essentially a bourgeois study which can only divert the attention of workers from real objectives. (But, in fact, it had a certain amount in common with the 'new sociology' of the time, particularly in its challenging of the taken-for-granted presumption that the school is a benevolent institution.) *Teachers Action* was particularly concerned to correct the mistaken analysis of education promulgated by other left-wingers; often, it claimed, the Right had a more acute understanding of what goes on in schools.

This analysis owes much to the anarchist-syndicalist tradition, although the Teachers Action Collective did not acknowledge this. Unlike the other radical groups of teachers (with the exception of *Libertarian Education*, which was ambivalent on the issue), *Teachers Action* did not believe in working within the union, relying instead on the self-organization of workers (unofficial strikes were the ideal). Its interpretation of vandalism and indiscipline as acts of class struggle might have come straight from Wilhelm Reich:

> Everything that is in contradiction with the bourgeois order, that contains the seeds of revolt, may be regarded as an element of class consciousness . . . The fundamental problem for a correct psychological approach is not why a hungry man steals, but why he doesn't steal . . .[17]

And *Teachers Action*'s idea of pupils as workers had been mooted some years earlier by the anarchist Keith Paton: 'the driver of a private automobile, the patient who submits to hospitalisation, or the pupil in the classroom must now be seen as a new class of employees'.[18]

Whatever the merits of the *Teachers Action* analysis, it offered three insights which were relevant to a radical theory of education. First, it accepted the idea that capitalism has implicit requirements of schooling, but pointed to the possibility that these requirements are not necessarily achieved.[19] While most left-wing theories assumed that the objective and the achievement of it were synonymous, *Teachers Action* pointed to the conscious refusal of school students – especially black youth in city schools – to comply with the process they were expected to go through. It ascribed conscious action to school students, seeing indiscipline, vandalism and classroom disruption not as 'mindless' action, but as behaviour with a sound rationale. It emphasized, to use Douglas Holly's words, 'human consciousness and the co-operation or revolt of *people* in . . . the educative process'.[20] And it counted children as people.

Second, it emphasized the custodial role of schooling – a role which other radicals tended to overlook. And third, it postulated mass collective action as the motor force of social change, independent of vanguard parties and trade union leaderships.

In all, 14 issues of *Teachers Action* were published between 1974 and 1981. Unlike other journals, it was not a forum for debate. The Teachers Action Collective had a line to proselytize, and most articles were discussed, revised and approved by the Collective as a correct representation of its views before being published. By issue no. 6 (Autumn 1976) it had relented to the extent of opening a letters column, but this was only for correspondents who agreed with the general position of the Collective. Articles in the journal were either restatements of its fundamental propositions, or interpretations of the issues of the day within its analytical framework, or reporting of incidents which supported its analysis.

I have not been able to ascertain the circulation figures of *Teachers Action*, but I do not think it had a large following within the radical movement. Whatever view one may take of its theory, the rigidity of its stance and its uncompromising language were hardly likely to win converts. But the fact that such a journal emerged and sustained itself for seven years in this period is in itself significant: it represents a serious attempt by radical teachers to understand their predicament and act in the world in order to change it.

Teachers Against Racism

For white radicals the question of racism in schools had been brought powerfully to their attention by Jonathan Kozol's book, *Death at an Early Age*, published in Britain in 1968. But the radical movement was slow to take up the issue. In 1971 a series of meetings was organized by London's New Beacon Bookshop to discuss racism in schools. There were two tangible outcomes: one was Bernard Coard's influential pamphlet, *How The West Indian Child is Made Educationally Subnormal in the British School System* (1972); the other was the formation of the Teachers Against Racism group (TAR) which, over the next two years, published four issues of a bulletin also called *Teachers Against Racism*. The group held regular meetings in London – and occasionally elsewhere – which discussed the questions of black studies, racism in children's books, African and Caribbean history, and the treatment of black children in schools.

Such issues were explored further in the bulletin. TAR made no attempt to offer a politically neutral approach to questions of race,[21] making it clear that it was part of the radical movement. Thus, the spring 1973 issue of the bulletin carried a long obituary of the Guinean revolutionary leader Amilcar Cabral who had been murdered in January of that year.

In 1973 *Teachers Against Racism* fell victim to the perennial problem of radical groups – lack of person-power to keep the group and bulletin operating. Its work was in part continued by the National Association for Multiracial Education and its journal *Issues in Multiracial Education* and, later in the decade, by the more militant All-London Teachers Against Racism and Fascism (ALTARF).

Although TAR was only a small group and its bulletin never achieved its circulation potential, it can perhaps take some satisfaction from the first sentence of the preface to the 1985 Swann Report, *Education for All*: 'The origins of this committee can be traced back to the concern expressed by the West Indian community during the late 1960s and early 1970s about the academic performance of their children.'[22] TAR can take some credit for having put the question of racism onto the agenda, not only of the radical movement but, eventually, of all schools.

The Right to Learn group

Unlike the other groups we have considered so far, the Right to Learn group did not publish a journal. It was a small group of London teachers which published two pamphlets – *The Right to Learn* in July 1973 and *School Does Matter* in May 1974. The concern of the group was that inner-city schools weren't working:

> We believe that the present staggeringly low standards of literacy in Inner London schools . . . are the results of poor expectations, poor teaching and working conditions, and poor organisation in the schools, rather than of any natural deficit in the children concerned.[23]

The group firmly rejected psychological and sociological explanations for working-class failure (such as low IQ, cultural deprivation, linguistic deprivation, 'bad homes', the supposed incompatibility of working-class culture and school knowledge). Instead, it asserted that just when working-class children were for the first time being

offered full educational opportunities – with the coming of comprehensive schools and the raising of the school leaving age – this
opportunity was being snatched back from them by the *Black Paper*
traditionalists, on the one hand, and 'community educationists' such
as Eric Midwinter, on the other. The group was scornful of the
progressives' cry for 'relevance' in the curriculum; this being, in its
view, no different from Geoffrey Bantock's case for a 'diluted'
curriculum for working-class children.[24]

The Right to Learn group did not share the radicals' critique of the
curriculum; it had no quarrel with the traditional curriculum, and
opposed the fashionable integration of subjects. Nor did it support
'children's liberation'. In its view, 'Children are not at the point of
being free to choose what they should learn; they don't have the
knowledge, experience and consciousness to give them that freedom''[25] but the group did believe in seeking and valuing children's
opinions on such matters.

What was radical about the Right to Learn group was its simple
proposal: it wanted the ILEA to give it a medium-sized comprehensive school to run in the way it thought necessary if working-class
children were to match the academic performance of middle-class
children. In its school it proposed to abolish hierarchy and division
of labour, which it saw as the bugbear of normal schools. Like Rank
& File, it considered teaching to be the most important job in the
school and therefore 'all functions of the school administration will
be shared equally by all the teachers; executive power will be in the
hands of the whole staff'.[26] Salaries were to be equalized. The driving
purpose would be to *expect* high achievement from every child in the
classroom.[27] Diversions from this purpose – such as pastoral care and
'socialization' – were frowned upon. The school would be un-
streamed, although setted in certain subjects, particularly mathema-
tics. Parental involvement would be encouraged.

In contrast to most radical groups, the Right to Learn group posed
a clear and realizable way forward. Whether it would have worked
or not we shall never know because, although there was a degree of
sympathy for the proposal in ILEA's County Hall, the ILEA could
not see its way through the administrative problems:

> To give one group of teachers, however admirable, the chance of
> running a school in their own way, the education authority has
> arbitrarily to dispossess another group of teachers of their right to
> teach in the school in question.[28]

Such niceties hadn't seemed to trouble the ILEA when it came to
closing Risinghill School.[29]

The Right to Learn group had much in common with the 'quanti-tist' position within Rank & File. It did not, however, sympathize with Rank & File because it did not share the political outlooks of the International Socialism group or the International Marxist Group. Equally, Rank & File did not support the Right to Learn group because the latter's strategy did not involve the union.

Resources Programme for Change in Education

The Resources Programme for Change in Education (RPCE) was a short-lived enterprise launched in 1973. Its initial statement described it as 'an extra-curricular college of education . . . for students and teachers who feel inadequately prepared to deal with the problems they face in teaching and who are willing to take an active part in helping themselves and others'. RPCE ventures were different in style from most other radical education meetings in that they drew on the encounter group/humanistic psychology/ therapy workshop techniques being increasingly imported from the USA at the time. RPCE called them 'interaction experiences'. If you went to a Rank & File meeting in those days, you sat in silence and listened to the speakers. ('Sitting in silence and lis-tening' was one of the things radicals criticized in orthodox schooling, but it took many radicals a long time to realize the contradiction between the form of their own events and the content of their message.) At a RPCE workshop you were more likely to end up with your shoes off punching a cushion.

For familiar reasons – lack of time, money and energy, and a failure to clarify aims – RPCE closed in July 1974. Its final newsletter reflected that 'it became increasingly vague and shapeless and failed to enable people to contribute and focus energy'.[30]

Socialist Teachers Alliance

By 1975 political tensions within Rank & File had reached breaking-point, and the International Marxist Group (IMG) teachers and a number of non-IS supporters of Rank & File formed the 'Socialist Teachers Conference'. Its bulletin explained that the Conference arose

> from dissatisfaction felt by certain delegates at the 1975 NUT conference over the performance of the Left as a whole. There was a feeling that Rank & File's politics were inadequate to the situation confronting the Left, and that the way that Rank & File

operated made it very difficult to challenge these politics from within.[31]

In 1976 the Conference became the Socialist Teachers Alliance (STA) which, in 1977, launched a new journal, *Socialist Teacher*. The editorial of the first issue said:

> The Socialist Teachers Alliance has set itself two main objectives. Firstly we seek to establish unity in action among the mass of teachers around a programme of basic demands, and, secondly, we hope to develop a coherent analysis of current educational practice and the role and position of teachers and the educational system within the present social framework.[32]

The STA and *Socialist Teacher* were effectively a remodelling of Rank & File, and those not versed in the subtleties of Trotskyist politics would find it hard to detect significant differences between the two. Yet there was a refreshing difference in that

> the Socialist Teachers Alliance does not pretend to have all the answers. There are many aspects of the wide-ranging debate about education on which socialists disagree, or have not yet come to definite conclusions, and there are many teachers who might be reluctant to accept the label 'socialist' who share our orientation . . . So we do not intend to produce a journal full of dogmatic assertions and black and white judgements . . .[33]

While following in Rank & File's footsteps in being primarily concerned with issues of the resourcing of the education service, teachers' salaries and conditions, and trade unionism, the pages of *Socialist Teacher* carried several articles in each issue on educational questions. These articles demonstrate a greater sophistication than anything the radical movement had been producing five years earlier; if the radical Left was still awaiting the 'coherent socialist theory of education' which *Radical Education* had looked for, it was clear that fragments of such a theory were beginning to be put into place. But there was a marked lack of any philosophical and psychological input. What was also absent was the perspective of 'seeing things from the point of view of the child', a perspective which had been emphasized earlier by writers like Neill, Holt, Dennison, Kohl and Mackenzie, and by the school students' movement and the children's rights campaigners (see next chapter). A critic of *Socialist Teacher* might think that its editors considered the interests of teachers to be more important than the interests of children. It is, of course, an explicit presumption of teacher trade unionists that what is good for teachers is *ipso facto* good for children (witness the NUT publicity poster 'Value Your Child – Value Your Child's Teacher'). But although this presumption was sharply challenged in the earlier years of the radical movement, it remained unexamined by *Socialist Teacher*. It is a measure of the entrenched 'oppositionism' that nowhere in *Socialist Teacher* (nor in Rank & File) is there any examination, critical or otherwise, of the notion of the public servant whose first duty is to the client. (Radical social workers, had, by contrast, taken this question seriously.)[34]

Society of Teachers Opposed to Physical Punishment

In concluding this discussion of teachers' groups, mention must be made of the Society of Teachers Opposed to Physical Punishment (STOPP). Founded in 1968, STOPP was never a large organization in terms of membership, but it included in its ranks some articulate and effective lobbyists. It was well organized and kept up a flow of well-produced reports and skilfully conducted campaigns which, in the long run, proved effective. Crucial to its success was its ability to make use of the media, which were never (apart from an unfortunate libel case in 1984) given the opportunity to tar STOPP with the brush it kept for other radicals.

This is not to say that STOPP's activists did not sympathize with the radical movement – they were, individually, involved in other radical groups. But STOPP set itself a single objective – the abolition of corporal punishment – and set out winning broadly-based support for this. It did not spurn the 'proper channels', promoting, for example, a Protection of Minors Bill which Baroness Wootton introduced into the House of Lords in 1973 (it was defeated on its second reading by 67 votes to 51). It did not alienate potential support by taking a stand on other issues, and only occasionally forayed outside the strict limits of its brief, for example when it presented the première in 1973 of Leila Berg's play about Risinghill, *Raising Hell*.

The reward for this has been that STOPP has been successful in a way that no other radical grouping can claim to have been. By 1986 it had largely achieved its objective, although it continues to campaign against the physical punishment of children in independent schools and elsewhere in society. Radicals might do well to ponder the lessons which could be learned from the success of this single-minded single-issue campaign.

CHAPTER 5

The school students' movement

The 'student revolt' of the 1960s in Britain can perhaps be dated from the formation of the Radical Students Alliance in 1966. But it first became visible to the public when, in 1967, student militancy (first manifested in California in 1964) reached Britain. In the spring of that year, students occupied the London School of Economics and, in December, the Regent Street Polytechnic. In February 1968 students held a four-day sit-in at Leicester University, protesting at their lack of representation on university committees. And then, in May 1968, student militancy erupted on many campuses and in many countries, including Belgium, Brazil, Canada, Chile, West Germany, Ireland, Peru, Spain, USSR and, of course, France. In Britain the event most celebrated by radicals was the occupation of Hornsey College of Art. As the book written by students and staff of the college begins: 'This book records the beginning of a revolution.'[1]

The radical school students' movement can be seen as a part of this 'student revolt'. On 13 December 1967 students in a number of Paris *lycées* (secondary schools) had staged a strike. *Comités d'Action Lycéens* (CALs) were formed. Strikes and demonstrations continued into the new year and, by March, 50 of the 60 Paris *lycées* had formed action committees.[2]

In March 1968 school students staged a strike in Manchester.[3] During that year a Manchester Union of Secondary School Students was formed, followed by the Swansea Union of Progressive Students, the Bristol Sixth Form Alliance and the Cardiff Union of Secondary Schools. In October 1968 the Free Schools Campaign (FSC) was begun in London. (This was a campaign for freedom in schools – not a campaign for 'free schools' as the term was later understood, as in 'Scotland Road Free School'). The Revolutionary

Socialist Students Federation, set up in the autumn to replace the Radical Students Alliance, had a school students' section with a considerable membership in some schools (there were 90 members at Camden School for Girls in North London). And in December the Secondary School Students Union, based in North London, was formed.

In January 1969 the FSC organized a conference in London which was attended by representatives of these groups, as well as of groups from Oxford, Leeds, Surrey, Hertfordshire and Middlesex, and delegates from the Libertarian Teachers' Association, the Labour Party Young Socialists, and from the French CALs. It was a hectic conference, the distractions including an ITV *World In Action* camera crew, a vociferous contingent of Maoists from Regent Street Polytechnic, an invasion by 15 National Front troublemakers, and an evident police presence. Nevertheless, a seven point programme of demands was agreed upon:

1. Freedom of speech and assembly and the right to organise inside schools; no censorship of school magazines, clubs and societies.
2. Effective democratic control of the school by an elected School Council, subject to instant recall, made up of representatives of students and staff.
3. The abolition of all exams in their present form.
4. The abolition of corporal punishment and all arbitrary forms of punishment, and of the prefect system.
5. A free, non-segregated (by class, race or sex), comprehensive education system.
6. Educational establishments to become local evening centres of educational and cultural activity and discussion.
7. Full maintenance grants to all receiving full-time education over school-leaving age.[4]

This 'action programme', as it was called, set the agenda (give or take some amendments) for the school students' movement in the coming years.

From that January 1969 conference two strands of the movement emerged. At a critical juncture of the conference Michael Duane had intervened, saying 'You have to decide whether you want education with a little politics or politics with a little education'. This pithily described the difference between the two strands. One strand was represented by the FSC, which wanted to be seen as 'apolitical'.[5] What this meant was that the FSC wanted to campaign on issues which immediately concerned school students, making no insistence on any 'correct' political line. Pitched against the FSC were those who argued that the school students' movement must have an explicit political analysis. This second strand crystallized into the Schools Action Union (SAU). A proposed umbrella organization, called 'Unison', was to be convened by the Manchester Union of Secondary School Students. Although one national meeting was called, Unison did not get off the ground, and in effect the two strands went their separate ways.

The Free Schools Campaign

FSC was a libertarian group in which adult anarchists played significant roles. It focused on the concerns expressed by its school student members – dictatorial headteachers, bullying teachers, boring lessons, petty rules, outdated attitudes to long hair, and so on. FSC produced four issues of a duplicated magazine, the *Free Schools Educational Supplement*. Although distinctly messy in appearance, it had the advantage over rival publications in covering questions of real interest to youngsters in a language they could understand.

By June 1969 FSC had groups in 16 towns and cities, from Belfast and Bristol to Aberdeen and Tunbridge Wells. The Swansea, Bristol and Reading unions already mentioned were affiliated to the FSC. It is hard to discover what these 19 groups achieved in terms of recruiting significant numbers of members or mounting significant campaigns. They certainly provided ready copy for local newspapers: headlines like 'Anarchy in City Schools: Pupils are Demanding Share of Control' or 'School Leaflet Campaign by Reds' were typical reactions to attempts by FSC activists to give out leaflets at school gates.

FSC lasted less than a year. Like the Libertarian Teachers' Association it eschewed organization on principle. Those FSC groups which were at all organized became Schools Action Union branches.

Schools Action Union

The SAU enjoyed a longer life and, on occasion, proved capable of some degree of organization. Between 1969 and 1973 SAU produced 13 issues of its newspaper, *Vanguard* (although eight of these were produced in 1969 alone), and four issues of the London region's broadsheet, *Rebel*. It published five issues of a theoretical journal, *Democratic Schools*; held four national conferences; maintained a national committee structure; printed and distributed hundreds of thousands of leaflets; organized several strikes and demonstrations;

raised petitions; took part in broadcasts, gave interviews to the media and issued press statements; supported many local single-issue campaigns; and provided a focal point for the school students' movement.

SAU's first venture was a demonstration held in London in March 1969. Some 500 school students handed in a petition to the Department of Education and Science calling for freedom of speech and assembly, co-educational comprehensive schools for all, the outlawing of corporal punishment, student and staff control of schools, more pay for teachers and the abolition of school uniforms. In June of that year 70 SAU supporters invaded Dulwich College in South London. Taking advantage of this prominent public school's 'open day', the incursors demanded an end to schools for the privileged. In the summer holiday of 1969 SAU organized a 'Living School' at London's Conway Hall.

In September 1969 SAU obtained office space in North Gower Street, London, which also housed Agitprop – a radical information agency – and the newly founded *Gay News*. Sharing the building with Agitprop meant that members of SAU came into contact with political activists from a variety of left-wing groupings. This helped them to shape their political attitudes. Older people in the building also helped them to learn concrete skills – for example, the preparation of artwork for litho printing.

Autumn 1969 was a period of teachers' strikes, and NUT officials were alarmed to find school students, carrying the SAU banner, joining their demonstrations. On 19 December SAU attempted its first London-wide school strike, intended to demand the right to organize and to oppose the victimization of SAU members which had been taking place. The strike was not successful, and nor was a demonstration called in July 1970. On each occasion less than 100 school students participated and it wasn't until 1972 that SAU again attempted large-scale actions. Energy was put, instead, into local group activity.

By the summer of 1969 there were some 27 SAU branches around the country (in addition to the 19 FSC groups). In numerical terms this was probably the peak of SAU's success. By September 1969 the number of local groups had fallen to 15, and the figure stayed at that level for the next two years. Local groups came and went like shooting stars, their existence usually depending on the enthusiasm of one or two activists, the group collapsing when they ran out of energy, left school, or were ordered to stop by their parents.

In its first years the membership of SAU comprised largely the children of middle-class parents – typically fifth- and sixth-formers in grammar schools and public schools. In 1971 and 1972, however, the membership became more working-class and based on comprehensive schools. This reflected a developing politics which more and more saw the problem of schooling as a class problem, rather than a predicament shared by all school students. Politically, the SAU embraced anarchists, Labour Party Young Socialists, the Young Communist League, supporters of the Militant Group, International Socialists and members of the International Marxist Group. Most SAU members, however, belonged to no group: their political views were forming as they joined SAU. It was clear, however, that as 1969 progressed the SAU centre was gravitating towards revolutionary Maoist politics.

By 1970 the various political factions in the SAU had begun to fall out and the subsequent history of SAU was marred by internal disputes at the centre, accompanied by dwindling contact with the grass roots. In the summer of 1970 the North Gower Street office was lost – a severe organizational blow. (One of SAU's problems was its constantly changing address which made it hard for would-be members to catch up with it.) *Rebel* was not produced after the summer of 1970, and *Vanguard* appeared only twice in 1970, twice in 1971 and once – the final issue – in May 1972. It stopped reporting what was happening at a local level; articles became longer, more didactic and less readable. In 1971 all 'Trotskyists, Anarchists, liberals and reformists' were expelled from SAU. The organization took an 'independent revolutionary line' which was, in fact, the very narrow Maoist line of the core of activists at the centre.

In April 1971 membership nation-wide was down to 338 (having topped 1,000 at an earlier stage). Six months later it was down to 87, but the leadership considered this to be an improvement since 'the calibre of cadres was higher'.[6]

Such real campaigning that SAU undertook was largely the work of local groups which carried on regardless of what was happening at the centre. SAU enjoyed a brief revival in May 1972 when it called a series of school students' strikes which culminated on 17 May with an estimated 10,000 taking part in a remarkable, if chaotic, march through the streets of London, pursued all the way by harassed police. However, enthusiasm died away as quickly as it had arisen, and another strike called for 26 May met with little support. This was in effect the death knell of SAU, although it continued for more than a year, pursuing ideological purity to the last.[7]

It would be easy to dismiss the SAU on the grounds that it never achieved mass support amongst school students. Even at its peak it did not involve more than a tiny percentage of school students. This can only partly be explained by the claim that most school students probably never heard of the SAU (or FSC). In fact the media gave considerable coverage to the 'pupil power' movement (as it was constantly dubbed) especially in 1969 and 1972. While it must have been the case that some potential supporters never found out how to get in touch with an SAU group, the experience was that even when a leaflet was thrust into their hands, the great majority expressed little interest.

SAU activists saw this as a problem of 'apathy', and they saw this as an indictment of our schooling system: bourgeois indoctrination was clearly having its effect, since most school students seemed to be complacent, listless, acquiescent. The SAU was probably right to reject the common psycho-biological explanation for this – 'teenagers just aren't interested in politics'. The evidence from France, where the CALs got a massive response from school students, suggested otherwise, as has more recent experience in Southern Africa and the Caribbean where teenagers have played leading roles in extremely courageous campaigns.[8]

Frank Musgrove has called the counter culture a 'revolt of the unoppressed'[9] and we must consider the straightforward possibility that the SAU did not evoke a mass response because most school students were happy with their lot. There is evidence to suggest that significant numbers of young people found the experience of school unpleasant or worse. Edward Blishen's book, *The School That I'd Like*, catalogued the complaints made by entrants to a competition run by the *Observer* in December 1967. And, once established, the SAU began to receive unsolicited mail which revealed varying degrees of anguish.[10]

SAU battled continually against great organizational handicaps. While a disproportionate amount of time was spent on political and theoretical debate, the grassroots work fell on the shoulders of school students who, in the main, lacked organizational skills and resources. Producing a leaflet can be a major task if you don't know how to do it and have no access to equipment. During the year that SAU had the North Gower Street office it offered duplicating facilities to local groups. College students and political groups also helped in this way, and in finding suitable venues for meetings. Money was a constant worry. Without the money for a bus fare or a few postage stamps – let alone the train fare to travel to a national conference – it must have been difficult to keep even a minimal organization together.

Communications within groups, between groups, and from groups to the centre, were always a problem for SAU, but the biggest source of disorganization was the high turnover of activists. Someone who became involved while in the fourth year at secondary school might leave school at the end of that year (the school leaving age was not raised until 1972); with little contact between school year-groups (unless the activist had a brother or sister in another year) there would often be no one to take over the SAU reins. Pressure of exam work was another reason why fifth- and sixth-formers often had to drop out of SAU activities.

However, it was from the fifth- and sixth-forms that the majority of SAU activists came; and the fact that fifth- and sixth-forms contain a greater proportion of middle-class youngsters (most 'early leavers' being working-class) than the school population as a whole helped to account for the strong middle-class representation in the SAU.

Activists faced constant hostility – from parents, teachers, police and the media. It seems that parental hostility was strongest in working-class families, except in those cases where parents themselves were active left-wingers. Many SAU activists were forced to give up their involvement by their parents; others could carry on only clandestinely.

Teachers responded unpredictably. If there was a liberal, willing-to-listen response in some schools, others reacted fiercely to SAU activities. Punishments, including physical assault, could be expected. Some headteachers considered student activism to be an insidious threat and went to great lengths to stamp it out. National attention was focused on Kingsdale Comprehensive School in South London when the headteacher suspended five pupils who had taken part in the SAU strike in December 1969. They were subsequently expelled by the governors. Other headteachers took a more covert approach; for example, secretly sabotaging the career or academic prospects of SAU activists.[11] Although there was nothing illegal in SAU activity *per se*, police were sometimes involved in discouraging school student activists[12] although policy seemed to vary from area to area.

What marked out the generation of schools activists in this period from earlier and later generations was that they dared to stand up and speak out. Indeed 'dare to struggle' was a slogan adopted by the SAU. But, of course, protest and dissent were fashionable at that time, which perhaps made it a little easier.

Considering all these conditions, the *TES*'s description of the SAU as a 'chaotic inchoate union of factions' was perhaps unfair.[13] It is possible to argue that the SAU did remarkably well considering the concrete problems it faced.

The ideas of the SAU

Although dubbed a 'pupil power' movement by the press, the SAU never sought this title. Its struggle, it explained,[14] was not against teachers, but against the system: 'We are not a pupil power organisation. We stand for working class power. If schools are to serve the people they must be controlled by the people.'[15] The SAU constantly demonstrated that it was not 'anti-teacher' by supporting teachers' pay claims. The fullest statement of the SAU view was set out in a long document, *Revolution in the Schools*, which was presented at its national conference in October 1970. For the SAU the school students' movement was part of the general struggle of the working class for socialism:

> What we seek to change in schools are not just some minor superficialities . . . we seek a socialist education that teaches self-reliance and respect, cooperation, production only for need and the liberation of man's desire for freedom, democratic practice, justice and the fulfilment of potential.[16]

Rather more specifically, a statement called *Schools' Charter* began:

> The fundamental aim of the Schools Action Union is to challenge the absolute power of the head and to place the day-to-day control of the school under the democratic authority of the school council.[17]

In this respect (and in others) the SAU's policy was similar to that of the Rank & File teachers' group; but there was never an active relationship between SAU and Rank & File.

In June 1970 the SAU put forward a five-point 'Civil Rights Programme' which called for the right to publish uncensored magazines; the right to organize meetings on school premises; the right to join school students' unions, and the right to strike; a committee of staff and students to decide punishments; and control of schools to be in the hands of an elected council of staff and students.[18] Several of these points were also being proposed at that time by the National Council for Civil Liberties.

It became a central tenet of the SAU that the reforms of schooling which it called for could not be achieved in any other than a socialist society. It saw the oppression of school students in school as a facet of capitalism, just as there were those who regarded the oppression of women, and racism, in the same light. But in fact many of the SAU's demands were for straightforward reforms which found widespread support amongst liberals: the abolition of physical

punishment, reform of examinations, the abolition of school uniform, and so on. These are nothing more than policies which had
been advocated by progressive educationists for many years. Even
the SAU's most radical demand – democratic control of schools –
became a *fait accompli* in Finland in 1971 (where corporal punishment
had been abolished in 1914 and there has never been school
uniform).[19]

Other SAU demands – for freedom of speech, freedom of publication (of students' magazines and leaflets) and freedom to meet and
organize collectively – did perhaps seem threatening to the established power structure. The fear, even perhaps in the heart of
progressive teachers, was possibly that things would 'get out of
control'. And yet, if leading SAU activists had had their way, things
would have been very far from getting out of control. After the
initial flirtation with libertarianism, the SAU's organization was
rigidly controlled. As it was expressed in *Rebel*:

> In order not to play into the hands of reactionary school author-
> ities, the revolutionaries must make their own position clear – that
> we do not stand for 'free for all' individual freedom, with no sense
> of responsibility, but we fight for a politically conscious move-
> ment with a high sense of discipline realised through democratic
> discussion and decision.[20]

Whether SAU would have been *capable* of controlling the mass
movement it sought to mobilize is, however, another question.

Like Rank & File, the SAU did not challenge fundamental assumptions about education. It continued to see education as a matter
of teachers giving lessons in classrooms, and did not address the
curriculum issue at all. This was a paradox because arguably the
greatest success of the SAU, and the other organizations of the
school students' movement, was the learning it provided for the
youngsters who were actually involved in it.

Adult manipulation?

A view often expressed by the local and national press, and by some
teachers, was that the school students' movement was created by
adult agitators bent on stirring up trouble in schools.[21] As a description of the school students' movement in general, this is quite
inadequate. It starts from the premiss that there was no 'real'
dissatisfaction among school students about their schooling; and it
goes on to assume that even if there was, school students would not
want to do anything about it unless they were stirred up by adult

agitators. These presumptions are not sustainable.[22] Adults were involved, but not many, and rarely in a manipulative way. There were some teachers who saw it as a legitimate part of their role to give help to school student activists. But in the main, the adult involvement comprised university and college students who were able to offer duplicating facilities and meeting spaces for school students' groups, and who were young enough to feel that the interests of school students were also *their* interests.

Assessing the SAU

The SAU (and the FSC) created a model of how school students can be an active collective force seeking to influence the shape of their education. Although not entirely without precedent, it was, in 1969, innovative in four respects. First, it added a new dimension to the emphasis of that time on children as *actors* in the world. Writers like John Holt and Herbert Kohl in America, and Keith Paton and Douglas Holly in Britain, were pointing out that orthodox practice treated children as material to be worked upon by teachers. Schools like Summerhill and Prestolee had pioneered a more active role for students. But these (with the possible exception of Summerhill) tended to stress the active role of students in their relationship to the subject matter of learning. The school students' movement went beyond this, raising broader questions of power and control and the organization of the schooling process.

Second, the SAU proposed collective action. From its earliest days, the SAU formed the view that polite representations to headteachers were unlikely to achieve its aims. It believed it would have to fight for its demands, and that only an organized union could defend activists from victimization.

This contrasts with Summerhill, or Prestolee, or the classrooms envisaged by Holt or Kohl, where an enlightened teacher enabled the student to take an active role. No role was envisioned for a school students' union.

The third innovation of the SAU was its overt association of the reform of schooling with politics. School pupils had gone on strike before[23] but had never generalized their specific demands in a political analysis. The SAU didn't just campaign for school students' everyday rights: it supported teachers' pay claims, took an active part in (for example) the 1969 Haringey 'banding' dispute and in the campaign in Barnet for comprehensive schooling. The SAU wanted to go beyond tackling single issues like corporal punishment. It saw campaigns on single issues like uniform or the right of boys to wear long hair 'as levers to mobilize school students and not, as the NUS sees them, the limits of our struggle'.[24] The political generalization was, as I suggested in Chapter 1, a feature of the radicals of this period. The SAU went from making specific complaints about schools to formulating a general critique of schooling and then a general critique of society.

Fourth, the SAU expressed its criticisms of schooling openly and defiantly and with a clear sense of entitlement to be doing so. It insisted on students' rights to make demands. No longer was it going to be a matter of progressive teachers inviting students to express their views: from now on, students were going to take the initiative and put their views forward – whether or not they were invited to.

The 1960s and early 1970s was a period of liberalization in many schools. Although few schools would want to be thought of as 'giving in' to SAU demands, the campaigns of the school students' movement gave added weight to the existing tendency to relax uniform requirements, phase out the cane, allow greater scope for student expression and establish school councils. Most notably, schools tended to make life more comfortable for sixth-formers. It was, indeed, in teachers' interests to do so, since more sixth-formers meant more scale posts for teachers. Schools had to compete increasingly for the over-16s with Colleges of Further Education which were considered to be more willing to treat these young people as adults. However, the liberalization of regimes for sixth-formers was not all good news for the school students' movement: if the sixth-formers were the ones most capable of organization and leadership, the granting of concessions to them could undermine their keenness to campaign for the interests of younger students.

It is very difficult to assess what impact the school students' movement had on schooling. It is not easy to pinpoint tangible reforms and say with confidence that these came about because of the pressures brought to bear by the SAU. It is just as likely that both the reforms and the school students' movement were a product of the same *Zeitgeist*.

Those who do not share the Maoist politics of the SAU's central core will find it hard to resist the reflection that that political orientation hindered, to say the least, the building of a mass organization which could campaign effectively for the interests of school students. To put these interests first, and politics second, was the reason for the formation of the second major school students' union, the National Union of School Students.

National Union of School Students

In March 1969 the National Union of Students (NUS), conscious of the growing school students' movement, launched a recruiting drive among sixth-formers. Although proposing to represent their interests to school authorities, the NUS's chief 'selling point' was the offer of cheap travel facilities to a targeted market of 25,000 sixth-formers. The NUS's Sixth-Form Campaign became, however, an embarrassment to the union and by the end of 1969 it was quietly dropped.

In 1972 the NUS again turned its attention to schools, agreeing to support the establishment of a National Union of School Students (NUSS). A number of school activists, by now disillusioned with the political direction of the SAU, were ready to take advantage of the opportunity. Holding its first conference in May 1972 – attended by some 200 school students – it adopted a series of policies which were amended later in the year into a 27-point programme. Many of these points were also policies of the SAU – for comprehensive, co-educational, schools, for democratic control of schools, against compulsory religion, for the abolition of physical punishment, for a school committee to handle disciplinary matters, for more pay for teachers, for the opening up of school facilities to the community, for the replacement of examinations, for a wage for students over 16, for freedom of speech and assembly and the right to produce uncensored literature; against uniforms; for freedom of movement during breaks and lunchtimes. But the NUSS added a number of further points to make its programme into a comprehensive package for the reform of schooling.

It was significant that the NUSS held its founding conference in the middle of the London school students' strikes of May 1972. The NUSS distanced itself from the SAU, hoping to project a more acceptable, 'moderate' image. It saw its aims as being achieved by a long-term process of pressure-group campaigning and by negotiation, rather than by militant action. It also distanced itself from the Rank & File teachers' group, fearing that too close an association would damn it in the eyes of the National Union of Teachers, with whom the NUSS were keen to establish cordial relations. In the event, however, the NUT steadfastly rejected the NUSS's overtures and never agreed to recognize the NUSS's existence. Communist Party and Labour Party left-wingers on the NUT executive were wholly in agreement with this stance.

Support from the NUS gave the NUSS organizational facilities which had been undreamt of by the SAU (and indeed most other radical groupings). As well as providing (rather humble) office facilities, the NUS paid a full-time salary to the NUSS president and provided printing and duplicating resources. Despite its considerable financial contribution, the NUS allowed the NUSS autonomy right through until 1979 when control of the NUSS fell into the hands of a combined Socialist Workers' Party[25] and International Marxist Group caucus, at which point the NUS decided to call a halt.

The NUSS's organizational resources allowed it to build up strong branches in some areas, and at one stage the union had a paper membership of around 15,000 – very much more than the SAU ever had. By the mid-1970s some teachers were able to countenance the idea of a school students' union without panic, and indeed in a few schools the headteacher acknowledged the NUSS as a legitimate negotiating body representing the interests of pupils. None the less, the overall climate remained one of hostility from parents, teachers, authorities and police. The problems which thwarted the development of the SAU were experienced by the NUSS in hardly less sharp form; the collapse of school branches when the prime movers left school; difficulty in finding venues for meetings; shortage of money for travel and local activities; parental opposition; and organizational inexperience. Internal political disputes were a bugbear for the NUSS, too, although until 1979 they were not as debilitating for the NUSS as they had been for the SAU.

It was not until 1978 that the NUSS launched a magazine. This was *Blot*, financed by a grant of £1,600 from the Gulbenkian Foundation. It had a circulation of some 10,000 copies. With a cheerful appearance and punchy style, which contrasted with the SAU's *Vanguard* and *Rebel*, it was received with outrage by some sections of the national press, particularly the third issue (1979) which mentioned masturbation.

Once the NUS withdrew its support, the NUSS quickly withered away, which demonstrates how important finance is for an organization of this type. And yet we might point to a discrepancy between, on the one hand, the financial problems of school students unions whose members sometimes 'couldn't raise the bus fare' and, on the other hand, the well-known increase in teenage spending power in the 1960s and 1970s. Maybe the school students who were interested in students' unions were not the ones who had money in their pockets; or maybe records and clothes (and the other big areas of the youth market) were a higher priority for youngsters than contributions to unions. Both student unions, and clothes and records, offer a sense of identity to young people, although of very different kinds. But clothes and records were socially approved while student unions were not, so the claims of each on teenage pockets were unequal.

Like other radical organizations which operated in the mid-1970s, the NUSS found that the social forces which gave rise to it, which we might summarize as the cultural upheaval of the 1960s, were dissipating even as it was founded. This is not to say that the reforms which the NUSS sought became any the less necessary, but that there was no longer a climate which encouraged talk of radical reform. The tide of social conservatism which has become so apparent in the 1980s was already coming in.

Other school students' groups

It would be an incomplete account of the school students' movement which recorded only the major national organizations. In addition to the FSC, SAU and NUSS, groupings of radical-minded students came together in schools and towns and cities all over the country. Very often their focus was the production of a magazine written by, and addressed to, school students.[26]

A good example of an independent school students' magazine was *Y-Front*, four issues of which appeared in London in 1972 and 1973. Anarchic in both form and content, it had humour and imagination which the more hard-edged political magazines lacked. Characteristically for the period, it made much use of *Beano* cartoons for graphics. *Y-Front* did not attempt to present its readers with any systematic analysis; taking a cheerful anti-authoritarian stance, its primary purpose was to entertain its readers. Like the other magazines, *Y-Front* did not last very long. They were produced because their creators enjoyed producing them (as evidenced by the heavy self-indulgence which was their hallmark). Once production became a chore, it was dropped. *Y-Front* printed 2,000 copies of its final two (litho-printed) issues, and had extensive contacts with similar ventures around the country. It published lists of other groups, recommended books and pamphlets, and carried news about free schools, making it clear that it was consciously part of a movement.

When children and young people protest about their conditions, they are protesting about conditions which are, for them, only temporary. Women will always be women, black people will always be black. But school students, like prisoners, are eventually 'let out', and although they may continue to sympathize emotionally and intellectually with those who remain behind, they no longer materially experience the oppression as they once did. Just when young people reach an age when they are able to articulate demands and start to organize to achieve them, they cease to be school students. It is for this reason that it is extremely difficult for school students to mount an impressive and sustained national campaign. Their only way out of this difficulty – to seek the active assistance of older people – calls forth immediate charges of 'adult manipulation'.

The absence of a sustained and impressive national campaign may too easily be taken to indicate that school students are satisfied with their lot. But it is more and more acknowledged in contemporary society that special-interest groups must somehow organize public campaigns if their needs are to be recognized – hence the multiplication of pressure groups of all sorts over the past 30 years. Few of these pressure groups suffer the kind of overt hostility and repression which the school students' movement experienced.

There is, therefore, I suggest, a particular moral onus on adults to examine critically how they treat children and young people. It was to take up this moral onus that the children's rights movement emerged in the 1960s. That movement, as well as some other radical groupings, is the subject matter of the next chapter.

CHAPTER 6

Children's rights and alternative education

This chapter will have something of a miscellaneous character about it, as I bring together the remaining radical groups: the children's rights movement; Schools Without Walls, the Campaign on Racism, IQ and the Class Society; the A.S. Neill Trust; Education Otherwise; radicals in fields allied to education; and deschooling. Finally I will look at the role of commercial publishing in this period.

Children's rights

> I'll tell you what I think. I think that since t'war they've played up this children job too much and t'children's taken advantage of it. I were brought up wi' t'boot and t'fist in my young days, but nowadays you can't touch 'em.[1]

There was a post-war current of liberalization in attitudes to children, exemplified notably by the writings of Benjamin Spock, whose influential *The Common Sense Book of Baby and Child Care* was first published in the USA in 1946. Spock's advice to parents was similar to that of A.S. Neill, although it took Spock to make Neill conscious of the significance of the child's earliest years.[2]

In the late 1960s this current swelled into a lobby for the rights of children. In 1967 the National Council for Civil Liberties (NCCL) published *The Rights of Children and Young Persons*, prepared by Nan Berger. The central propositions were that children were being denied human rights which are taken for granted by adults in our society, and that the place where these rights were most comprehensively denied was the school.

In 1970 and 1971 the NCCL published a series of six broadsheets under the heading *Children Have Rights*. The first of these was concerned with children in schools. It argued for modification of the *in loco parentis* concept, for the establishment of advisory school councils, for the abolition of corporal punishment, for the right of children to organize themselves in school unions, for uncensored magazines, against compulsory religion, for freedom of personal appearance and clothing, for freedom from discrimination, and for the right to a good education. These were, of course, similar to the demands made by the school students' unions; but the NCCL was arguing not for revolution but for reforms in the law. The publication of the six broadsheets culminated in an NCCL Conference on Children's Rights in October 1971.

A rather different approach came from the book *Children's Rights* published in 1971.[3] In this book Nan Berger quoted words ascribed to William Morris: 'Children have as much need for a revolution as the proletariat have'.[4] Although the book endorsed the law reform strategy of the NCCL, it was more concerned with the broader place of children in society. A central concern was the repression of children's sexuality: the psychological authority to whom all the contributors referred was Wilhelm Reich, and the practical ideal the supposed customs of the Trobriand islanders.[5]

The book was more than a plea for the rights of children: it was also a manifesto for an alternative revolutionary outlook, and in this sense it brought a new dimension to the radical movement. Instead of the Marxist view that class is at the root of social problems, it argued that sexual repression and patriarchy were a deeper source of evil:

> The sickness inducted into the child is that of our society: anti-sex, anti-life, the giving of greater importance to power and money than to love . . . The importance of the rights of children is that by recognising them we will break the chain of continuity.[6]

The question of child and teenage sexuality touches some of the rawest nerves in our social psychology. Any suggestion that young people have, or would like to have, an active sexuality, under conditions of their own choosing, seems to raise public hackles. And there was plenty to raise public hackles (and the salacious rage of Fleet Street) at this time: in 1971 both the editors of *Oz* and the publishers of *The Little Red Schoolbook* were on trial on charges of corrupting the morals of minors. And there was something of a furore in the same year over Dr Martin Cole's sex education film, *Growing Up*, which showed people masturbating.[7]

The contributors to the *Children's Rights* book, joined by John Holt and, by chance, one of the contributors to *Oz* issue no. 28, launched a new magazine called *Children's Rights* in December 1971. From the outset the magazine's purposes seemed unclear. Among several strands running through it was the sexual liberation theme:

> All the people involved in *Children's Rights*, book or magazine, will carry on the Freudian and Reichian formulation by stating that the integration of sexuality in the life of persons of any age is one of the major objects of our fight for the rights of children.[8]

Alongside this was an interest in deschooling and freeschooling. At the same time, there was an apparent attempt to win a readership among school students. And then again the third issue, which dealt with childbirth, seemed to be addressed primarily to parents and parents-to-be. In among this mixture was some anarchism with a hard edge. In the first issue a brief 'Children's Angry Brigade Communique' asserted:

> We are tired of being a repressed generation. Our generation is repressed by censorship laws, age regulations, schools (prisons?), and sadly our own parents. No longer shall we accept this repression. We are angry. The only hope for a future society lies in us . . . The reprinting of an uncensored 'Little Red School Book' for free distribution was our first act. We shall not limit ourselves to non-violent acts if the school situation persists . . . All sabotage is effective in hierarchical systems like schools – unscrew locks, smash tannoys, paint blackboards red, grind all the chalk to dust – you're angry – you know what to do.[9]

This upset several of the magazine's backers, but more was to come. In the fifth issue (May 1972), alongside articles by John Holt and Michael Duane attacking examinations and testing, and an account of the hidden curriculum by Ian Lister (shortly to become Professor of Education at York University) was 'Children's Bust Book Part 1', intended as a guide to young people on what to do if they got into trouble with the law. In among some fairly standard legal advice were comments like 'The first indication of an arrest is when a copper has got hold of you. What happens next depends upon your speed, strength and fighting spirit.'[10] This upset the magazine's backers even more. Holt resigned from the editorial advisory board; so did Neill, although it caused him anguish to do so.[11] The advisory board sacked editor Julian Hall; the name of the magazine was changed to *Kids*, and the format altered. However, the magazine, even though claiming a circulation of 10,000, still didn't find an identity and it ceased publication after the seventh issue in 1972.

The problem of *Children's Rights* was one shared by many radical educational publications: to whom should they address themselves? Those who believe that teachers are in a position to implement radical reforms can address themselves to teachers. And those who believe that children can win their liberation by their own action can address themselves to school students. But between these and the direct political lobbying of local and national government is a yawning chasm. In this chasm are all the people who deal with children (which means most people) whether as parents or in their working capacity. Radical books or magazines which sell 5,000 or even 10,000 copies clearly aren't reaching this great mass of people. Although the occasional book will achieve a mass circulation – Dr Spock's *Common Sense Book of Baby and Child Care* is an example – even those reach only a minority of the population.

Radicals had no clear answer to this problem. Putting their faith in the proverb 'from little acorns great oaks do grow', they published their ideas in a small way hoping that they would, somehow, 'catch on'. But not all little acorns grow into great oaks, and the radical movement could have done with clearer hypotheses about how public consciousness might be changed. *Children's Rights* was unique among radical education magazines in trying to address itself to the generality of people – but this was its downfall: in the jargon, it failed to 'locate its readership'. Looked at another way, it did not identify a 'power base' on which it could build.

The most extreme statement of the children's rights position came in John Holt's book, *Escape from Childhood*, in which he argued that children, however young, should have all the same rights and responsibilities as adults – to vote, to choose their place of domicile, to own property, to enter into contracts, to drive a car if they can pass the test. Whatever the merits of Holt's case, it cannot be said that it received wide acceptance, even among radicals.

Children's Rights Workshop

Out of the ashes of *Children's Rights* magazine, the Children's Rights Workshop (CRW) was established in London in February 1973. The workshop offered an advice and information service, handling the substantial quantity of mail which the magazine had engendered, and acted as a pressure group for legal and social change. CRW became one of the focal points for the freeschooling and deschooling movements in England. It also supported the growing number of parents who were thinking of educating their children at home (see page 84).

CRW's most successful project was its analysis of children's books. In August 1974 it published a statement together with a list of books which were recommended as 'useful, because in some way they escape from the narrow and distorted view of the world found in most children's books'. CRW was not, in fact, the first in this field. A Children's Books Study Group had been formed in London in Autumn 1971; with a feminist orientation, it developed into the Campaign to Impede Sex Stereotyping in the Young (CISSY). Their pamphlet, *CISSY Talks to Publishers*, published in 1974, generated a good deal of public debate.

CISSY's initiative, taken up by CRW, in proposing a thorough-going review of children's books was important because it was one of the few projects of the radical movement which gained momentum after 1976 and went on to make a significant nation-wide impact. The CRW children's books project eventually developed into a periodical, *The Children's Book Bulletin*, which reviewed new children's books and became influential – at least in progressive circles. It also helped to generate a useful literature on the matter.[12] In time this would lead to more and more schools and libraries reviewing their stocks of books, weeding out those most guilty of racism, sexism and other prejudices. Many publishers were also encouraged to take a more critical look at their lists.

The connection between this project, and the earlier conception of 'children's rights' was a little tenuous. It illustrates, perhaps, the difficulty of the *concept* of children's rights[13] which easily – if not unavoidably – becomes a matter of adults adjudging what is good for children and what is bad for them. There was a prima-facie conflict between the CRW's campaign against sexism and racism in children's books and the school students' campaign against censorship. This was not lost on the right-wing press, which held up the critical review of children's books to some fairly predictable ridicule.

In common with many other radical projects the CRW eventually foundered in a sea of too much work being attempted by too few people with inadequate resources. If the CRW had been launched in the golden years of GLC funding, ten years later, things might have turned out differently.

The pursuit of rights for children has continued, largely in the form of pressure group lobbying – by, for example, the Children's Legal Centre – for reform of the law. Although some progress has been made, much remains, in the view of those who champion the cause, to be done.[14]

School Without Walls

School Without Walls (SWW) described itself as follows:

> We are a small group of people (including teachers, architects, librarians, a film-maker etc. as well as parents) who have been meeting irregularly since 1967 to concentrate on our belief in 'education as a life-long process in which children and adults are inter-dependent'. In our 1969 Pulborough statement, we said that we 'no longer believe that the schooling system is the most appropriate way of educating children', and although this statement is now ripe for review, our basic position remains the same. Since 1970 we have attempted to provide a meeting point for new educational experiments, particularly those that go beyond the classroom and aim to draw on the untapped resources of the general environment, local people and facilities. Apart from the SWW Mobile Learning Bus which was much used by local community groups as well as schools, SWW provided a mobile exhibition for conferences, exhibitions, a register of experimental/alternative education projects and resources, and regular meetings which publicised these experiments and provided a forum for further discussion. [15]

SWW was initially established as a working party of the New Education Fellowship (or the World Education Fellowship, as it was renamed in 1965), the long-standing progressive education grouping which had published *New Era* since 1921. As we can see, SWW were examining the possibilities of 'deschooling' before Ivan Illich coined that phrase in 1971 and popularized the idea. As its name suggests, SWW wanted to promote learning outside educational institutions. Its 'Learning Bus', obtained in 1972, has been imitated in a number of areas. SWW also promoted learning exchanges which were an alternative favoured by deschoolers. It supported a project which examined how the press treated educational questions. [16] And in 1974 it produced a pack, *Learning Not Schooling*, which was a fairly comprehensive catalogue of the radical education movement in England, and provided lists of organizations, magazines, pamphlets, books, free schools, films and resources for learning.

SWW also submitted evidence to the Taylor Committee on the Government and Management of Schools, [17] a rare example of a radical grouping participating in such official consultations.

In 1976 SWW folded, for the usual reason: the people involved had too many other commitments and they could not find 'new blood' to take on the workload. Some members of SWW went on to establish the Corner House Bookshop in London's Covent Garden which specialized in radical education and continued the function of SWW (this closed in 1983).

Bootstrap Union

The most intriguing thing about the Bootstrap Union, which published the *Bootstrapper's Charter* in 1974, was its name. Its founder, Peter Norwood, said:

> The Bootstrap Union works to bring working class parents and teachers together in campaigns, using whatever means are needed to get something *done* about urban schools. Schools must be made to fit the children. They must be democratised to bring in parents, to respond to their wishes . . . Teachers and parents at the coal-face must take upon themselves the job of reform.[18]

The Bootstrap Union saw itself as becoming a working-class equivalent of the Confederation for the Advancement of State Education (CASE). Started by one man, it did not have the resources to bring itself to the attention of many people, and its supposition that working-class parents would want to be involved in a mass campaign for the radical reform of city schooling was never put to the test.

Campaign on Racism, IQ and the Class Society

The Campaign on Racism, IQ and the Class Society (CRIQCS) was established in 1974 to campaign on the specific issue of intelligence. There had been a long-running effort, since the 1950s, spearheaded by Brian Simon, to demolish the idea of intelligence as a fixed attribute.[19] It was to the credit of Simon and others that by the 1960s their campaign was bearing fruit, and doubts were growing in the minds of educational administrators and policy-makers about the validity of intelligence testing. But this success was only partial. Many teachers still believed in fixed intelligence; the majority of educational psychologists believed in and used IQ tests; many local authorities were reluctant to abolish secondary school selection based on 'intelligence' until forced to do so (by the 1976 Education Act); and belief in IQ remained potent in the public mind, as evidenced by the continuing popularity of books like Hans Eysenck's *Check Your Own IQ*.

A revival of academic support for the IQ concept in the late 1960s and early 1970s[20] coincided with an increase in violent racism on the streets of Britain. CRIQCS argued that this racism was underpinned by the 'scientific' notion of IQ which claimed to demonstrate the 'innate superiority' of white Anglo-Saxon peoples over almost everybody else, especially blacks and Irish. As if to prove the point, the first major conference held by CRIQCS, in London in March 1974, was invaded by a group of youthful National Front members who chanted 'long live the pure Anglo-Saxon race' before being ejected.

CRIQCS was also concerned to draw a link between the belief that blacks are 'genetically inferior' and the argument that working-class children do badly at school because of their low average innate ability – a view which had been given a thorough airing in the *Black Papers*.

The approach which CRIQCS took may be described as a public information campaign: it published a series of leaflets and argument sheets which succinctly covered the main issues. It also reprinted an (American) Progressive Labor Party pamphlet, *Racism, IQ and Class Society*, which dealt with the issue from historical and political as well as scientific angles.

This 'public information' approach taken by CRIQCS marks it out as rather different from the other radical groupings we have been considering. First, it was a single issue campaign (like STOPP). Rather than seeking to make general assertions about education, it concentrated on one question. Second, it was confident that on this question it could marshal the facts to substantiate its case. Third, it could make an appeal to the public (although it focused its attention on teachers and others in the education service) without requiring from them a prior commitment to, or at least inclination towards, radical politics. However, the tagging of 'Class Society' onto its title indicates that CRIQCS couldn't quite resist the radical propensity to widen and generalize. But the core of its case against IQ rested on scientific grounds; there was an implicit belief that a wide spectrum of people would accept firmly-based scientific evidence regardless of their political sympathies. Firmly-based scientific evidence was not, in general, available for most radical propositions about education.

In producing argument sheets and speakers' notes, CRIQCS clearly had a long-term programme in mind. This, too, differentiated it from much of the radical movement which, as I pointed out in Chapter 1, was characteristically in a hurry.

CRIQCS organized a series of demonstrations outside the venues where its chief adversaries – notably Hans Eysenck and Arthur Jensen – were due to speak.[21] Such demonstrations annoyed some academics – not to mention Fleet Street editors – who saw them as 'bully-boy' tactics which disrupted the process of legitimate scientific discourse. Defenders of CRIQCS replied by querying just how far this particular discourse was scientific and asking how far scientists may be permitted to detach themselves from the social consequences of their work.[22] In fact, CRIQCS shared the London premises of the British Society for Social Responsibility in Science which had the aim of raising just that question.

CRIQCS succeeded in putting the question of IQ high on the agenda for radical educationists. But its efforts to achieve a shift in public opinion ended when, after little more than a year of activity, it ceased to function.

The A.S. Neill Trust

The A.S. Neill Trust was founded in January 1974, defining its objectives as:

> To promote the freedom of children, irrespective of age, race, colour, creed or sex, to live as they choose, subject only to the right of others to similar freedom.
> To provide help and advice (legal or other), training, encouragement and finance to individuals, groups or organisations whose work and aims seek to foster freedom for children.
> To seek to persuade people in other countries to work towards these ends and to co-operate with them.
> To launch appeals for funds as and when necessary and to administer those funds through Trustees appointed for the purpose.[23]

Neill had died in September of the previous year, and it was to commemorate his work and ideas that the Trust was formed. Over the next few years the Trust held a number of conferences, published a newsletter, and sought to raise funds for disbursal to projects which shared the objectives of the Trust.[24] However, the Trust was not successful in raising substantial sums of money. There was a tension within the Trust, characterized by one participant as being between 'hippies' and 'straights'.[25] The 'hippies' tended to preponderate, but they were not good at fund-raising.

In the five or six years from 1974, the A.S. Neill Trust and its newsletter served mainly as a means of communication between people involved in freeschooling and similar projects. It is unlikely, however, that this was the chief interest of the Trust's 400 or so members who (judging by the variety of well-known names on the membership list) would have seen the implications of Neill's life and work extending far beyond freeschooling.

Education Otherwise

In the early 1970s opponents of compulsory schooling began to take note of section 36 of the 1944 Education Act:

> It shall be the duty of the parent of every child of compulsory school age to cause him to receive efficient full-time education suitable to his age, ability, and aptitude, either by regular attendance at school or otherwise.

Education Otherwise was inaugurated in 1977 to give guidance and support to parents who wished to choose this 'otherwise' option. There had been a number of celebrated cases where parents had had to fight for their right to educate their children out of school.[26] Some LEAs held that it was impossible for an 'efficient full-time' education to be provided outside school and, taking advantage of ambiguities in the 1944 Act, prosecuted parents who wanted to educate their children at home. Education Otherwise aimed to establish the right of parents to choose the 'otherwise' option and to shift the burden of proof from parents having to demonstrate that the education they were providing was 'efficient' to LEA's having to demonstrate that it was not.

By and large, Education Otherwise has been successful in this respect; through the late 1970s and 1980s its membership expanded as more and more families opted out of formal schooling. It should be noted that not all members do so for reasons which might be described as 'progressive' or 'radical'.

Clearly the number of parents who are in a position to exercise this option is limited, and Education Otherwise has been criticized, possibly unfairly,[27] for being an organization of middle-class people who have withdrawn their energies from the campaign to improve schooling. On the other hand, I have noted the general absence of parents *qua* parents from the radical movement; Education Otherwise is a rare example of a parents' initiative (although we should not overlook the Confederation for the Advancement of State Education and the National Confederation of Parent-Teacher Associations) and it is perhaps unreasonable to expect parents *qua* parents to become involved in campaigns without having the immediate interests of their own children in the forefront of their minds.

Radicals in allied fields

It is important to recognize that radicals in education received moral, if not material, support from other radicals working in related fields.

I listed these in Chapter 1 but some of them merit a little more attention here.

In the field of psychology there was a good deal of radical activity. As Liam Hudson has noted, in the mid-1960s

> confidence in the scientific approach to psychology began to falter. A shift in the *Zeitgeist* had occurred, unmistakable if unexplained. What had seemed self-evidently true suddenly became a matter of personal opinion, even of prejudice.[28]

Red Rat (subtitled 'The Journal of Abnormal Pychologists') was a magazine devoted to radical critiques of psychology. It first appeared in Summer 1970 and five more issues were published over the next four years. 'Red Rat' was, of course, a satirical reference to the way orthodox psychologists do experiments with rats and then attempt to draw conclusions about human behaviour.

More immediately relevant to education was *Humpty Dumpty*, which was also produced by radical psychologists, but with an emphasis on educational psychology. Several of its editors worked as educational psychologists. *Humpty Dumpty* declared that its aim was 'to question the role of the expert in psychology'.[29] Although there was a fashionable distrust of experts at the time,[30] many of the articles in *Humpty Dumpty* were in fact written by people with very specialized knowledge. Supporters of *Humpty Dumpty* saw the Association of Educational Psychologists (AEP) as a bastion of reactionary psychology and attempted to make radical interventions at AEP conferences.

Seven issues of *Humpty Dumpty*, selling an average of 2,000 copies each, were published between 1972 and 1975; among the issues of particular concern to educational radicals which they discussed were special schooling, behaviour scales, ESN assessment, IQ testing and behaviour modification.

The radical psychologists' critique was most fully spelled out in a much praised pamphlet, *Rat, Myth and Magic*, published in 1972. It stands as a clear manifesto of the positions taken at that time.[31] Other journals which touched on questions of interest to radicals in education included *Self and Society* (published by the Association of Humanistic Psychology), and the journals of the Mental Patients Union, *Cope-Man* and *Heavy Daze*.

It is a paradox that of all the radical critiques which burgeoned in the 1960s and 1970s, that of psychology was one of the most coherent, and yet made, in the long run, little apparent impact on the mainstream. For example, behaviourism, which radicals argued against in great detail, remained highly influential in educational psychology. Nor, it must be said, did much of the radical psychology make a deep impression on radical teachers: we have seen, for example, how *Socialist Teacher*, for all its attempts to elaborate a socialist theory, paid scant attention to questions of psychology.

In the world of psychology, the establishment seemed peculiarly impervious to the critiques mounted in the 1960s and 1970s, and radical psychologists usually had to go outside the orthodox canons of their subject to make their critiques. This was not the case in sociology, which has had a reputation of fostering radicalism, and radical sociologists were able to claim a certain academic legitimacy for their work which was not available in psychology. It was not always necessary, therefore, for radical sociologists to adopt a fiercely oppositional stand, and much of the radical work can be found in mainstream journals and books. In the field of sociology, we have already discussed *Hard Cheese*, and acknowledgement must also be made of two journals, *Cultural Studies* (published by the Centre for Contemporary Cultural Studies) and *Schooling and Culture* (published by the Cultural Studies Department of the Cockpit Theatre), both of which sustained a high level of theoretical debate, especially on the question of culture which has become, for radicals, a key concept in their analysis of education. Mention might also be made of *Screen Education*, whose advocacy of the value of the study of film and television has for many years had a markedly radical edge.

Radical Philosophy, launched by the Radical Philosophy Group in 1972, aimed to publish 'philosophical work contributing to the development of radical theory, and to the exposure of the social and political assumptions in orthodox philosophy'.[32] Although the journal has maintained a high standard of debate over the years (and is one of the few radical journals to have survived and thrived), it did not make an important contribution to the growing interest among educational radicals in philosophical questions, for two reasons. First, it continued the tradition of mainstream British philosophy in that it gave little attention to the philosophy of education: the journal has very rarely carried articles about education as it is thought of by people interested in schooling. Second, it did not share the aspiration of other radical journals (such as *Humpty Dumpty*) which tried to break down the barrier between 'expert' and 'layperson'. Most articles were written in a language which few non-specialist philosophers could understand. Sadly, it probably contributed to the myth, all too easily accepted by teachers, that philosophy is a secret garden best left to philosophers. Perhaps significantly, the two most valuable contributions to radical educational philosophy were made by students: David Adelstein's *The Wisdom and Wit of R.S. Peters* and Keith Paton's *The Great Brain Robbery*.

In contrast, the work of historians in this period made a big impact on radicals in education. The most notable contribution was made by the History Workshop, which held stimulating conferences (the 1972 conference on 'Children in History: Children's Liberation' at Ruskin College, Oxford, was particularly well received), published pamphlets – such as Dave Marson's *Children's Strikes in 1911* – and published *History Workshop Journal*. I have noted elsewhere in this study other contributions made by historians to radical thinking on education.

Many radical groups were committed to 'demystifying' their subject and to breaking down the barriers of expertise and professionalism. *Needle*, for example, was

> a radical magazine for *all* those working in, or concerned with, the hospital services. It appears about once every six weeks and we expect sales of this latest edition to reach 2,000. It is produced by an editorial collective of technicians, nurses, doctors and medical students who meet every Thursday . . . ANYONE, from ward maid to consultant is welcome to come along to these meetings.[33]

Yet in reality there was an ambivalence about this. Some people clearly knew a great deal more about their subject than most other people, and it was not clear what might be gained from hiding their light under a bushel. The ambivalence was also seen in a tension between the awareness that theory was important, often requiring abstract and necessarily difficult work, and a feeling that theory excluded ordinary people from important debates.

Deschooling

Although the notion of deschooling was widely discussed by radicals in the 1970s, it is not my intention to discuss it at length here. The literature on deschooling[34] certainly added to radicals' armoury of criticism of schooling. But, as was widely acknowledged, it did not offer any practical strategy for its implementation. There were a number of educational alternatives which considered themselves to be pioneering deschooling: some free schools thought they were doing so (although Ivan Illich felt that they weren't); School Without Walls had already embarked upon a number of 'deschooling' projects before the term had been coined; and a number of small-scale attempts were made to establish the 'learning exchanges' advocated by Illich, for example at Centerprise in East London. The small,

London-based, Deschooling Society attempted to establish a learning network with the aim of 'broadening the social experience of
children by putting them in touch with interesting and interested
adults', and to act as a centre for general information on alternatives
in education.[35]

Possibly the idea of deschooling prompted the formation of a
variety of non-institutional, community-based, learning programmes which appeared in the 1970s.[36] One example was World
Education Berkshire, which had a bus which travelled to schools to
promote world development education.[37]

But the effect of such small-scale initiatives could well have been
to complement, and even improve, schooling rather than contribute
towards its abolition – the aim of the deschoolers. It might also be
suggested that deschooling took away some of the impetus from the
radical movement for the reform of schooling. Illich's clarion call
during a speaking tour of Britain in October 1971 split the libertarian
movement down the middle, leaving libertarians arguing among
themselves rather than pursuing a united campaign for school
reform. However, the fact was that of all the radical groupings and
journals we have surveyed, most flatly rejected deschooling. As we
have seen, School Without Walls was already working along deschooling lines, but it did not take up the abolition of schools as an
objective. *Libertarian Education* was lukewarm about deschooling.
The A.S. Neill Trust, Children's Rights Workshop, Education
Otherwise, the Resources Programme for Change in Education, and
some free schools, can all be said to have taken on some of the
thinking of the deschoolers but none of them unambiguously advocated the abolition of schools.

At one level, the flaw in the deschooling argument was a political
one. It offered no suggestions as to how the task of abolishing
schools might be undertaken, and it appealed to no discernible
interest group in society. (But, in terms of the political currents of
the 1980s, deschooling might be an attractive idea for the 'libertarian'
wing of the New Right.) The curiosity was that Illich's *Deschooling
Society*, a turgid, repetitive, almost unreadable little tract, was one of
the best-selling education books of this era: by 1985 it had sold over
80,000 copies in the UK. Clearly it had *an* appeal, but it is hard to
categorize those to whom it appealed.

Commercial publishing

The sheer number of radical books about education which appeared
in this period was remarkable. Few of these books were published by

houses which considered themselves to be radical publishers; in fact the radical publishers of that time were quite slow to appreciate the possibilities of the education market.

The late 1960s and early 1970s saw the emergence of a considerable number of radical bookshops and bookstalls around the country which provided a ready outlet for these books. And, for those who were not close to such a bookseller, they could be obtained by mail order from agencies such as Agitprop and Rising Free.

The radical books published in this period are listed in the bibliography. No less than 18 of them were published by Penguin. There were two editorially separate Penguin imprints: Pelican (with the familiar blue covers), and Penguin Education. The Pelican imprint published books like Leila Berg's *Risinghill: Death of a Comprehensive* and the early John Holt books. Penguin Education was started as a separate division of Penguin in the early 1960s. The editor who was probably most responsible for the radical flavour of the lists was Martin Lightfoot, who joined the division in 1966. The most creative sector of Penguin Education was the school books: the Voices and Connexions series were highly regarded by teachers. But the general reader would have been more aware of the Penguin Education Specials which came out from 1968 onwards. The majority of these were British editions of American books: they had the commercial advantage of being cheap to publish (the school books required a large investment). This was the main avenue by which British readers got to know of Jonathan Kozol, George Dennison, Neil Postman and Charles Weingartner, Herbert Kohl, Everett Reimer and Paolo Freire. The sales figures indicated that there was considerable interest in these writers.

But the Penguin Education titles brought forth a sharp reaction from right-wing critics. Conservative MP Angus Maude (a contributor to the *Black Papers*) wrote in 1970:

I hope I am not alone in being thoroughly alarmed by the editorial policies of Penguin Books in the field of education . . . What is horrifying is that such a large and influential sector of educational publishing should have become a propaganda vehicle for the partisan views not of its authors but of its editors.

These lamentably influential censors clearly do not believe that there can be any alternative viewpoint to the one – 'progressive', egalitarian, permissive, anti-academic, and occasionally straight Marxist – which they themselves so glibly and consistently propound. This kind of blinkered partiality has not, surely, anything in common with the ideals that once inspired

Penguin and made it an important and respected institution.[38]

Oxford philosopher Anthony Flew was also much exercised by the output of Penguin Education.[39] Lightfoot pointed out that Allen Lane had founded Penguin as a left-wing publishing house:[40] indeed, during the 1930s Penguin editorial policy had amounted to a sustained critique of the Conservative governments of that decade. The implication in Maude's and Flew's attacks on Penguin, that there is something illegitimate about publishing radical books, was puzzling to those who believed that freedom of speech and publication was an entrenched right in the United Kingdom.

In 1974, following the takeover of Penguin by the Pearson Longman empire, Penguin management made an abrupt decision to close down the Education division. Charges were made that Pearson Longman was a right-wing corporation and that the closure of Penguin Education was politically motivated. Penguin management asserted that the decision had been taken on purely commercial grounds. The 42 staff made redundant disputed this. It is to be hoped that the truth about this episode will one day be uncovered: in the meantime, suspicions linger on.

Although Penguin continued to publish education titles after 1974, commissioning of new books by radical writers dwindled virtually to zero, as did the reprinting of American titles which had been such an exciting feature of Penguin Education. No doubt this contributed to the loss of impetus which the radical movement was experiencing by 1974. The right-wing critics were surely correct when they observed the influential role of Penguin Education, and they may well have felt a quiet satisfaction when this role was snuffed out.

Individuals

It may have been noticed that in the last few chapters I have rarely named the individuals involved in the various groups. I decided not to do so for a number of reasons, not least of which was that it would be invidious to mention some people and not mention others. But, of course, the key roles played in each group by particular individuals ought to be recognized.

I do want, however, to refer to a few people who played particularly significant roles. There has been a line of radical headteachers in the post-war period – from Alex Bloom and E.F. O'Neill through Michael Duane, R.F. Mackenzie and Tim McMullen, to Philip Toogood, many of whom got into trouble by trying to reform specific schools.[41] More than any others, perhaps, they laid their heads on the line (if the pun may be forgiven) for the radical cause, and in most cases suffered for it. The contribution of these individuals to British education has been important, but they have not been rewarded by public acclaim or seats in the House of Lords.

But pride of place must surely go to A.S. Neill. In any account of education in the twentieth century, he must be afforded a prominent position. Because at several points in this book I take issue with Neill, I would like here to record my enormous admiration for him. But I find myself agreeing with Bruno Bettelheim that, while Neill was an intuitive genius with children, when it came to explaining his methods in writing 'he is often woefully inadequate and naive'.[42] I do not think Neill should be elevated to 'guru' status, and I hope it does nothing to detract from the greatness of his life's work to disagree with some of the things he wrote.

CHAPTER 7

Free schools

The history of alternative schools is a long one. There have been several significant traditions: the enterprises of the great innovators – Froebel, Pestalozzi, Montessori, Isaacs, for example: the European libertarian tradition – Robin, Tolstoy, Faure, Ferrer,[1] the German movements,[2] and, most familiar to us in Britain, the independent progressive schools.[3] There is another British tradition which has not been so well chronicled. While the independent progressive schools were fee-paying, residential, rural and served a middle-class clientele, there have also been radical schools intended for the children of ordinary working people. Robert Owen's school at New Lanark is well known; less is known about Barbara Bodichon's Portman Hall venture in the 1850s,[4] the Liverpool Communist School and the International Modern School in the years before 1914.[5] In the inter-war years the Burston School was a *cause célèbre* for radicals, but it was essentially an anachronism, rather than an exemplar of a continuing tradition.[6]

In the main the energies of reformers within the working-class movement had gone into striving for state provision of a full schooling for all. Voices which asked whether such provision would necessarily serve working-class interests were muted.[7] It was not until the 1960s that schooling for all, up to the age of 16, looked likely to be fully achieved. There was some irony in the fact that this was the decade when a new wave of criticism emerged which asserted that state schooling was thwarting, if not deliberately denying, working-class educational aspirations.

There was a growing belief in the 1960s that the mantle of progressivism had been taken over from the independent schools by the maintained sector.[8] State schools were thought to be capable of accommodating any desirable innovation.[9] Freeschoolers rejected both of these propositions and started planning independent schools which would be radical and serve working-class children.

Origins of free schools

'Free universities' have from time to time been set up – most notably by the syndicalists in Paris in the early 1900s.[10] The idea was taken up in the United States by radical students in the 1960s, and spread to Britain. A venture along these lines began in London in 1966, called the London Free School. It aimed to set up counter-cultural educational opportunities for people in the Notting Hill area of London. It hoped to break down the distinction between teacher and student; it saw the 'Free School as an agency of community education and action through attempts to tackle real community problems'.[11] The project hardly got off the ground, and did not really involve children. Its most notable outcome was the establishment of a weekly newspaper, *IT (International Times)*, widely read by hippies in the late 1960s.

The first free school for children was established in the United States in 1962, but it took a long time for the idea to cross the Atlantic. A Free University in Bristol in 1968 (accompanying a student sit-in at the University) gave rise to a number of summer holiday play projects which were known as the Bristol Free Schools. They entertained up to 200 children a day for several weeks.[12] They did not lead, however, to any provision for children during term-time. A Birmingham Free University did lead to the establishment in 1972 of St Paul's Community School in Balsall Heath, but the first free school proper to be established in Britain was the Scotland Road Free School which opened in Liverpool in 1971.[13]

There are three senses in which schools have been called 'free' schools: free in the sense that they do not charge fees; free from the constraints laid down by church, state or other authority; and free in the sense of adopting a philosophy of maximum individual freedom for the children. The original use of this latter sense is usually attributed to Kristen Kold who set up his school in Denmark in 1852.[14]

The free schools of the 1970s were free in all the three senses. But what counted as a free school, and what didn't, was a matter of dispute. The Children's Rights Workshop suggested 'at the risk of general disapproval' the following criteria:

a) these schools are small, have a flexible non-hierarchical structure, and are housed in non-specialist premises; they cater for a

Table 1 Free schools in Britain[1]

	Opened	Closed	Number of children at peak	Ages of children	Premises	Registered with DES as an independent school?
[2]Kirkdale School, Lewisham, London SE26	1965	Still open	60	3–12	Suburban villa	Yes
Scotland Road Free School, Liverpool 5	1971	1974	94	10–16	Youth Club, then Church Hall, then disused primary school	Yes
[2]Durdham Park School, Redland, Bristol 6	1971	1978		5–16	Suburban villa with spacious grounds	
South Villas Comprehensive, became Freightliners Free School, Camden, London NW1	1972	1976	22	6–15	Basement of private house, then disused goods yards	Yes
[3]Parkfield Street, Moss Side, Manchester	1972	1973	10	10–16	Dilapidated house	?
Manchester Free School, various Manchester locations	1973	1979?	36		Various	Yes
[4]St Paul's Community School, also called Balsall Heath Community School, Birmingham 12	1972	Still open	35	11–16	Community centre	Yes
White Lion Free School, Islington, London N1	1972	Still open	50	3–16	Ex-hostel for homeless	Yes (until 1982)
Brighton Free School	1972	1973	16	5–15	Hired rooms, then Church Hall	Yes

School	Founded	Closed	Pupils	Premises	Registered
Leeds Free School, various Leeds locations	1973	1982?	40	Disused chapel, private houses	No
Barrowfield Community School, Glasgow 40	1973	1978	24		Scottish Office
[5]Bermondsey Lamp Post, Bermondsey, London SE16	1973	1977	20	Rented room in Christian mission	Yes
[6]The New School, also known as The Buxmoor Centre, later called Sundance Free School	1973	1976?			No
Vauxhall Free School	1973	1974	20	Dilapidated shop	No
Delta Free and Community School, Southampton	1974	1978	8	Rented terraced house	Yes
[5]North Kensington Community School, London W11	1975	1978	10	Adventure playground hut, rented rooms, dilapidated house, space in community centre, hut	No
Bronte Free School, Liverpool 3	1976	1980	14	Small workshop	Yes

Notes: 1. It is by no means certain that this list is complete or accurate. (Criteria for inclusion: offering full-time provision for five or more children, and surviving for more than one school term.) The Children's Rights Workshop tried to keep a register of free schools, and when it closed the task was taken over by White Lion Street Free School. Since the onus was on new schools to notify themselves to these registrars, we cannot know if any did not do so. While some free schools attracted publicity, others were almost secretive (for example Meadowside School in Lancaster, which closed after one term). Sutton Park School in Dublin (1957–72), run by Ruarc Gahan, might be included in this list. (Details in *Libertarian Education*, no 11.)

2. Kirkdale and Durdham Park are included for the sake of completeness, although both were fee-paying.

3. Parkfield Street Free School is described in David Head, *Free Way to Learning*.

4. St Paul's Community School was a 'free school' only in its first years. It subsequently developed away from the free school model.

5. Bermondsey Lamp Post and North Kensington Community School ceased to be free schools when they were taken over by the ILEA as truancy centres, in 1977 and 1978 respectively.

6. I have not been able to discover any information about the New School/Sundance Free School.

small number of children – never more than 100 – and practise a
high ratio of adults to children; b) these schools have a child-
centred approach to learning and child-care and encourage maximum access to choice in the learning process; c) these schools are
urban and serve inner-city populations; d) these schools have been
set up as clear alternatives to the state controlled education
system.[15]

To this list we can add further characteristics of free schools in the
1970s. They were mostly independent schools, set up on small-scale
local initiatives. Most were committed to democratic control involving parents, children and staff. All stressed openness in a number of
senses – they were non-selective in their admissions, open to parents
at all times, offered their resources to the local community, and
tended to open longer hours and more often (including weekends
and vacations) than conventional schools. They were open, too, in
the sense of avoiding closed meetings and not keeping secret files.
Few of the free schools made lessons compulsory, and all were
committed to non-coercive arrangements. They tended to stress
informality and equality between staff, children and parents. In
many cases they cut across orthodox age ranges. And they avoided
division of labour, with children as well as staff involved in school-
keeping, maintenance, cooking, cleaning, administration, and so
on.

Much of the inspiration for these schools came from A.S. Neill's
Summerhill and, to a lesser extent, John Aitkenhead's Kilquahanity,
and Monkton Wyld in Dorset. But, as we shall see, they were very
different from these fee-paying rural boarding schools. Although by
this time Neill was feeling very old, and was not able to give much
active support, he did write to the *Guardian* hailing the opening of
Scotland Road Free School:

> For 50 years I have regretted that, because of finance, I could take
> middle-class pupils only. It is a joy to read that John Ord [co-
> founder of Scotland Road] has taken freedom to the children of the
> poor . . . I wish John all the success in the world but advise him to
> throw away that fag in his mouth and take to a pipe.[16]

It has been said that many free schools were established in the
1970s.[17] Many towns and cities did have groups who planned to set
up a free school. Sometimes they would get something going, with a
handful of children, but typically the venture would founder within
a few weeks. In fact only 14 or 15 free schools can be said to have been
properly established in Britain (see Table 1; the criteria for inclusion

are schools which offered full-time provision for five or more children and lasted for longer than one school term).

The contrast with America is marked. There, by 1967, there were 30 free schools. Fifty more were established in 1967 and 1968, 60–80 more in 1969, and in 1970 over 150 further free schools opened.[18] The boom peaked in the early 1970s.[19]

A distinction may be made, although it is not absolutely clear-cut, between free schools and other alternative education projects which sprung up in the 1970s. These belong to a tradition of their own (Homer Lane's Little Commonwealth, the Farmhouse Schools, Finchden Manor, Hawkspur and Barns, Otto Shaw's Red Hill and Howard Case's Epping House) which has specialized in providing for children designated as 'problems' – persistent truants, 'disruptive pupils', 'maladjusted children' and other categories judged to be better served away from the normal school. Just as the free schools broke with the rural boarding tradition and set up in inner cities, so did these other new alternatives. Many of them were barely distinguishable from free schools. Often staffed by people who were sympathetic to free schools, they would even be called 'free schools' by the children who attended them. Some of these projects were funded by local authority Social Services Departments; others by LEA Schools Psychological Services; yet others from Intermediate Treatment funds. Some were set up or adopted by LEAs and designated 'special units'. Some were voluntary bodies raising their funds from charities.

Some excellent accounts of such alternative education projects have been published[20] and the phenomenon of 'special units' has been studied by the DES.[21] I have excluded these projects from my study because they considered themselves to be working 'within the system' whereas free schools saw themselves as outside, if not against, 'the system': staff in these alternative education projects usually received Burnham salaries whereas staff in free schools often received no salary at all or at best received very much less than Burnham rates.

Having said that, the distinction is not a watertight one. Two of the free schools listed in Table 1 – Freightliners and North Kensington Community School – received funding from the ILEA as truancy projects, and a third – Bermondsey Lamp Post – eventually did so. The first two of these originated in adventure playgrounds where play-leaders who found themselves with a group of truants hanging around during school hours resolved to lay on alternative provision for them. In the sense that they targeted a specific group of youngsters from the start, they were not typical of free schools.

More common was a group of adults with radical ideas who went to look for children with whom their ideas could be put into practice.

The practical problems of free schools

The extent of the interest in free schools may be gauged from the fact that a booklet written by Alison Truefitt and published by White Lion Street Free School, *How to Set Up a Free School*, sold some 6,000 copies. Why were free schools so much talked about yet so rarely established? And why did those that did get started often close down quite quickly? The answer lies largely in the practical difficulties: resources, finding support, obtaining premises, the hostility of LEAs, problems of planning and the burdens on the people involved.

Few planners of free schools ever got beyond the first hurdle – finance. The obvious sources - jumble sales, donations from well-wishers, even the life savings of members of the planning group – did not begin to meet basic costs. Grant-giving bodies, such as charitable trusts, were reluctant to commit scarce resources to schemes which were only at the planning stage. For many groups the problem remained unsolved.

Light is thrown on the free school movement by their approach to the money problem. In America 80 per cent of free schools charged fees,[22] but in Britain this was unthinkable. We have here an example of the paramountcy of principle which I discussed in Chapter 1. Fees would have restricted access to families who had money and would think of spending it on schooling. English radicals, identifying themselves closely with the working-class movement,[23] were interested only in 'the children of the poor', as Neill had put it. Even the compromise made by most American free schools (and by Kirkdale, Durdham Park and Monkton Wyld in England) of charging fees on a sliding scale, so that poor families needed to pay very little, was generally rejected. Better, it seemed, to have no free school at all than one which compromised on a basic principle.

In fact a free school which was well established, well run, and administered by people with public relations skills *could* raise money in Britain. There were moments in the history of White Lion Street Free School when it had so much money that special meetings were needed to work out how to spend it. But in this respect White Lion was quite exceptional.

Free schools which did get started found it relatively easy to obtain resources in kind. Local firms would happily donate materials (quantities of paint in discontinued colours explained the bizarre colour schemes in several free schools). People were always ready to donate books, and LEAs, reluctant to help in other ways, seemed glad to part with unwanted furniture. Creative use of scrap materials gave a sound conservationist edge to free school projects.

Just as difficult as raising money was finding premises. Table 1 shows the kind of premises those free schools managed to find. Scotland Road led a nomadic existence from YMCA to Church Hall to the disused primary school which was eventually made available by the City Council. The commonest solution was to find a private house scheduled for demolition. Such premises were likely to be dilapidated and often unsuitable. A building that felt like a home (rather than an institution) had its advantages, helping to cultivate the kind of family atmosphere which free schools sought. But the snags were serious: the lack of any room big enough for large-scale activities like meetings, dinners, drama, games; the dominating presence of the staircase; inappropriate plumbing; fire and safety hazards; the lack of space for specialist activities like science. For those free schools lucky enough to find any premises at all, such problems conspired to make their work all the more difficult.[24]

The lack of substantial public support for free school projects can be traced to the fact that no appreciable class, power group or interest group was attracted to free schooling – in other words, free schools lacked a power base.[25] This, perhaps, was where the free school movement's lack of strategy was most keenly felt. In the words of Samuel Bowles and Herbert Gintis, the free school movement 'has presented its ideals as universal; it has remained puzzled by its lack of acceptance by other social groupings – among which oppressed minorities and the traditional working class are only the most obvious'.[26] People who wanted to start free schools, or support them, are hard to classify. In the view of the founder of one free school, they were just 'people who didn't fit in'.[27] Although I have located free schools within the radical movement, ironically they lacked the support of any significant grouping even within that small movement.[28] Freeschoolers spurned their most likely constituency – 'trendy' middle-class people who might have been hippies five years earlier. But they were not welcomed by the labour movement. Trade unions were wholly uninterested in free schools; so were the political parties, the churches and ethnic organizations.

The most tangible support for free schools came from the mass media. There was a great deal of coverage of free schools (Scotland Road especially) in the press and on television, much of it, perhaps surprisingly, favourable. Even the *Daily Mail* praised Scotland Road. Support did come, too, from progressive academics.

However, neither of these sources of moral support was sufficient to help free schools over the practical hurdles they faced.

Curiously, a 1979 survey by the Institute of Community Studies of attitudes to schooling in the London Borough of Hackney found that 20 per cent of respondents would have liked a free school for their child had there been one available in their locality.[29] This suggests the possibility that had LEAs offered parents a variety of educational alternatives for their children, in the way that the city of Toronto does,[30] they might have been agreeably surprised by the take-up. Notwithstanding the efforts of pressure groups like the Campaign For State Supported Alternative Schools,[31] no British LEA rose to this challenge. If indeed there was a pool of latent support for freeschooling among parents at large, the free school movement did not succeed in tapping it.

Most free schools experienced frostiness, if not hostility, from their LEA:

> The day prior to opening we had been to see the CEO [Chief Education Officer] and his deputy in response to their request to do so. The discussion proved of greater use to them than us since it involved going over many of those all too familiar objections to free schools as well as some necessary clarification of the limits of the 1944 Education Act . . . Within a week both these gentlemen had called to see the school for themselves and we await with interest their verdict and subsequent moves. In spite of this not too promising first encounter with officialdom we remain hopeful that in the long run some sort of rapport might develop which will, no doubt, be hastened by our demonstrating our capacity to survive and prosper.[32]

Some LEAs took the view that free schools were not a serious attempt to provide education for children and insisted that children attending them were absent from school. The parents of these children could therefore be prosecuted for failing to ensure their child's education in accordance with the law.[33] An example was the case of Theresa Beer who joined Leeds Free School in April 1978, having truanted persistently from her previous school. The Leeds LEA attempted to prosecute her parents and Leeds Free School mounted an energetic campaign in their defence.

Within the LEA, it is the job of the inspectorate to form a judgement as to whether a child is receiving an adequate education. In practice, then, the free schools' relationship with their LEA hinged upon the kind of understanding they were able to reach with their local inspector. Inspectors ranged from the implacably hostile to the sympathetic – it was 'the luck of the draw'.

Most free schools opted for the legal status of being independent schools[34] although they made problems for themselves if they did not do this until after they had opened, which was often the case. The school has to register with the Department of Education and Science, which automatically grants provisional registration. This is followed by a visit from Her Majesty's Inspectorate (HMI), which must satisfy itself that certain minimal requirements[35] are met before registration proper is granted.

Once a free school was registered as an independent school the LEA needed no longer to concern itself. (But some free schools unwisely thought that they needed no longer to attempt to cultivate constructive working relationships with the LEA.) Responsibility for keeping an eye on the school now rested with HMI. As A.S. Neill discovered on a famous visitation,[36] HMI is capable of breadth of vision, and free schools often found inspectors more open-minded than their LEA counterparts. Scotland Road was inspected by HMI in June 1972, and registration proper was withheld only on the grounds that the premises were unsuitable. White Lion Street Free School came out unscathed from a full inspection in January 1974. Up until 1978 the DES could award independent schools the accolade 'recognized as efficient'. No free school ever sought this status (nor did Summerhill) and it is unlikely that they would have achieved it.

If LEAs did little to help free schools in their early days, some came gradually to help in limited ways, most notably in agreeing to pay for school dinners and to make various other resources available. But to achieve even this minimal level of co-operation required a degree of diplomacy and negotiating ability which did not come easily to every freeschooler. The founders of Delta Free School, for example, did not think to contact their LEA until the day before they opened. LEAs could hardly be blamed for a frosty attitude if free schools failed to take elementary steps to prepare the ground for their venture.

To get a free school established required a considerable degree of competence in planning, organization and negotiation. But some of the people who wanted to set up free schools came from a milieu which placed a fairly low valuation on competence, efficiency, planning and organization: such things were considered to be characteristic of an impersonal, uncaring, inflexible and bureaucratized system which was precisely what they wanted to get away from. Sometimes the attitude was that the LEA needed to be attacked, not negotiated with.

Having got a school started, the pressures on staff were heavy. Most free schools were reliant on one or two strong and competent people, a fact which somewhat belied the ideals of equality and power-sharing. Once these key people left, the schools were in danger of falling apart. Every freeschooler experienced exhaustion:

> it was shattering all the time. You never got time off. You couldn't divide your day between us and them – or even space between us and them. There was constant interaction, which is exhausting. It was a very close, very intense, and very exhausting process for everyone.[37]

Even resilient personalities (and not everyone who was attracted to work in a free school was resilient) soon experienced 'burnout'.[38] The few free schools which survived the departure of key staff nevertheless suffered from high staff turnover. Exhaustion and staff turnover meant that things that needed doing were often left undone – a common problem of free schools.

Free schools weren't able to pay their workers proper salaries (apart from the two which were funded as truancy centres). Indeed, very few of the free schools paid any salaries at all to their workers, who had to subsist on unemployment benefits or supplementary benefits. In general there was a marked discrepancy between the emphasis which free schools gave to the rights of children and the scant attention they gave to the rights of workers. Everyone who worked in a free school was willing to make sacrifices because of a commitment to the school's ideals, but there was an unwillingness to ask what are the limits to the sacrifices adults can be expected to make for the benefit of children. Free school staff worked long hours under poor conditions, constantly struggling against the destructiveness and sometimes hostility of children. It is not certain that this was good for the children, let alone the workers. In passing, we might offer the hypothesis that the willingness of free school staff to work under such conditions made them unacceptable as role models to the children attending the schools: in the words of several White Lion children, they were 'mugs'.

There are two further comments to make on free school staff. First, despite the fact that free schools were adamant that they did not require formal qualifications of their staff, the majority of people who worked in free schools were university graduates and/or trained teachers. Second, despite the fact that free schools would appear to owe more to the anarchist tradition than anything else, very few of the people who set up free schools were anarchists. It is, in fact, very hard to find a political label which describes the assortment of people who worked in free schools: perhaps 'libertarian socialist' would describe a number of them, although in general their preference for 'prefigurative' politics, as against 'organizational' or 'strategic' politics (see page 156) would make such labels inappropriate.

If the practical difficulties of free schools help to explain why so few free schools were established in Britain, they do not explain why free schools were so *late* in coming. The first free school in America opened in 1962, yet Britain's first free school did not open until 1971. It was as if what was needed was a trigger to set off a British free school movement; and Scotland Road acted as that trigger. But the delay in starting up free schools was to prove a handicap. By 1971 the spirit of the 1960s – the romanticism, radicalism, idealism, iconclasm, inventiveness – which gave rise to free schools was already fading. A 'new realism' (or perhaps a weary resignation) was taking over. 'Be realistic: demand the impossible' had been a slogan of the 1960s, but by the 1970s economic recession was biting deep into European social structures. The freeschoolers' dream, that 'a hundred flowers would bloom', with free schools opening in every town and village until they provided a nation-wide alternative to state schooling, remained just a dream.

The philosophy of free schools

So far I have defined free schools in terms of the organizational and administrative characteristics which they had in common. When we come to consider their educational philosophy, it gets more difficult. Free schools were much clearer about what they were against than what they were for. Their starting point was a critique of existing schools; the one thing they were certain of was that they weren't going to be like *them*.

One of the more positive statements of philosophy was made by Barrowfield Community School. Here is an extract from its *Progress Report*:

> The running of the school is based on three straightforward principles.
> The first is our belief that education is a natural process and is intrinsically interesting. We feel that the onus should be on the teachers to present it in such a way as to be interesting and directly relevent to each child's experience, interests and prospects. (Because of this we often work in much smaller groups than is normal in other schools.)

Each activity and course of study is in the last resort a matter of choice to each pupil and it is up to the teachers to find out each pupil's interests and develop both the interests and the skills needed for this development.

Secondly, responsibility for the pupils' general welfare, rather than strictly educational needs, is assumed by the school. This means that teaching at the school is much less of a nine to four profession. In fact, the times of activities range from 9.30 am until the early evening, although the teachers are frequently involved in school or school related community matters in the evenings, at weekends and during the holiday periods.

The third educational principle involves the school's relationship to the community and specifically to an inner-city deprived area such as Barrowfield.

Firstly the school's attitude towards responsibility involves the teachers in community affairs – usually in the organisation of activities that involve not only the school's pupils but other people in the area – perhaps older brothers, sisters, parents etc.

We feel that the child's education consists not only in the understanding of his environment and the problems of living in a deprived area but also in learning how to cope with them and beginning to solve them.

Community activities not only involve children in this but also, on another level, relieve enough of the pressures of living to make an educational process possible.

Hence while the school, through activities and educational experiences, opens up to its pupils a whole avenue of opportunities, which at the moment are not available (in any meaningful sense of the word) to residents of the area, it, at the same time, tries to make it apparent that the solution to the lack of resources, amenities and activities so often lies in action as a community and co-operation with people in the same situation.

We believe that if we can reach a situation where these three principles are followed successfully then the school will produce people who, on the one hand, can reach a level of self-fulfilment whilst living in a difficult environment and, on the other hand, have the confidence and knowledge to do something about those conditions.[39]

Note the characteristic appeal to 'natural', 'interests' and 'relevance'; the central place given to the community; and the absence of anything specific about what children will learn in the school, and how they will learn it. In contrast to some free schools, however,

Barrowfield clearly envisaged a role for the teacher.

Leeds Free School stated its position in this way:

Underlying all our ideas about a Free School is the concept that children are *not* objects whose only need is to be rationalised into society, nor should they be treated as such; rather they are all human beings, each with differing needs and abilities. Yet this tendency to reification is inherent in the nature of a State School, with its large classes, fixed syllabuses, compulsory attendance, etc., and even the best will in the world cannot overcome it.

In a school, however, which is run directly by the children, parents and teachers – where they themselves decide what is relevant; in a school which is small, has a high adult to child ratio, a school which is, in its essence, decentralised to allow maximum flexibility for each person's needs, this tendency may be overcome. Such is the nature of a free school. It is a school where the children tailor *their* education to *their* own needs.

We firmly believe that only in such a school can each child's creativity and capabilities be developed to a maximum. In a State School there is so much 'wastage', so much talent ignored, so many 'products' (and in many cases this is the correct word to use) lacking in confidence and ability to stand on their own two feet. The adults coming out of a Free School, however, would, we hope, be confident, aware, and capable of building a better world.

The majority of Leeds children are victims rather than beneficiaries of the State education system (Leeds is the second worst borough in the country for expenditure on books per pupil). This system produces exceptionally high absentee rates in the secondary modern schools and a bored elite in the high schools suffering from a cramming of useless information bearing little relation to the problems of modern life.

A Free School in one of the communities of Leeds will provide a working practical alternative to the centralised system, an alternative that will allow the community to work with and for its children in a framework that is under community control. It is the organisational structure of a Free School that provides this framework.

What Is A Free School?

(a) *Self-government*

This means that the school is controlled and run by its members on an equal basis. Children, teaching staff and those who in general cater for the welfare of the children have an equal say, all decisions being taken at a General Assembly. This principle virtually abolishes the concept of 'pupils' and 'staff' as two separate entities, with separate aims and interests.

(b) *Lack of coercion*
This relates to the principle of self-government. However, it is possible under extenuating circumstances that the General Assembly will impose disciplinary measures on any person in the school who is constantly interfering with the freedom of others there.

(c) *Education as self-fulfilment*
It is fairly obvious that, in the type of school which we have outlined, there will be no rigid curriculum. The relationship of academic learning to practical activity (by which the children may learn a great deal, incidentally) will not be compulsory, but the idea, practice and feeling of genuine democracy will, we feel, encourage members of the school to participate in such meetings.

Attendance at lessons will not be compulsory, but attendance at the school is compulsory by law. This is really the only basic compulsion at a Free School.[40]

The emphasis here (in addition to the organizational proposals and the repeated criticisms of 'State Schools') is on old progressive tenets – the importance of the individual, child-centredness, tailoring education to individual needs, creativity, developing capabilities to the maximum. Like Barrowfield, Leeds Free School appeals to 'relevance' and 'needs' without defining them. And even more than Barrowfield, Leeds is highly unspecific when it comes to saying what children will actually *do* in the free school.

Scotland Road, in its preliminary announcement, was rather more outspoken:

Only those who are educated in the fullest sense of the word, imaginative and creative; mature and tolerant; aware and concerned can cope with the pressures and complexities of modern society. It is only those schools that consciously create an atmosphere of understanding and tolerance that best allow these qualities to develop.

The ultimate aim of the free school is to bring about a fragmentation of the state system into small, all age, personalised, democratic, locally controlled schools which can best serve the immediate needs of the area in which they are situated.

It is felt that the state system in contemplating change considers only innocuous reforms which do not question the total structure. We are obliged therefore to step outside the system in order to best demonstrate the feasibility and fulfilment of the free school idea. Having achieved this demonstration we are sure that society will enforce the adoption of the free school idea by the state system.[41]

There is not much sign in these statements (or in any of the other statements of British free schools) of a coherently worked-out philosophy of education. In particular, little thought seems to have been given to the general question of the *aims* of education, to the matter of content of learning, and to how children learn. If their preliminary pronouncements gave little indication of what free schools were actually going to do when they got started, descriptions of what happened once they were established showed that they were floundering – in some cases badly.[42] I will discuss three issues raised by the statements we have looked at: the relationship between the school and the community; the emphasis on organizational structures; and the place of free schools in society.

The free school and the community

The notion of 'community' was important to free schools. Often they incorporated the word into their names. It was the same in the United States, where most of the free schools called themselves community schools. Of course, at that time 'community' was a fashionable word. At its simplest, 'community' expressed a commitment to a specific locality; free schools limited their access to children living nearby. And they wanted to build organic links within the neighbourhood. Many free schools took on neighbourhood functions: Bermondsey Lamp Post ran a 'shop' which helped people with housing, legal and social problems; Freightliners ran a lunch club for old-age pensioners; Scotland Road ran, among other things, a community transport scheme; St Paul's was part of a much larger community project; White Lion ran an open youth club. But there may have been a rather romanticized image of community – in virtually every case, as it happened, the actual local community was in a state of chronic decline: the image of South Wales pit villages or Coronation Street bore little resemblance to the places where free schools set up.

There is little evidence that the high-minded principles enunciated by freeschoolers struck a chord with ordinary local people. This is not to say that free schools failed to recruit working-class children. Some were flooded with applications and had to turn children away.

But this represented a desire to get away from an unpleasant experience (local schools) rather than a widespread approval for libertarian ideas. The *intention* of free schools to set up in inner-city areas, to charge no fees, to admit all-comers and to invite democratic control was a distinctive break with the independent progressive tradition. But while the independent progressive schools offered an ethos which harmonized with that of their pupils and parents (why else would they pay the fees?) the free schools often found themselves defending their values in the face of scepticism from parents and children.

The free schools' appeal to community had another significance: there was an implicit distinction made between 'community interest', on the one hand, and the 'national interest' on the other. The latter was thought to be only 'ruling-class interest' in disguise, and so the appeal to 'community' could be interpreted as saying 'conventional schools serve *their* interests, but free schools will serve *our* interests'. [43]

There was an attempt, too, to get away from notions of 'community care' in which professionals attempt to solve a community's problems for it. [44] Free schools stressed community self-help and *action* by indigenous community groups themselves. This underlies the much stronger concept of community found in the opening paragraphs of Scotland Road's first statement:

> There will be set up in the Scotland Road–Vauxhall area of Liverpool, an alternative type of school to be known as Scotland Road Free School. The school will be a community school which will be totally involved in its environment . . . The nature of this involvement will be such that the school will be in the vanguard of social change in the area. By accepting this role, the school will not seek to impose its own values, but will have as its premise the total acceptance of the people and the area. . . [45]

We find here the idea of schooling-as-social-action, going decisively beyond a mere sensitivity of the school to its community [46] and giving the school an integral role in taking social (and political) action. In Europe the idea had been pioneered by the *doposcuola* movement in Italy from 1968. [47] It is an idea which has been widely discussed, both in its overtly political forms [48] and in 'community action' terms. [49]

Scotland Road's stance was more explicitly and aggressively political than any other free school. This gave it a driving sense of purpose which other free schools lacked. Most free schools (whatever the private intentions of their founders) couched their public statements in terms of an appeal to consensus: they tried to present themselves as a sensible response – which no reasonable person could ignore – to an appalling crisis in schooling. Those who didn't agree with them were perceived as doing so because they hadn't read the situation correctly, which in part explains the emphasis which freeschoolers placed on criticizing orthodox schooling.

Scotland Road's stand won it friends – and enemies. Clearly the idea of engaging children in social and political action (Scotland Road took children to join trade union picket lines, for example) is controversial. As long ago as 1943 Margaret Mead had warned, apropos of the view that it is possible by education to build a better world:

> When small children are sent out by overzealous schoolteachers to engage in active social reforms – believed necessary by their teachers – the whole point of view becomes not only ridiculous but dangerous to the children themselves.[50]

Scotland Road Free School attracted nationwide interest. The press and TV gave it an extraordinary amount of attention, and in the year 1973–4 it received some 2,000 visitors (creating an impossible burden).[51] Although notoriety brought some pleasures and benefits, it ultimately placed too much strain on the school, which closed in 1974. The bitterness and recrimination lasted for several years. But Scotland Road was outstanding among free schools in building real links with local people and helping to develop a collective sense of community purpose.

It is not possible to say that free schools successfully pioneered the practice of education as social action. They did not last long enough to demonstrate how it might work, nor to develop the theory.

Structures

While orthodox schools thought mainly in terms of curriculum and pedagogy, the free schools emphasized *structures*:

> The whole significance of the Free School lies in its pioneering of new structures, both in relation to the community, and in terms of 'curriculum', the role of teachers, parents and students, and of day-to-day organisation . . . words like structure and curriculum acquire a new meaning in our situation.[52]

Teachers usually think of 'structure' as referring to a well-planned, tightly organized, well-controlled classroom where everyone is clear what they are supposed to be doing. This is not what free schools had in mind. Rather, they used the term 'structure' to refer to the environment in which learning was to take place. Three insights were relevant: first the notion that children learn from the 'hidden curriculum';[53] second, that form, content and method are indivisible; and third, a sensitivity to the *conditions* of learning, drawn to popular attention by writers like John Holt, George Dennison, Jonathan Kozol and R.F. Mackenzie.

Free schools held that it was the whole environment from which children learn: thus they claimed that 'our school *is* its curriculum': 'the Free School curriculum is the total experience which it provides for its children'.[54] Hence the democratic structure of free schools was not just an organizational matter to involve parents and children in decision-making: from this structure children would learn things like the practice of democracy and the skills of public speaking. From the open and equal relationships between the staff, children would learn to model their own relationships likewise. By making no lessons compulsory, and by neither rewarding successful students nor penalizing unsuccessful ones, children would learn that their own valuation of their learning was the most important one.

This emphasis on the educative power of structures has a long pedigree in the libertarian tradition. As Michael Smith puts it: 'For the most part libertarians did not see their ideals as being taught formally through the curriculum but rather as being expressed through the way in which education was conducted.'[55] While we need not doubt that structures – in the sense in which freeschoolers referred to them – are an influential component of learning (although this is not universally recognized)[56] what may be questioned is whether it is *enough* to get the structures right and then just hope for the best. It is arguable that the free schools' concern to get their structures 'right' distracted them for giving attention to other questions which are equally important – such as curriculum or how and why children learn.

The place of free schools in society

We can detect in the freeschooling literature (especially in the statements made by free schools) an ambivalence about their relationship to society. On the one hand, there is a considerable amount of talk about *changing* society, particularly at a local level. On the other hand, there are signs of a desire to withdraw from any acknowledgement of obligation to society. In this respect they followed Neill, who 'never considered that education should acknowledge any duty to society to ensure that the new generations were trained for its purposes'.[57]

Despite their rhetoric, free schools tended to fall back on the formulation of the progressive tradition – that their contribution to society would be to bring up children to be 'emotionally free and well-balanced';[58] if only schools could produce healthy individuals, then society's problems would be solved. What was lacking from the free school literature was any attempt to grapple with the question of the relationship between schooling and the economic life of society. Even under capitalism, life must go on, and so people must work to produce the necessities which sustain our existence. Radicals find this proposition difficult to cope with, the more so in the face of statements of this kind: 'If the non-competitive ethos of progressive education is allowed to dominate our schools, we shall produce a generation unable to maintain our standards of living when opposed by fierce rivalry from overseas competitors'.[59] If the economic life of society – production – is presented as necessarily a matter of competition and rivalry, it is easy to see why radicals wanted nothing to do with it. But ironically, by discouraging their pupils from participating in the 'rat race' (as they saw it) free schools ran the risk of producing young people who were equipped to do nothing but the most menial jobs.

It would be unfair to suggest that freeschoolers were alone in not facing up to the question of the relationship between schooling and 'the world of work'. As G.D.H. Cole pointed out in 1952, this has long been a feature of the socialist movement:

> Technical education has always . . . attracted but little attention from the educational idealists . . . The cultural teachers who played a large part in framing Socialist educational policy were apt to look askance at any attempt to give schooling a vocational basis, because they thought of such attempts as meaning so much subtracted from 'culture' and alienated for the benefit of employers who, they felt, should see to the training of their workers in their own time.[60]

'Technical' or 'vocational' training is, however, only part of the problem I'm pointing to. There is the wider issue of bringing children to an understanding of the crucial role of production in sustaining human existence. Free schools backed away from tackling the question 'what is to be the relationship between school and economic production?'.[61] In doing so they deprived their schools of the chance of finding – and conveying to their children – a fundamental sense of real, concrete, purpose. And, lacking such a sense of purpose, they found – to their chagrin – that they were encountering very similar problems to teachers in conventional schools: in a nutshell, children who 'didn't want to know'.

The strategy of freeschooling

Many radicals were sceptical about freeschooling. In particular there were doubts about their part in a general strategy for change:

> If these alternatives are to contribute to a better social order, they must be part of a more general revolutionary movement – a movement which is not confined to schooling, but embraces all spheres of social life . . . What this requires is the development within the [free school] movement of an analysis which rejects any notion that schools are independent of society, an analysis which places schools concretely in their social and economic context.[62]

and

> the 'free school' movement is not so much an agency of social change as an example of social changes in society impinging on education from without. Assuming this is so for a moment, then it would appear that the 'free school' movement is a transitional, if not a transitory phenomenon, useful as a critique of the educational system as it is at present, but without the power to provide either long-term solutions or the institutional framework for their enactment.[63]

Such charges did not disconcert every freeschooler: some made no claim to be changing the world: they were merely getting on with what they wanted to do. They wanted to work with children, but they did not want to work in the restrictive and authoritarian environment of conventional schools. Some free schools – Freightliners, for example – had the modest and specific aim of helping a small group of youngsters keep out of trouble.

But some freeschoolers did consider themselves to be changing the world:

> The basic reason for starting a free school is that our western society, internally and in relation to the Third World, is grotesquely unjust and inhuman. This injustice is focused in the schools, among other places, since they are one of its chief instruments.[64]

or

> free schools *do* point the way to a totally new society. Free schools

reveal the authoritarian basis of society, and the way in which this is buttressed by fear and aggression. Free schools reveal that this basis for social and economic activity stunts and warps the development of humans, confining their horizons to the pillars that support the rat-race . . . If the principles upon which free schools are organised were carried on into the larger society, the growth of individuals and their opportunities for individual and communal development would be virtually unlimited.[65]

or

the school will be in the vanguard of social change in the area.[66]

The freeschoolers' strategy had two elements. First, they envisaged an ever-growing number of free schools taking more and more children away from the maintained sector until eventually conventional schools would become obsolete. And second, they wanted free schools to serve as models whose practice was so manifestly successful that other schools would be obliged to imitate them. This strategy is characteristic of 'alternative society' politics: change is not sought by legislation nor by revolution but by encouraging people to start creating in the here and now the forms which the envisioned society will ultimately adopt.[67] Other examples are the movement to replace the nuclear family by communal living, the replacement of 'junk food' diets by organic and 'natural' wholefoods, and the move towards the various alternative forms of medicine.

As we now know, the freeschoolers' ambitions were not realized. For a start, very few free schools were set up. Even those free schools which were established closed – with one or two exceptions – before they could make much impact on public consciousness. And it has to be said that those free schools which did survive were not demonstrably successful in the way they needed to be if society was to 'enforce the adoption of the free school idea by the state system'.

But these are not the only reasons for the failure of the free school movement. The freeschoolers' strategy lacked an understanding of why conventional schooling *is* as it is. It grossly overestimated the level of public dissatisfaction with orthodox schooling. The whole reason for the emergence of free schools was that freeschoolers disagreed profoundly with what most people considered 'good education'. If most people thought of good schooling in terms of quiet orderly classrooms where a teacher, firmly in charge, teaches a traditional curriculum; where the ultimate objective is passing exams; and where conventional values are passed on to the rising generation; if this was most people's idea of 'good practice', why should they be driven to imitate a free school which 'abolishes the concept of "pupils" and "staff" as two separate entities', where the traditional curriculum is rejected as 'irrelevant', where exam passes receive low priority, and where conventional values are flouted at every turn? And it is even less clear why the state should want to implement such reforms.

Free schools belong much more to the tradition of American radicalism than the English tradition. Almost without exception,[68] American radical writing about education assumed that the only thing stopping schools from changing was that people – teachers, administrators, parents – hadn't yet heard the good news which radicals were bringing:

> It is not because of any inner depravity that educators follow such a self-defeating system. It is quite literally because they do not know any feasible alternative. It is in the hope of letting teachers know that it is not *necessary* to follow the conventional pattern that I am going to present three different examples . . . of new ways.[69]

Thus even when John Holt rather belatedly noted that American society contains rich people and poor people and that it might be in the interests of the former to keep it that way,[70] he was still unable to see that this might have significant implications for a strategy of educational change.

Whatever arguments may be summoned by freeschoolers in support of their strategy, recent history has proved it to have been unsuccessful. But it does not follow from this that freeschooling is, from a radical point of view, a bad thing. If free schools have failed to change the face of British schooling (let alone British society) it is still possible to hold that they served a useful function. First, they did offer the taste of an alternative education to a small number of children. The charge that freeschooling diverted energy from the broader attempt to change schooling is barely sustainable, because the numbers of people involved were so small. Second, even if free schools were not demonstrably successful, they at least nourished the idea that it might be possible to go about schooling in a thoroughly different way. And third, they offered a potential 'laboratory' in which radicals could put their theories to the hard test of practice.

CHAPTER 8

Radical perspectives on learning

It would require nothing less than an encyclopaedia to catalogue and analyse all the radicals' ideas about education. The next two chapters have the modest aim of taking just one topic – learning – and examining critically some of the radical ideas which were current in the 1960s and 1970s. At the end of Chapter 9 I will suggest a framework for a radical theory of learning.

Some sections of the radical movement were not interested in the question of learning. For 'quantitists' (see page 40), learning was not problematic. Their emphasis was on teaching. When the study of education was split into separate disciplines,[1] learning came to be regarded as the province of psychologists.[2] With certain exceptions, radicals in the 1960s and 1970s were not greatly interested in psychology. But, as we shall see in this chapter, there is much to be said about learning which is not strictly psychology.

By learning I mean the acquisition of knowledge and abilities. These need not be narrowly defined as propositional knowledge, cognitive abilities and practical skills; there is also the whole domain of emotional learning and the development of awareness and sensibilities.

I take it as axiomatic that learning should be at the heart of the purpose of any school.[3] Although this may seem obvious, there is a view that learning is not as important as 'being'. In Pestalozzi's words: 'The reading, writing and arithmetic are not, after all, what they most need; it is all well and good for them to learn something, but the really important thing is for them to *be* something'.[4] I would reject this opposition between 'learning' and 'being', for the simple reason that one can learn and be at the same time.[5] A similar, and in my view equally mistaken, opposition often occurs in radical writing: 'The proper concern of a primary school is not education in a narrow sense, and still less preparation for later life, but the present lives of children'.[6] But you can, of course, be preparing for something *and* have a present life: they are not mutually exclusive.

Another confusion appears frequently in A.S. Neill's writing: 'I have no interest in how children learn'.[7] Or again: 'Parents are slow in realising how unimportant the learning side of schooling is. Children, like adults, learn what they want to learn'.[8] Or again: 'The notion that unless a child is learning something he is wasting his time is nothing less than a curse.'[9] But Neill is using 'learning' here in a very narrow sense – the sense he associated with traditional schooling: what Neill would call 'book learning'. He took his cue from the 'New Education' of the 1890s – 'education which aims not at learning, but at developing through self-activity'.[10] (Once again we have an unnecessary opposition, between 'learning' and 'developing'.) Neill was against the systematic organization of learning (this was at the centre of his disagreement with Maria Montessori);[11] he considered it an unwarranted interference in the life of the child. However, if we accept the broad definition of learning, the whole point of Summerhill was to create a particular type of environment in which children could *learn*, not bookish things, but 'the art of living' as Neill saw it.

I want now to consider a statement made by White Lion Street Free School. It is very representative of radical thinking. The ideas it embodies will form the subject matter of much of this chapter

> For us learning is defined as the development of the capacity for choice and control. It is an expansion of the learner's own scope for action. It is not something which can be taken out of the hands of the learner, but can only take place when the learner is taking the initiative himself. Defined in this way learning is not compatible with a situation in which the choice of subject matter and teaching method is made by the teacher.[12]

Epistemology

For a while in the 1970s radicals became interested in the theory of *knowledge*, and this is reflected in the White Lion statement. We are reminded of Kant's view that

> knowledge is not a collection of gifts received by our senses and stored in the mind as if it were a museum, but . . . it is very largely the result of our own mental activity; . . . we must most actively

engage ourselves in searching, comparing, unifying, generalising, if we wish to attain knowledge.[13]

or of Froebel when he remarked that 'the purpose of education is to bring more and more out of man rather than put more and more into him'.[14]

The radicals wanted us to stop 'reifying' knowledge, to stop thinking of it as a *thing*. As George Dennison put it: 'There is no such thing as knowledge *per se*, knowledge in a vacuum, but rather all knowledge is possessed and must be expressed by individuals.'[15] In the radical view, knowing must be seen as an act of creation:

> whatever we tell the learner, he will make something that is all his own out of it, and it will be different from what we held so dear and attempted to 'transmit'. He will build it into his own scheme of things, and relate it uniquely to what he already uniquely holds as experience. Thus he builds a world all his own, and what is really important is what he makes of what we tell him, not what we intended.[16]

Once we stop thinking of knowledge as a thing to be put into learners, like liquid to be poured into jugs, and start thinking of it as something created by each learner for himself or herself, the implications for schooling are far-reaching. If 'teachers started acting as if their students were meaning makers, almost everything about the schooling process would change', announced Postman and Weingartner.[17] Out would go pupils sitting attentively in rows; out would go fixed syllabuses and curricula, the traditional teaching role, separate subjects, examinations and tests, marking, grading and streaming and the rest. The outcome of education would now be necessarily unpredeterminable.[18]

At the same time, radicals lambasted the belief that knowledge can be ideologically 'neutral'.[19] And they pointed to the alienation of young people from the knowledge offered them in schools. In a striking passage, George Dennison observed:

> José could not believe that anything contained in books, or mentioned in classrooms, belonged by rights to himself, or even belonged to the world at large, as trees and lamposts belong quite simply to the world we live in. He believed, on the contrary, that things dealt with in school belonged somehow to school, or were administered by some far-reaching bureaucratic arm. There had been no indication that he could share in them, but rather that he would be measured against them and found wanting.[20]

The radical project, then, was 'to re-establish the status of learning itself as a part of the person rather than an alienated activity which goes on, frequently against the will of the learner',[21] which reminds us of Jean Piaget's famous dictum 'the child must be the agent of his own learning'.

My caveat about all this is that, in reacting against the rigid objectification of knowledge, there is a danger of slipping into a view of knowledge as a purely individual creation. What each one of us 'knows' can not be simply a matter of individual choice. What makes human society is a set of *shared* understandings and *shared* meanings. Language is a good example. And education is surely concerned with such shared meanings. It seems obvious that the 'expansion of the learner's own scope for action', to use White Lion's phrase, is largely dependent on developing an understanding of the *shared* world which makes up human society. One's scope for action, and one's capacity for choice and control, will be increased as one's knowledge increases,[22] but only if one's knowledge is true – if, for example, it accords with the facts. Knowledge, or rather belief, which does not accord with the facts does *not* increase our scope for action: a person who 'knows' that you draw unemployment benefit from the RSPCA is in for disillusionment.

It was Paolo Freire who suggested a way forward:

> One cannot conceive of objectivity without subjectivity. Neither can exist without the other, nor can they be dichotomized. The separation of objectivity from subjectivity, the denial of the latter when analysing reality or acting upon it, is objectivism. On the other hand, the denial of objectivity in analysis or action, resulting in a subjectivism which leads to solipsistic positions, denies action itself by denying objective reality. Neither objectivism nor subjectivism, nor yet psychologism is propounded here, but rather subjectivity and objectivity in constant dialectical relationship.[23]

A radical theory of learning needs a theory of knowledge which avoids two extremes: one is knowledge seen as a 'thing' which must somehow be pumped into passive learners; the other, knowledge seen as a purely individual creation.

Initiative

I turn now to the third sentence of the White Lion statement: Learning 'is not something which can be taken out of the hands of the learner, but can only take place when the learner is taking the initiative himself.' The truth of this was questioned by a Conservative opponent of freeschooling who remarked that during his national service he had been made to learn many things he didn't want to know – the initiative was entirely out of his hands. The possible response that such learning would not have developed his capacity for choice and control seems to me to be difficult to substantiate. However uninterested he may have been at the time to learn, say, how to use a rifle, it is arguable that his enforced learning would enable him to choose later in life, if he wished, to use a rifle – a choice which someone who had not learned how to use a rifle would not be able to make.

In point of fact, the experiments of behaviourists have shown that learning can take place when the learner is taking no initiative. Indeed, we have a colloquial expression – 'learning the hard way' – to describe things we learn without taking any initiative to learn them. (Thus 'Vera learned the hard way that dogs can bite'.)[24]

There is a weak sense in which all learning requires the initiative of the learner, in that the learner's mental faculties do have to be minimally engaged. I sometimes have the radio on, but am only half listening to it; and I sometimes learn things this way. Yet I am not 'taking the initiative' in any meaningful sense in this situation. Dr Johnson's opinion that 'what is learnt without inclination is soon forgotten'[25] may sometimes be true. But sometimes it is not: when I learned from the background radio that John Lennon had been shot in New York, I didn't soon forget it.

It may be possible to defend the White Lion statement by drawing a distinction between the accidental learning of discrete bits of information (dogs bite, John Lennon is dead) which can be learned without taking any initiative, and much more complex learning tasks (such as learning French, or how to play the piano) which may require much greater efforts on the part of the learner. But I suggest that the only truth we can wring out of the White Lion sentence as it stands is the unremarkable one that children may not learn very much in boring lessons.

The White Lion statement goes on: 'Defined in this way, learning is not compatible with a situation in which the choice of subject matter and teaching method is made by the teacher.' If we remove the qualification 'defined in this way', the proposition is clearly false. If it were true, no one would ever learn anything in traditional classrooms. But there are many people who will vouch that they *did* learn something in such classrooms. Even if we do not remove the qualification, it is far from clear that the White Lion proposition is true.

Teaching and learning

Enshrined in libertarian educational thought is a sentiment which might be summed up in the motto 'learning good, teaching bad'. I am not sure where this sentiment originated. Rousseau gave Emile's teacher a central place. Godwin criticized teachers but did not seek to diminish their role. Cobbett, however, had this to say about the schoolteacher in his day:

> He is their [the pupils'] overlooker; he is a spy upon them; his authority is maintained by his absolute power of punishment; the parents commit them to that power; to be taught is to be held in restraint; and as the sparks fly upwards, the teaching and restraint will not be divided in the estimation of the boy. [26]

Libertarians, as Michael Smith has pointed out, are always uncomfortable when talking about teachers. [27] This was well illustrated by the decision in 1972 to change the name of the magazine *Libertarian Teacher* to *Libertarian Education*. A.S. Neill was notoriously – in fact, comically – uninterested in whether his staff could teach or not. For libertarians in the 1960s and 1970s the slogan was 'put learning back into the hands of the learner' which I take to be the kernel of the White Lion statement we are discussing. At its sharpest this sentiment turned into bitter attacks on teachers in general.

This libertarian stance, as Doug Holly has noted, [28] compounds two separate issues: how children learn; and the power relationships between teachers and pupils in conventional schools. Teachers in conventional schools justify their authority over children by claiming that they use it to get children to learn. Libertarians, rejecting this authority, seem sometimes to leave the teacher with no part in helping children learn.

Libertarians, like the deschoolers, place great emphasis on 'incidental learning', meaning all those things one learns for oneself in the course of daily life. The ideal model is portrayed in William Morris's *News From Nowhere*: a utopian society where all economic difficulties have been eliminated and everyone lives together in love and friendship. The children pick up what they want and need to know without any formal schooling. The adults all have plenty of time to help children, who also learn from each other and from doing things in the real world.

Now it is the case that one can learn things without a teacher. Infancy offers particularly striking examples, and John Holt has shown, from his observation of childrens' sports, how they learn without any teaching. [29] But two errors can arise from this recognition of incidental learning. One is to make an opposition (as libertarians do too often) between incidental learning and *organized* learning, as if one had to do one or the other but couldn't do both. The other error is to deduce that teachers are superfluous.

There are many things which one can't learn without a teacher; there are many things one is unlikely to learn without a teacher; and there are many things which are much more easily learned with a teacher than without. For example, it is inconceivable that any one person could discover for themselves the knowledge and skills of acupuncture which have been developed by the Chinese over many centuries. You might, perhaps, with enormous dedication, learn them solely from books, although you would need ample opportunity for practice – an opportunity which few patients would want to grant to a 'self-taught' acupuncturist. But books (including the misnamed 'Teach Yourself' books) don't do away with a teacher. They merely put the teacher, who writes the books, into a different relationship with the learner, in the same way as other forms of distance learning like Open University courses.

As several critics of deschooling argued,[30] it is wholly improbable that 'incidental learning' could equip most people with the knowledge and abilities which are required if a complex society like ours is to be sustained. Some radicals were so disenchanted with our complex society that they saw no case for sustaining it. The contradiction was that this view did not prevent them from 'stooping to pick up the golden apples dropped from the tree of industry': if one accepts things like reliable supplies of food, telephones, electric power, record players, air travel and all the rest then one is *de facto* accepting the need to sustain a complex society.

Here, once again, we need to get away from a false opposition: 'remember, it is learning, and not teaching, that we are interested in'.[31] I suggest that we should be interested in teaching *and* learning. What radicals need to find is the proper role for the teacher, which will be somewhere between no role at all (as in some free schools) and the domineering role which radicals regarded as an oppressive feature of traditional classrooms. This question of the proper place of the teacher was explored by several radical writers[32] and has been the subject of some sensitive investigations by researchers over the past decade.[33] White Lion's statement that 'learning is not compatible with a situation in which the choice of subject matter and teaching method is made by the teacher' is, apart from not being true, too sweeping a statement to be helpful. The relationships between teacher and learner, between learner and content, and between teacher, learner and their context will surely be subtle ones which cannot be reduced to simplistic formulae.

Infant learning

Radical ideas about learning drew heavily on the model of infant learning. Infant learning demonstrates the enormous capacity for learning with which almost every human is endowed, and a curiosity which seems so remarkable that it seems right to call it 'natural'. The acquisition of language is a particularly marvellous achievement. Moreover, the infant displays an amazing degree of motivation, both instinctive and conscious. Infants set themselves learning tasks and learn a great deal from experimenting on their own. All this 'and not a professional teacher in sight', remark Colin and Mog Ball.[34]

Clearly if learning of this intensity and quality could be sustained throughout childhood and into adulthood, many of the problems of schooling – such as the problem of 'underachievement' – might disappear. Some radicals held that it was only schools and teachers which prevented this.[35] Often quoted was John Holt's assertion that 'if we taught children to speak, they'd never learn'.[36] (The same assertion had been made 50 years earlier by Edmond Holmes.)[37] It is possible to slide from here into a belief that if we did away with schools and teachers and just left children to themselves, all would be well. But there are four reasons for doubting this.

First, there is the matter of developmental stages. It may be a mistake to presume that the infant stage *could* be sustained indefinitely. Piaget's researches suggested a series of developmental stages. Second, to say that children learn to talk, or walk, without teaching is to define 'teaching' in highly restrictive terms. In learning to talk and walk there is much interaction between helpful older people and the learning infant. The 'wild boy of Aveyron', who encountered no other humans, did not learn to walk; perhaps it never occurred to him to try.[38] There are many recorded cases of children brought up in silent homes who, of course, don't learn to talk. (There are, however, some cases which suggest that siblings in such an environment can develop a private language. But the inadequacy of such a private language for any purpose other than communicating with each other goes to demonstrate that there needs to be a shared or generally accepted element in knowledge and abilities learned.) Rather than accept the bland assertion that no one teaches children to talk, perhaps we should ask whether the part which older people evidently do play in helping children learn to talk might not be taken as a paradigm of good teaching. Perhaps Margaret Mead got it right when she said:'When a child is learning to talk, the miracle of learning is so pressing and conspicuous that the achievement of the teachers is put into the shade.'[39]

Third, the question of content is surely crucial. Infant learning is all well and good as long as the infant is choosing his or her content (but we should carefully note that this content can only be chosen from what is presented to the infant by his or her environment: English children normally learn to speak *English*; infants can't learn to fly). But there is an increasingly *social* content in what *needs* to be learned. It is simply impossible for infants, once past the first few days of life, to go on learning only those things which take their fancy at any moment. They have, for example, to learn to start taking solid foods, and there are many parents who will testify that this is not quite as serene a process as the idealized model of infant learning would have us believe.

Motivation

Which takes us, at last, to the matter of motivation. While it is reasonably clear that most infants want to, and need to, learn to get about and communicate and much else, it is less clear that these same organic needs and wants lead everyone to learn other things – to share toys with other children, say, or to read and write. There comes a point at which the egotistical drives of the infant become insufficient for learning to live in human society. Learning takes on a social dimension. And this takes us on to the central concern of this chapter.

If A.S. Neill was not interested in how children learn, one of his great admirers, John Holt, was extremely interested and published two remarkable books on the subject in the 1960s – *How Children Fail* and *How Children Learn*. Based on close observation of children, they are full of highly perceptive insights which earned the books a place on many College of Education reading lists, Holt's radical conclusions notwithstanding. But I would take issue with Holt on a number of points, and we can begin by considering the following statement:

> . . . in our struggle to make sense out of life, the things we most need to learn are the things we most want to learn . . . curiosity is hardly ever idle . . . When we learn this way . . . we learn both rapidly and permanently . . . Birds fly, fish swim; man thinks and learns. Therefore, we do not need to 'motivate'

children into learning, by wheedling, bribing or bullying.[40]

In *Freedom and Beyond* Holt returned to the question of motivation with a characteristically vehement statement: 'Talk about motivation or innovative courses or inspiring kids to learn is simply dishonest nonsense.'[41]

One need not favour bullying or bribing (I'm not sure about wheedling: defined as 'persuading by coaxing words' it may have its merits; what, after all, is poetry?) to discern positive virtues in motivation. Let us consider the example of children learning to swim.[42] Some children, when first taken to the swimming pool, recoil in terror. But adults can use various methods (including, no doubt, wheedling) to show them that, despite first appearances, swimming can be fun. This teaching role has long been recognized: 'gifted educators are precisely those who can get children going on activities which have no initial appeal to them'.[43] It would be a happy thing if every child took readily to water as soon as they saw it. But they don't.

Holt returns to the example of swimming in a later book, still arguing against any adult persuasion:

> The child might in time have learned to swim on his own, and not only had the pleasure of swimming, but the far more important pleasure of having found that pleasure for himself. Or he might have used that time to find some other skills and pleasures, just as good.[44]

I know adults who can't swim and who are afraid of water and who regret not having been helped over this hurdle in childhood. They would disagree with Holt's position. But then Holt makes a further point. If swimming were an isolated instance, he might accept the worth of 'motivating' a child to swim. But it isn't an isolated instance. This kind of thing is happening all the time because

> there are dozens of adults, each convinced that he has something of vital importance to 'give' the child that he would never get for himself, all saying to the child 'I know better than you what is good for you'.[45]

It is this cumulative effect which, Holt argues, deprives children of a sense of being in charge of their own lives and is so harmful. The same point was made by Neill: 'The brilliant teacher diminishes the child's autonomy by the *continuous* exercise of the powers of persuasion.'[46]

The strength of such radical arguments is that they reject the view that motivation is a quality (perhaps genetically determined) *which some children have and others don't*, like big feet or red hair.[47] In this view, 'if students are not interested in learning what the teacher insists they learn they are said to "lack motivation" '.[48]

Where Holt goes wrong – and he has this in common with conservative educationists – is that by focusing on the individual learner,[49] he overlooks the fact that motivation has a crucial *social* dimension. What individuals are motivated (or not motivated) to do is critically influenced by their social (and natural) environment. Just as an animal born into the hot desert does not need to seek ways of keeping warm, so a child born into a society where no one swims will have little, if any, motivation to learn to swim. And, likewise, a child born into a society where there is no written culture will, of course, grow up without literacy, blissfully unaware of the joys and sorrows of reading.

Children may be intrinsically motivated to walk and talk, but they start learning to walk and talk only because they see, hear and interact with other people doing it. Similarly, it is superficial to claim (as some have)[50] that 'left to their own devices' children will learn to read and write. Children are never 'left to their own devices'. They grow up into a human society.[51] In some sections of human society, reading and writing is a commonplace activity, and it has frequently been observed that children from these sections rarely have difficulty learning to read and write. If they do, it may be diagnosed as an illness, and given a name like 'dyslexia'. There is a whole continuum of environments in which reading and writing is less and less commonplace, through to non-literate societies. Although we may accept that all children have ample innate ability for the task, in this continuum children will have less and less *social* motivation to acquire literacy, and in the non-literate societies no motivation at all. This is the reasoning behind Michael Duane's comment that

> The solution to the literacy problem lies not in better techniques for teaching reading . . . but in social changes that will have the effect of making reading as essential to the normal lives of all people as it is, at the present time, for the middle classes.[52]

The operation of social motivation is clearly visible in the periodic 'crazes' which sweep our nation's youth – hula-hoops, Yo-Yos, clackers, skateboards, Rubik cubes, and so on. Suddenly 'everybody's doing it' and everybody *wants* to do it. But these examples should not lead us to think that social motivation is a trivial or ephemeral thing. My contention is that it is the most powerful single determinant of what children learn and what they don't.

Necessity and motivation

The proverb 'necessity is the mother of invention' reminds us that necessity is a powerful source of extrinsic motivation. (I am using the phrase 'extrinsic motivation' to make a distinction from the purely internal drives which Holt suggests are all that are needed to sustain learning.) It is easy to see how necessity works by thinking of primitive societies.[53] It is from primitive societies that textbooks on learning often draw their examples. Children must learn how to build boats, control fire, build huts, gather food, and so on, if the society is to survive. Whether they want (in the sense of 'feeling like it') to learn these things is neither here nor there, although we might speculate that since these things are so commonplace – like walking and talking – it is unlikely that they would not want to: they are so much part of the warp and woof of daily life, and children learn them by being involved in *doing them*.[54]

But in complex contemporary societies the necessities of survival are much more difficult to appreciate, being in large measure removed from daily experience.[55] For example, it is not part of the everyday experience of city children that food has to be produced by people working the land. Importantly, survival comes to be perceived as an individual problem (where will I get my food from?) rather than the shared collective problem familiar to primitive societies (how will we produce the food we need?) Thus an important collective social motivation to learn has been dangerously undermined.

I am not saying, of course, that complex societies do not have mechanisms to ensure that the necessities of life are produced. Only that these mechanisms are obscured from children's experience, and that therefore they will only learn about them if specific steps are taken to bring them to children's attention. Unfortunately, the mechanisms are all too easily presented as a bewildering array of 'jobs' (the farm worker, the builder, and so on), and the children's relationship to the mechanisms as a matter of 'getting a good job' – a matter of purely individual ambition. The social aspect of 'getting a job' – that we all have to acquire skills needed for our collective survival – may be perceived by youngsters as mere moralization, if it is perceived at all. In times of mass unemployment even the *individual* motivation to 'get a job' is weakened.

Free schools, and similar radical programmes, which encourage children to pursue their own interests (in the sense of things they find interesting) do nothing to overcome this problem. Indeed, they may reinforce the problem by encouraging children to conceive of their future place in society *only* in the individual terms of 'self-realization'. Rejecting even the 'mere moralization' of persuading children that they should get a useful job, they make no contribution to the fundamental task of preparing the next generation to do what needs to be done to ensure its survival.

Putting children face-to-face with necessity has, however, been a feature of some educational experiments. A good example was the Forest School which existed from 1930 to 1940.[56]

Just how far youngsters may be detached from the need to play a part in the collective human struggle to survive is suggested in one of Paul Goodman's most moving passages. He recollects asking some young people what they wanted to work at, if they had the chance, after they left school:

> all of them had this one thing to say: 'Nothing'. They didn't believe that what to work at was the kind of thing one *wanted*. They rather expected that two or three of them would work for the electric company in town, but they couldn't care less. I turned away from the conversation abruptly because of the uncontrollable burning tears in my eyes and constriction in my chest. Not feeling sorry for them but tears of frank dismay for the waste of our humanity . . .[57]

The other side of the coin of not comprehending how our society ensures our daily survival is that children do not themselves feel necessary. George Dennison compares the peasant children at Tolstoy's school at Yasnaya Polyana with his children at the New York First Street School:

> Where the peasant children acquired the skills of farming and carpentry and dozens of other necessary occupations, and therefore knew that they were indeed necessary persons, ours had acquired nothing and could do nothing, and did not at all feel necessary to the inner life of labour that sustains a country.[58]

The next chapter will look at the question of growing up in society.

CHAPTER 9

Learning in society

In this chapter I will continue with the theme of learning, first putting it in a social context and then examining the radical proposal for education as critical re-evaluation.

Growing up in society

In order to become a member of any community, the growing child has to learn – and make his or her own – the ways of that community. This process, sometimes called socialization or acculturization, is a fact of human life. There is a tendency among radicals to consider it as an oppressive imposition upon the child – a matter of 'conditioning', if not 'brainwashing'. Neill and Holt, for example, see socialization as a matter of interfering adults imposing their whims on the growing child. But such an 'imposition', if we must call it that, is an inevitable part of growing up into any human society. Socialization need not be viewed as something done to the child: it may be viewed as a process in which the child learns to find a viable *modus vivendi* of some sort within society – something everyone has to do. Take the example of language acquisition. There are, in fact, laws of language and the growing child has to accept them. This is not a matter of 'brainwashing'. Here is a concrete example:

> There are always hundreds of things that are not true, but we are forbidden by the laws of communication from expressing them, unless someone believes otherwise: we cannot go around saying, however truthfully, 'You don't have three heads', or 'the ceiling isn't purple', or 'that dress you're wearing isn't mine'. Instead we have to wait until someone either declares the reverse or acts as if

the reverse is true. From a surprisingly early age, children are sensitive to that unwritten law and seem to understand the conditions under which one can and cannot produce a negative statement.[1]

John Holt tells the story[2] of an 11-year-old who, asked if she believed in God, replied 'Yes, I suppose so. After all, what choice do we have?' Holt offers this as an example of the adult brainwashing of which he disapproves. But to call this 'brainwashing' is to slide over important and difficult questions of *culture*. Culture is a set of socially constructed ideas, values, beliefs, customs, conventions, behaviours, established practices, and means of communication. In most societies these include religion. But it is an inadequate view to hold that people are entirely free to pick and choose from all these as they wish.[3]

Actually culture may be viewed as a necessary pre-emption of choices. It saves each individual from the quite impossible task of deciding every little thing for himself or herself. Without culture, human society would be impossible. Now culture *is* coercive, just as much as the heat of the sun or gravity is coercive. The difference is that it is within human power to change culture, which is where problems begin. In a static society where the culture has been unchanged for generations, and where the fundamentals of culture are unquestioned, education might be a straightforward task.[4] But a society where the culture is under challenge, where conflicting cultures compete, presents profound problems for humanity which cannot be reduced to a facile notion of 'adult coercion'. The coerciveness of culture in fact acts every bit as much upon adults as it does on children.

In any case, the answer to the girl's question 'what choice do we have?' is 'plenty: millions of Americans don't believe in God'. On that ground at least American society is presumably to be commended: Holt's 11-year-old would have had much less choice, on this matter, if she had been brought up in, say, Iran.

Holt and Neill err because they do not see growing up in society as a dialectical process between the growing child and society. It is not sufficient to see growing up either as a mechanistic process of imposition on the child, or as a process in which the child can freely choose whatever she or he likes. In Freire's words: 'This process of orientation in the world can be understood neither as a purely subjective event, nor as an objective or mechanistic one, but only as an event in which subjectivity and objectivity are united.'[5]

The central problem for radicals is that children have to grow up into a society of which radicals, to a greater or lesser extent, disapprove. As Neill put it, 'the child must from the start be forced to fit himself to our insane society'.[6] There is a conflict between the need to maintain the culture and to change it. In Jules Henry's words: 'Another learning problem inherent in the human condition is the fact that we must conserve culture while changing it: that we must always be more sure of surviving than adapting – as we see it'.[7]

Growing up involves learning unexceptionable things – walking or talking, for example – but also things which radicals find exceptionable – 'ruling-class ideology', competitiveness, gender roles, for example. A standard textbook describes the necessary learning of each growing child as follows:

> Clearly, since the inherited accumulated wisdom of mankind is manifested not through hereditary biological mechanisms, but instead is embodied in the material of the social environment and in the laws and customs of organised society, each baby is faced with problems of learning or, in other words, of developing adequate behavioural patterns, to ensure satisfactory adjustment to the complexity of social living . . . He is not born with the ability to make boats, to control fire, or even to use a spoon.[8]

For radicals, however, problems are raised by such phrases as 'the inherited accumulated wisdom of mankind' (like how to make nuclear weapons?), the 'material of the social environment' (like poverty?), the 'laws and customs of organised society' (like the Official Secrets Act?), 'adequate behavioural patterns' (like 'boys don't cry'?), and 'satisfactory adjustment' (like not arguing with an unjust teacher?). The danger of anthropological definitions of education – such as the one just quoted – is that they leave such concepts unexamined. Culture and society are taken as fixed givens into which the child has to grow willy-nilly. Even a famous progressive educationist, Sir Fred Clarke, found it possible to say: 'It is the first business of education to induce such conformity in terms of the culture in which the child will grow up.'[9]

Faced with the problem of children having to grow up in a culture of which radicals disapprove, three possible approaches suggest themselves. One is *insulation*. Rousseau, in his imagination, tried to isolate Emile entirely from society, the source (for Rousseau) of all evil. Summerhill and other progressive boarding schools tried to insulate children by bringing them up in an isolated rural community. Rousseau wasn't keen on letting Emile play with other children; Neill, by contrast, had such confidence in the goodness of children that he was sure that they would, left to themselves without

adult interference (the source of all evil), work out among themselves the best way of living together. Another example of the
isolationist approach can be seen in the Education Otherwise movement. The free schools, however, rejected the isolationist approach,
partly because rural isolation is beyond the financial resources of
most working-class parents, but partly because they sought to draw
on the positive aspects of the local community rather than dwell on
the harmful aspects of its culture.

A second approach starts by attempting to distinguish between
the acceptable parts of the culture and the unacceptable parts. The
difficult question here is who is to decide what is acceptable and what
is not – and on what grounds? There is also a problem of whether we
can divide culture into 'parts' in this way. [10]

A third approach involves the concept of 'critical re-evaluation'
and I propose to discuss it in some detail.

Critical re-evaluation

The third approach starts with the recognition that culture is not a
static thing, but is constantly in a state of change and conflict – at least
in most parts of the contemporary world. A series of radical books
published in the early 1970s took this up. The first to appear was
American – Neil Postman and Charles Weingartner's *Teaching as a
Subversive Activity*. It was followed, in England, by Douglas Holly's
Beyond Curriculum and Gabriel Chanan and Linda Gilchrist's *What
School Is For*. To this group we might add Chris Searle's *This New
Season* and Colin and Mog Ball's *Education for a Change*, although
they had rather different approaches. All these writers agreed that
there was much of value in our culture – whether arts, skills,
knowledge, concepts, ethics or traditions. All accepted that to grow
up in society children have to come to terms with these. All were
opposed, however, to any insistence on *conformity* to the given
culture. All agreed that schools have a role in systematically making
the culture available to children. And all rejected the simplistic
opposition which posits that either the learner must be in control of
the learning process or the teacher must be in control.

What these writers proposed was that schooling should engage the
learner in a continuing process of critical re-evaluation of the culture.
(Postman and Weingartner, borrowing from Ernest Hemingway,
called this process 'crap detection', but I will stick with the longer
term, clumsy as it is.) Critical re-evaluation stresses two things: as
regards content, it rejects the notion of a fixed body of knowledge to
be transmitted from teacher to learner; and as regards method, it

stresses the active and autonomous involvement of the learner.[11]
Critical re-evaluation not only involves helping children to look at
the culture with a critical eye, but also encourages them to participate
in the action of *changing* it. And it involves an acknowledgement of
those aspects of the culture which are commonly discounted by
educational institutions – for example, popular culture[12] or the
history of working-class struggle.[13] And, finally, it involves giving a
central place to the child's own experience.

I wish to raise a number of problems with this idea. My purpose in
doing so is not to suggest that it is a 'non-starter', but that a good deal
more thought is needed if critical re-evaluation can be put forward as
a workable programme by radicals.

The first problem is that all the writers who propose it are
concerned with children over the age of 11. But it may well be that
by this age the greater part of the 'damage' (in terms of acculturization into an unacceptable culture) has been done. For much younger
children the possibility of critical re-evaluation – which is essentially
a rational process – is more doubtful. It may be that very young
people do engage in critical re-evaluation of their own, but if they do
so they might be labelled as 'naughty' or 'disturbed'. And indeed,
critical re-evaluation requires a sophisticated approach: it does not
mean that you reject things just because *you* don't like them; it does
involve a sensitive and discriminating respect for other people's
values; and it should not involve the adoption of behaviours which
bring individuals into unsustainable conflicts with others. These are
difficult enough things for teenagers – and adults – to deal with. I am
not at all sure they can be within the abilities of a five-year-old.

The second problem is that all the proponents of critical re-
evaluation pin their faith (not without heart-searching) on state
schools as the right place for the transmission of culture and its
critical re-evaluation. Even if it were assumed that all schools are
staffed by people dedicated to the radical cause of critical re-evaluation (and they are not), there remains the possibility, often expressed
by progressives, that *all* adults are 'tainted'. As the co-founder of
Kirkdale School put it: 'We wanted children to produce their own
brave new world. We (the older generation) are already flawed.'[14]
Free schools appeared to go some way towards meeting these two
problems. They often took children from the age of three, they were
to be staffed by the 'right' kind of people – critical re-evaluators all –
and they tried to minimize the directive role of adults. They hoped to
create an environment which embodied the best aspects of our
culture, and it would be in this environment that, in the school hours
at least, the children would grow up. This proved to be more

difficult to put into practice than freeschoolers had envisaged.

But it seems to me that the most serious weakness of the critical re-evaluation scheme is this: *why should children want to engage in it?* In other words, where is their motivation to come from? We are forced back to the question of why children learn, or refuse to learn.

I have argued that acculturization is the process whereby children learn to make their way in the culture into which they are born. I have pointed to the insufficiency of the view that children are 'naturally motivated' to learn and that therefore there is no problem about learning. Children are motivated to learn to do the things that other people do: we may say that they want to be like other people. Thus, for example, they have 'role models'. If critical re-evaluation were so commonplace in our society that everyone did it, then it might well be that children would willingly participate. But the whole basis of the radical critique is that critical re-evaluation is *not* commonplace, though it ought to be. It seems possible, then, that children will perceive it, not as something 'everyone does', but as something quite eccentric. A well-known attempt at critical re-evaluation was Johnny Speight's television series *Till Death Do Us Part*. Speight claimed that the aim of this series was to hold up Alf Garnett for inspection, so that we could all see how foolish his racist and sexist prejudices were. And indeed the scripts are full of splendid examples of the folly of Alf's prejudices. But during my years as a teacher I found that it was rare for a white child to see it this way. What they saw was a racist and sexist white man who was quite normal. What Alf Garnett actually gave them was a recognizable (if comic) role-model who armed them with an ample vocabulary to express their own prejudices.

It may be that there are certain moments in history – moments of major cultural upheaval – when critical re-evaluation becomes commonplace, and children perceive it as such. At such moments children may be swept up by the impetus so as to be engaged, for their own part, in the process. The cultural revolution in China in the 1960s may be a case in point. So perhaps was Grenada after the 1979 revolution on that Caribbean island.[15] The 1960s in Britain (as elsewhere) were, to a lesser extent, a period of cultural re-evaluation and evidently children, or at least teenagers, were involved in that. However, the younger the child (or perhaps we might say, the more immature the child) the greater the need for an enveloping sense of security and stability. For them cultural turmoil may seem perplexing, if not distressing.

Before continuing, it may be helpful to summarize the argument so far. My concern in the last chapter was to question Holt's analogy between humans learning and 'birds flying and fish swimming'. While accepting that humans have an instinctive ability to learn, I have argued that human *motivation* to learn, once past infancy, has a powerful social dimension. This social motivation cannot be reduced to a notion of coercive adults or coercive schools forcing children to learn; it is a necessary part of growing up into any human community, and would be so even in an ideal world.[16] The problem for radicals is that the culture which is the source of this motivation is, to a greater or lesser extent, disapproved of. Some radicals therefore proposed that children should be engaged in a process of critical re-evaluation of the culture. But I have now asked the question: where is the motivation for this critical re-evaluation to come from, except in times of cultural upheaval when critical re-evaluation itself becomes a central feature of the culture?

Schooling and the class struggle

An answer to this question was offered by those radicals who believed that this motivation would come from the struggle for liberation into which working-class children are pitched historically and which is inexorably bound up with *their* cultural heritage. Acculturization is now seen as the process of learning the ways of working-class life and culture, of assimilating class perspectives, and participating in the class struggle. The motivation will come from the drive to 'be like others' in the context of working-class traditions and the class struggle, which itself may be viewed as a continuing process of critical re-evaluation. A prominent exponent of this programme in England was Chris Searle, who argued that

> we must re-establish culture in its organic, democratic sense, linking it to the real world of people who are working and struggling for control over the conditions of their lives. As teachers, it is only by completely committing ourselves to their struggles that we can commit ourselves to a truly educational consciousness. The 'Problem of Education' cannot be isolated merely as a problem of the schools, or of teachers. It is a problem of politics, and the economic domination of one class over another. It has to be solved politically, in the schools as in all of society.[17]

Describing his own attempts to put this into practice in the classroom, Searle says:

> it was important to look to tradition and history, to find prece-

dents in the past where individuals and masses of East End working people have similarly resisted or organised, or achieved advances which now benefited the children and their families. And so local history often pushed its way into the present, as a base for contemporary action and syllabus.[18]

This motivation differs sharply from another motivation – the motivation of the 'bright working-class child' to get on and out of the working class.[19] The new plan was to 'teach the working class assuming that they will stay working class but that they will nevertheless be struggling for equality and for greater fulfilment – as a class'.[20]

The programme put forward by Searle stressed the need for action in the real world as part of the learning process – 'actional education', as Frantz Fanon had called it. It was not something which could go on behind closed classroom doors. In Freire's words, it 'is brought about not through an intellectual effort alone, but through praxis – through the authentic union of action and reflection'.[21]

Two currents of thinking can be seen to come together here. The first is a view of class, culture and society which owes a good deal to Richard Hoggart and Raymond Williams.[22] The second is a much more combative conception of class which was reinforced by the renewed interest in Marxism in Britain after 1968.

Searle got some exceptional writing out of his pupils[23] and it did look as though he had succeeded in tapping a fierce motivation to learn which orthodox schoolers had overlooked, or, more likely, fought shy of for political reasons. He came in for intense criticisms, not only from the political Right, but also from progressives.[24] It was, however, ironic that after Searle was sacked by his school governors for publishing *Stepney Words* he was reinstated by Secretary of State Margaret Thatcher.

I want to raise five problems here. First, the presumption that the working class is the historical agency of social transformation is open to some doubt these days. If we look at the movement for the liberation of women, which has promoted one of the most significant critical re-evaluations of the post-war era, we find that it is not a working-class movement – rather the reverse, in fact. The women's movement provides us, by the way, with an excellent model of how the process of critical re-evaluation can be socially motivated. Young people – girls at any rate – have been actively involved in this process. The women's movement has generated an enormous amount of learning (even by men, who were hardly 'taking the initiative', if I can hark back to the earlier discussion). And we may note that a great deal of this learning has taken place outside the formal educational institutions – in women's groups, women's centres, women's campaigns, through feminist magazines and books, and so on.

Although the women's movement certainly lends weight to the thesis that *conflict* is a great source of learning, it cannot easily be explained within a class-conflict model of social change. Nor is the women's movement an isolated example. The 'green' movement, taking this in its broadest sense – concern for the environment, post-industrial economics, non-militarism, ecology, alternative medicine, alternative nutritional patterns, and so on – provides another case in point.

My second worry about the 'working-class struggle' programme is that it relies upon what some would see as idealized notions of the working class. These notions are given substance by events like the 1984–5 miners' strike; and both Searle and Scotland Road Free School seemed to draw on their pupils' real experience of working-class community solidarity. But the question remains whether such class solidarity, and such a sense of community, are typical of contemporary capitalist society or whether they are lingering remnants of a past era. My question is not whether communities and solidarity are things of the past, but whether they can any longer be identified with a mass working class engaged in a conscious historical struggle to transform society.

Radicals of the Left assume that the causes they hold dear will find their natural constituency in the working-class movement. Anti-imperialism is an example. In *Classrooms of Resistance* Searle's pupils deal not only with local community struggles – around dockland redevelopment, the closure of Poplar hospital, the Metal Box factory dispute – but also the 1973 coup in Chile and the black struggle in Southern Africa. Profoundly important as such struggles are, their relationship with British working-class culture is, unfortunately, uncertain.

If working-class culture is to provide the social motivation for learning, that motivation must come from the culture as it is experienced and perceived by working-class children, not as it ought to be in the minds of left-wingers. For many working-class children lessons about Chile or Southern Africa may seem no more consonant with their experience than, say, Henry VIII's squabbles with the church. I am not arguing that children should not learn about Chile or Southern Africa: only that it doesn't fit very easily into the theoretical programme we are discussing. If left-wingers hold that children should be *made* to learn about Chile and Southern Africa, they share the same epistemology, the same theory of learning, the same model of the relationship between teacher and taught, as the traditionalist who holds that children should be made to learn about, say, the British constitution or the Bible. It is worth reflecting on this comment on the Italian *doposcuola* movement of the late 1960s:

> They teach in the 'doposcuola' by replacing the traditional heroes with socialist ones; they try to treat the children like friends and ask them 'what would you like to do?' or 'what would you like to talk about?' and always end up talking about fascism, resistance, Vietnam and the Middle East no matter what the children's requests are. They talk on these topics just as the school teachers used to, and although the 'doposcuola' pupils are somewhat noisier than the ordinary pupils their participation remains passive.[25]

The third problem can be expressed as an often-asked question: what is the relationship between working-class culture and the *common* culture?[26]

The fourth problem is that when we think of working-class struggles we are usually thinking of struggles against opposing forces (city financiers, Area Health Authorities, employers, imperial powers). But we must ask whether the lifestyle of permanent dissension which characterizes left-wing activists is a viable, or even a healthy, perspective into which children might be acculturized. George Dennison warned: 'Teachers who are radicals should refrain from foisting their attitudes on children, especially their highly rationalised sense of alienation.'[27]

The final problem is a practical one. There is little evidence that working-class parents in general want an education for their children which is based upon the premise of working-class struggle. I suspect that the parent described in this memory of the socialist Sunday Schools is quite rare nowadays:

> My father was a strong socialist . . . Dad sent me right away to the Partick Socialist Sunday-school . . . I was taken down at four years of age to the Sunday-school and that was the happiest time of my life right up until I was fourteen . . . It was very well organised in Glasgow and all of the socialists – the Labour voters as you would call them nowadays – they were really early socialists who wanted a change in society and their children to learn as much as possible about these things . . . They wanted their children to learn that socialism was a good way of life and what was good for one was good for all, and so this was the moral attitude they had.[28]

But without the support of parents for the programme, it is hard to see how it can be justified. Possibly a case could be made for separate schools for the children of radicals and socialists, but this is an idea fraught with hazards.

It may be that radicals can find answers to these problems. My hope is that they will try to do so.

Relevance

Much of the foregoing discussion might have been presented as a discussion of 'relevance'. This was a major concern of radical critics of schooling in the 1960s and 1970s.

It was common for critics of schooling to 'prove' its irrelevance by pointing to specific items on the curriculum: Latin, perhaps, or quadratic equations (which Neill had a thing about), or Boyle's Law (R.F. Mackenzie's favourite target). Now it is easily shown that we can't pick out irrelevance by pointing to any specific item of content: what is irrelevant to one person may be relevant to another; and what is irrelevant to me today could become relevant to me tomorrow. I will consider, therefore, two other approaches to the matter suggested by radicals.

John Holt[29] suggested that children shouldn't be asked to learn something until they need to know it. Samuel Butler once said the same thing: 'Never try to learn anything until the not knowing it has come to be a nuisance to you for some time'.[30] But the moment that not having learnt to swim, for example, becomes a nuisance to you could well be the last moment of your life. Parents rightly instruct their children in a large number of things ('don't run out into the road', 'don't pull the dog's tail') in advance of their being needed. While this most obviously applies to matters of safety, there is also an element of wise preparation for all kinds of contingencies.

Of course, there has to be some limit to this: no one can be prepared for all contingencies and some 'preparation for contingencies' arguments are less persuasive than others: few people would be unduly alarmed by the threat that if they don't learn Latin they may one day come across a word whose etymological derivation escapes them. Nevertheless, the blanket injunction never to learn things until they are needed is unsatisfactory. Reaction against an over-emphasis on children's learning as a 'preparation for life' can lead to the opposite extreme of denying that learning has any preparatory function. There needs to be a balance.

A second approach to relevance poses it purely as a matter for each individual child to decide. The founders of White Lion Street Free School offered an example of this:

> Real learning, as any pre-school child will demonstrate, is a process in which each individual creates his own unique 'curriculum'. He asks and seeks out answers to the questions raised for him by his own unique experience. [31]

I have already discussed the difficulties of taking infant learning as a paradigm for all learning. But there are three other weaknesses in this approach.

First, by stressing the individual, this statement, like others I have quoted in this chapter, fails to address the question of the relationship between the individual, on the one hand, and the social and natural environments, on the other. It would be equally incomplete to claim that the curriculum is fixed for every individual by the natural and social environment. What we need to stress is the dialectical relationship between the learner and the environment. The much used term 'individual learning' can be misleading if it posits the lone individual as the basic unit in the educational process. In the words of Bowles and Gintis:

> Human development is not the simple 'unfolding of innate humanity.' Human potential is realised only through the confrontation of genetic constitution and social experience. Dogma consists precisely in suppressing one pole of a contradiction. The dogma of repressive education is the dogma of necessity which denies freedom. But we must avoid the alternative dogma of freedom which denies necessity. Indeed freedom and individuality arises only through a confrontation with necessity, and personal powers develop only when pitted against a recalcitrant reality. [32]

It should be clear, then, that the concept of relevance has a social dimension as well as an individual dimension. This is readily appreciated if we return to our image of learning in a primitive society: each individual must learn to perform the tasks necessary for group survival. In such primitive societies it is probably easy for the growing child to see how the social relevance of learning coincides with the individual relevance. The fact that this is not so easily seen in complex contemporary society should not lead radicals to retreat into defining relevance in purely individual terms.

The second weakness of the notion that each individual creates 'his own unique curriculum' was pointed out by Vygotsky in his critique of the early libertarianism of Soviet education after the 1917 revolution. [33] It is, simply a recipe for 'no change'. It leads inevitably to a concentration on what the child can do and offers no mechanism for taking her or him on to what she or he cannot yet do. In Vygotsky's words: 'Instruction was orientated to the child's weakness rather than his strength, thus encouraging him to remain at the pre-school stage of development'.[34] If the child 'asks and seeks out answers to the questions raised for him by his own unique experience' there is no guarantee that the child will move *beyond* his or her own experience. To put it bluntly, the exclusive emphasis on the 'uniqueness' of individual learning leaves children wallowing in a vortex of their 'own experience': it can too easily resemble, and remain stuck at, the pre-school stage of development.

The third problem with the prescription that each individual should determine his or her own relevant curriculum was discovered quickly at White Lion Street Free School. It doesn't work. Within three years of making the statement above, White Lion was forced to concede:

> There has been a lot of talk recently about letting children decide for themselves what they want to learn. As anyone who has tried it will know, this is not a straightforward alternative . . . At White Lion Street we discovered early that though a few children knew what they wanted to do, most didn't, beyond a (usually) guilt-ridden conviction that they ought to do reading, writing and numbers.[35],

An analytical framework

To conclude my discussion of learning I want to sketch out a framework which will, I hope, enable us to perceive the problem more clearly. Let me pose the 'problem of learning' in this way: it is the problem of finding the right relationship between three factors: children; the content of learning; and society. Each of these factors is related to the other and may be considered in a triangular relationship as shown in Figure 1. Like all triangular structures, you can't change one of the factors without changing the others. This model helps us to see where many theories of learning go wrong. First, let us consider theories which tend to neglect one or other of the three factors.[36]

A.S. Neill disregards *society*.[37] While he is very strong on children, he is quite inscrutable on the matter of content: at one time he says he's not interested in what children learn, at another he says they have to learn not to gratify themselves at other people's expense. In general, concepts of 'child-centred learning' run the risk of giving

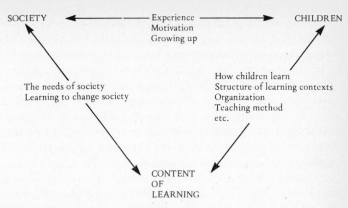

Figure 1 The problem of learning

insufficient attention to society and content. As Douglas Holly puts it: ' "pupil-centred learning" is as much a dogmatism as "subjects", "disciplines", "academic rigour" and the rest. A humanist-material-ist approach is concerned to erect criteria which link the individual and society, the child with the learning.'[38]

Traditionalist educationists – for example, many of the *Black Paper* contributors – neglect *children*; they tend to consider only the relationship between society and the content of learning. Certain radicals also make this error when they talk of, for example, 'the kind of curriculum we need for the building of a critical socialist democracy'.[39] Both leave children out of the equation and 'render the act of learning . . . a mere accident'.[40]

One consquence of this omission is the well-known fact that very many children don't actually learn the content which schools are supposed to teach them. (This doesn't worry everyone: those who despise the content aren't bothered; and those who favour a stratified society see it as a convenient way of sorting the sheep from the goats.)

It is more difficult to find clear examples of those who talk exclusively in terms of society and children, and who ignore the *content* of learning. But a definite tendency in this direction can be found in certain free schools and in the writings of the deschoolers who emphasized children's learning in society without giving attention to what the content of this learning might be. The fact that deschoolers advocated no serious arrangements for learning any specific content suggests that they did not regard any specific content as important.

We can now turn to a second set of errors which take the linkages between society, children and content to be only *one-way* linkages when they must be seen as *two-way* linkages.

Making the linkage 'society' to 'children' only one-way requires children to take society as given and to conform to it.[41] It does not see children as contributing to the formation of society. At its extreme, children are simply ignored. A small example is the way that local authorities, until quite recently, built swimming pools which were too deep for young children to stand up in. The children's badge 'children are people too' sums up their response to this error.

The two-way relationship between society and children must be appreciated if a correct understanding of motivation is to be reached; if we are to recognize that children's experience (often emphasized by radicals) is experience-in-society; and if we are to accept that children have somehow or other to grow up in society – which includes the possibility that they change society in doing so.

Making the linkage 'children' to 'society' only one way is to think of a quite artificial 'world of childhood' in which children may be 'left to themselves'. I have dealt with this elsewhere.[42]

The conception of a purely one-way linkage 'content of learning' to 'children' is exemplified by an expression which has become common in recent years: the *delivery* of education. This piece of jargon, conjuring up the image of people delivering milk or letters, rests on the conceptualization of education as a *thing*. It takes no account of how and why children learn, and why they do not. Children, in this view, are seen as empty jugs waiting to be filled up.

It is not only contemporary technocrats who make this mistake: in 1983 the ILEA published a paper entitled *Delivery of the Authority's Initiative on Multi-Ethnic Education in Schools*. The same mistake can be found in the *Black Papers*[43] and in radical writings: 'The core of a defence of mixed–ability teaching . . . should centre on its ability to deliver an understanding to the great majority of students of the main concepts and principles of the various disciplines.'[44]

Conversely, to make the linkage 'children' to 'content' only one-way leads either to the idea that it is sufficient for children to choose their own content, or to the construction of a false opposition between 'being' and 'learning'. This is what happened in certain free schools which were happy to just 'let children be' without concerning themselves with what, if anything, the children learned.

Making the linkage 'society' to 'content' only one-way again rests on a static conception of society into which children can only fit in. It excludes the possibility that what children learn may cause them to change society.[45] This possibility lay behind nineteenth-century fears that universal education would lead to revolution. Certain conservative educationists seek to prevent this possibility by insisting on a 'neutral' curriculum, by which they mean a curriculum which does not question the prevailing ideology. Hence, for example, they oppose anti-racist and anti-sexist curriculum developments.

On the other hand, making the linkage 'content' to 'society' only one-way ignores the social (and historical) location of education. It promotes an idealized curriculum ('education for its own sake') which could, if it prevailed, lead to a threat to the collective survival. Education conceived of purely in terms of 'self-realization'[46] comes into this category. Carried to its logical conclusion (which, however, I do not think it could be) it could produce children quite unable to make their way in society and also quite unable to *change* society.

I suggest that the problem of learning can only be solved by putting the three factors into a workable relationship with each other. But a situation may arise where, unless something is changed, there is no possibility of any workable relationship. In this situation, dysfunction occurs. It may help to consider a hypothetical example. Let us imagine a society which from an early age imbues its children with a competitive ethos – a society which motivates children, from infancy, to 'get on top', to seek advantage over others, to put themselves first. This may be represented by a particular linkage, as shown in Figure 2. Now let us further imagine that this same society,

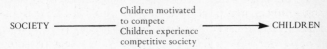

Figure 2

to be sustained, requires children to learn a particular content: work for the common good, put the 'national interest' first, play the role assigned to you, accept your station in life. This constitutes another given linkage, as shown in Figure 3. When we now turn to the third

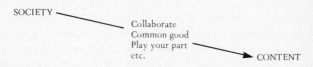

Figure 3

linkage, between children and content, we can see that there is going to be a dysfunction. What children are motivated to learn does not match up with the content they are required to learn. This is sure to be manifested in problems in schools – teachers struggling vainly to get the children to learn their lessons, for instance. Such dysfunctioning has been observed by Jules Henry:

> The multiplicity of techniques used by teachers to maintain discipline in American schools is related to the severity of the disciplinary problem; the severity of the disciplinary problem is related to the fact that the children are not interested in being educated; the children are not interested in being educated because of the lack of unity between education and the rest of the social sphere.[47]

Although I have used the term 'dysfunction', other writers have preferred the term 'contradiction', and an analysis of the contradictions of schooling along the same lines can be found in *Schooling in Capitalist America* by Samuel Bowles and Herbert Gintis.[48] In a similar vein this interesting statement was made by the Big Flame group in 1977:

> Progressivism [I would say radicalism – NW] put into question what school is for, but it could not bridge the chasm between school and society. For running counter to progressive reform were the material changes in the class structure and labour market we have previously described. The more the internal school experience was made 'relevant', the less relevant that became to changes outside the school gate. It is precisely this weak point which the traditionalists have exploited. For they have a simple answer: functional education.[49]

I do not, however, agree that 'functional education' is a simple answer, for reasons I will explain in the final chapter.

Where there is dysfunction, something has to be changed, unless of course the problems caused by the dysfunction are just left to fester. (And in my view, 'just left to fester' is an accurate description of the problem of learning in English schools in the post-1945 era.) Different views of the immutability of each factor will give rise to different formulations for a resolution of the dysfunction. Some might suggest, for example, that children should be thrashed until they learn the content which established society wants them to learn. Others will advocate 'curriculum reform'. And yet others will insist that society must be transformed. This latter was a common radical view and I wish to consider it a little further.

The central thesis of Paul Goodman's book, *Growing Up Absurd*, was that 'There is no right education, except growing up into a worthwhile world',[50] and he held that contemporary society does not constitute a worthwhile world and hence the problem of learning cannot be resolved within it. The same sort of idea was expressed in much more specific terms by Ken Coates: 'To see things the right way up, and begin the pursuit of education, we must ask "what sort of factories do our schools need?" '[51] I would prefer to pose the question as 'what sort of factories do our children need?' since schools are only one possible form of the linkage between children and content.

Now, of course, radicals take as their starting point the belief that society needs changing. Those who don't share this belief will seek other solutions to the problem of learning. But the possibility exists that there may be no such other solutions, and this possibility will increase as children and content, and the linkage between them (how children learn, the structure of learning environments, the organization of school, pedagogy, and so on) are taken as given. For example: the work of Piaget suggests that children are not infinitely manipulable but have certain definite characteristics; these characteristics place constraints on the solution of the problem. Similarly, every bit of content which we wish to hang on to – the 'accumulated wisdom of mankind' as it is sometimes called – constrains possible solutions.[52]

The model framework which I have been suggesting has a further important implication for radicals. In blue-printing the kind of society they would like to construct, and the means of getting there, they will have to give the problem of learning – the problem of finding a workable accommodation between society, children and content – central rather than peripheral attention. Marxists, for example, tend to draw up their blue-prints in economic terms, focusing on the economic and social relations between adults. We can now see that certain economic formulations might prove unworkable, not in economic terms, but because they make dysfunctional demands on children and the content of learning.

There is hardly any need for me to point to the simplicism of the framework as I have suggested it. As it stands, it does not pay any attention, for example, to the question of class, or of sub-cultures. And again, it does not suggest how changes can be made in, and between, the components in order to move towards the elimination of dysfunction. But in principle I do not see that such considerations could not be accommodated using a more complex framework.[53]

Conclusion

The model I have outlined reinforces my earlier argument. That argument may be summarized as being that radical ideas about learning tend to be misleading; they are misleading because they are incomplete; and they are incomplete because they focus on one particular feature of the learning process and ignore its relationships with the whole. This matters because radicals do make proposals about how schooling should be done (or, in some cases, how it should be abolished) based on these ideas. In some cases they attempt to put these proposals into practice (as in free schools) though more often they propose that others should be putting the ideas into practice. My simple contention is that such radical proposals will not work if they are based on unsound theory.

In making a critique of radical theories, I do not wish to suggest that we return to a satisfied acceptance of conventional methods of schooling. They, I believe, can easily be shown to be just as defective – if not more so – than the radical ideas. My view is that the radical theories mark a step in the right direction; but they require much more work.

This chapter and the last were intended as a case study in the sense that I have taken just one topic and looked at what radicals had to say about it. It will be clear now why an encyclopaedia would be needed to deal with the whole range of radical theories of education. And yet I believe that work of that scale needs doing. That is why, in the final chapter, I will be proposing a radical research programme.

CHAPTER 10

Radical dilemmas

The left is well known for its 'sects' and 'splits', which seem, from a distance, irrational, self-defeating. Yet issues of debate in society at large reproduce themselves even in the smallest and seemingly most homogeneous groupings, and it is therefore sometimes the most seemingly subtle differences that are the most decisive. Every left-wing group has its own left and right wings, every right-wing group has its; churches have their agnostic tendencies, atheists their spiritual; terrorists their humanitarians, charities their hardliners. Indeed, one might say that the whole spectrum of political opinions has a tendency to reproduce itself not only in each group *but in each individual*.[1]

In this chapter I will explore debates within the radical movement which, on occasion, turned into open feuds. While some radicals felt certain which side of the debate they were on, others were conscious of the pull of both sides. It is because these debates remained, and remain, unsettled in the minds of many radicals that I have chosen to call them *dilemmas*.

What kind of reforms are needed?

I referred in Chapter 3 to the division between 'quantitists' and 'qualitists' as it emerged within the Rank & File teachers' group. Quantitists maintained that the radical changes which were needed in the field of education were a matter of access, resourcing, and better teaching: 'We want more education for more people, leading to more democracy . . . nearly all children could benefit from the quality of education at present reserved for an elite at the public and grammar schools . . .'.[2] This view tended to be held by those whose primary allegiance was to the working-class movement: 'The hard evidence suggests that if we could open education as freely to working-class children as we have done to middle-class ones, we would double – and double again – our highly talented and highly educated groups.'[3] A typical quantitist statement is this description, in *Rank & File*, of the 'crisis in education':

> A generation of expansion has come to an end, to be replaced by contraction into the indefinite future . . . teacher training colleges closed . . . school building stopped . . . teachers arbitrarily transferred . . . early retirement . . . salaries under attack . . . nursery expansion halted . . . supply and part-time teachers sacked . . . capitation allowances stretched . . . school meals cut back . . . new buildings empty . . . oversize classes . . . 20,000 teachers unemployed.[4]

For qualitists, by contrast, the 'crisis in education' had a very different meaning. It concerned a deep crisis of confidence about the aims, forms, methods and content of schooling.[5] The qualitists believed that, with or without more resources and increased access, what was required was a radical rethinking of what education was for and how it should be done. For them, what happened to middle-class children in public schools and grammar schools was no model for the kind of education they were seeking: 'It is time we stopped using the word 'education' honorifically. We must ask, education how? where? for what? and under whose administration?'[6] Mackenzie bluntly declaimed: 'The education system is irrelevant to our educational needs.'[7] Paton attacked 'the crazy idea of bottling up thirty kids in one classroom with someone in charge'.[8] Qualitists held that 'the story of education is the story of unexamined assumptions'.[9] In challenging the taken-for-granted understandings of 'education', 'learning', 'schools', 'school knowledge', 'teaching', and so on, they considered that they were the true radicals. The quantitists regarded this as treachery – an attempt to rob working-class children of the opportunity to have the good education which most radicals had themselves enjoyed.[10] In the words of NUT General Secretary Edward Britton, qualitists were 'educational quislings'.

It was left to the deschoolers to wonder aloud whether any nation could ever afford the level of resourcing envisaged by the quantitists:

> According to an educational law of eventually diminishing returns increased investment leads to increased failure and, in its turn, to arguments for yet more investment. This creates an exponential increase in the cost of failure. A developed country

is one that can afford failure at the highest per capita cost.[11]

For revolutionary socialists, the demand for more resources was part of a strategy of exposing the inability of capitalism to meet basic social needs. Whether any imaginable socialist society would ever be able to provide the kind of resourcing demanded was a moot question.[12]

At the root of this debate lies at least one empirical question: why do so many working–class children fail at school? Is it, as the Right to Learn group insisted, simply that they are not being given the provision which middle-class children receive? Or is it to do with the way that 'success' and 'failure' are conventionally defined? This brings us to the second dilemma.

A class analysis?

Closely related to the foregoing was a debate about the degree of emphasis which ought to be placed on social class in educational questions. Those radicals who gave primacy to a class analysis (Marxists, socialists and certain anarchists) regarded schooling as a systematic mystification by which the working class was purported to be offered a good education but was not. They considered the radical movement as an integral part of the struggle of the working class.[13] Other radicals – and this was particularly true of most American radicals – believed that the evils of schooling affected all children more or less equally. Gabriel Chanan and Linda Gilchrist argued that both were correct:

> there is a certain amount of confusion between the criticism of schools as teaching middle class values and as simply failing to teach effectively . . . Our legitimate criticism of schools is a compound of two distinct criticisms, the first a criticism of what school does to those who fail in it and second of what it does to those who succeed.[14]

There were certainly signs that middle- and upper-class children experienced their own schooling as oppressive. The school students' movement, at least in its early stages, attracted youngsters from grammar and public schools as much as from comprehensive and secondary modern schools. And we may take it that the kinds of criticism catalogued by Edward Blishen in *The School That I'd Like* came largely from middle-class children.[15] And we should not forget that the radical movement itself was a middle-class movement: it was not born out of any indigenous working-class resentment against schooling. The issue was whether or not the education problem was part of the class problem.

There has been an ebb and flow of class analyses as the central preoccupation of progressives and radicals. In the post-1945 period the early works advocating a new look at schooling[16] hardly mentioned class as an issue. Although interest in class was revived as an educational issue in the early 1960s by historians and sociologists,[17] the early publications and statements of the Libertarian Teachers' Association made no reference to the class question and even the first issues of *Rank & File* (1968 and 1969) made no suggestion that class might be an *educational* issue. It was not until the very end of the 1960s that class became a major concern of educational radicals. Until that time, radicals had tended to take as their starting point not class but 'the youth rebellion': 'These youngsters are truculently questioning our whole civilisation; and our civilisation is not standing up very well to their questions.'[18] Then, from the mid-1970s, class once more moved into the background (which is not to say that it was forgotten) as radicals made the issues of race and gender their primary concerns.

For radicals, class was not just a sociological concept for explaining social phenomena. British radicals were strongly influenced by the Marxist view that only the working class is capable of overthrowing capitalism (and its attendant evils). Therefore the 'mobilization of the working class' was fundamental to their strategy. But there were alternative ideas of the motor force of social change. As we have seen, there were those who believed that it was *young* people who would transform the world: 'Young people represent the most potent force for change in our society'.[19] Obviously, radicals who held this view had a particular reason for being interested in schools.

Reform or revolution?

For radicals of the late 1960s 'reform or revolution?' was a burning question. What was at issue was whether the social changes which radicals sought could be achieved through existing political structures and established institutions, or whether these would have to be swept away if radical changes were to be made. It was not only revolutionary socialists who eschewed 'reformism'; many anarchists did too, as well as sections of the non-Marxist Left such as that represented by *Peace News*, which declared itself (and continued to do so until 1989) 'for non-violent revolution'.

Revolutionists[20] were actively involved in the radical education movement, particularly in Rank & File and the Schools Action

Union. But when it came to educational debates it was never clarified what the implications of the revolutionist perspective were. It was hard to talk about education without talking in terms of reforms, but reforms were precisely what revolutionists had ruled out: 'The objective is not to have better schools within capitalism, but how to reconstruct education in a worker's state.'[21] An attitude taken by some revolutionists, which had the merit of simplicity, was that there was no point in proposing educational reforms until after the revolution because the fundamental constraint on education is the structure of prevailing social relations and 'it is impossible to change the social relations of education without a workers' state'.[22] Actually this view can be traced back to the eighteenth century (if not earlier):

> The art of forming men is in all countries so strictly connected with the form of government, that, perhaps, it is impossible to make any considerable change in public education, without making the same in the constitution of states.[23]

In this view any attempt to improve education under capitalism could only work to the advantage of capitalists.[24] Those involved in education could only agitate and organize as workers against their employers and link up with similar workers' struggles. Thus questions of 'education' became questions of teachers' salaries and conditions and so on. The *Teachers Action* group held that pupils, too, were workers (albeit unwaged) and encouraged them to join the struggle. But since they did not have employers it was unclear who they were to struggle against. (There would seem to be a better analogy between students and *unemployed* workers, and the Left has always had difficulty in specifying a clear role for the unemployed in the class struggle.)

At a time when educational matters were being widely debated the 'wait till after the revolution' stance was hard to maintain and revolutionists were inevitably, if reluctantly, drawn into proposing reforms. The clearest example of this was Rank & File's proposal for the democratization of schools (see Chapter 3). On the whole, revolutionists, unable to develop a distinctively revolutionary strategy on educational matters (apart from the stillborn idea of turning schools, colleges and universities into 'red bases'), were content to give their support to progressive reforms like comprehensive schooling, mixed-ability groupings and the abolition of corporal punishment. Even here, however, the fear of being labelled 'reformist' was evident, for example in the International Marxist Group's statement that it was opposed to corporal punishment, not because it was morally or educationally indefensible ('liberal' sentiments) but only because 'it divides pupils and teachers in their common struggle against capital'.[25]

The belief that the reforms thought desirable by radicals could not possibly be achieved within capitalism (this was the view of the Schools Action Union) is open to doubt. Many radical reforms have been implemented in, for example, Finland in recent decades. There may, perhaps, be a darker side to revolutionism in the feeling that any reforms which improve the people's lot are a setback for the class struggle because they diminish people's inclination to struggle for the overthrow of capitalism: in this view 'better means worse'. If revolutionists believe this, they should say so.

Related to the 'reform or revolution?' debate was the question of how far and how fast it was right to go at any time. There were those who held that if you attempt to go 'too far too fast' you alienate potential sympathy and end up in an isolated position: the correct tactic is to make proposals which move in the right direction but which are capable of carrying popular opinion with them. (Thus, for example, the best tactic for supporting a teachers' pay claim is to propose infrequent half-day strikes rather than all-out strikes of indefinite duration.) Characterizing this view as 'gradualism' or 'Fabianism', its opponents argued that gradual approaches are too easily negated, ignored, compromised or appropriated by the status quo[26] and can even be counter-productive. Such arguments were often invested with suspicions about the motivations of those taking the opposing view: perhaps the 'gradualists' don't *really* want there to be changes; perhaps there are some among the 'whole hog' brigade who don't *really* care whether they succeed or fail. It is hard to see how such arguments might be resolved. It may be that the heady days of the 1960s gave young radicals an unrealistic notion of the tempo of social change: if they didn't think that 'the world can be changed overnight', they did feel that it could be changed within a few years.

There was a similar debate about whether the best tactic was a frontal assault on an objective or whether subtler forms of man-oeuvre were more effective. Within schools, for example, groups of radical teachers debated whether it was better in staff meetings to attack the headteacher and his or her policies openly or to try to win ground by making proposals which pretended to be only designed to further those policies.

One further matter to be discussed in connection with reforms and revolutions is the question of 'single-issue' campaigns. In Chapter 4 I described the success of the Society of Teachers Opposed to Physical

Punishment (STOPP), which campaigned assiduously for 20 years to achieve its objective. Revolutionists tended to spurn single-issue campaigns except as vehicles for 'putting across' their political message (and, it must be said, as fishing-grounds for new recruits). Their view was that such campaigns deal with symptoms not causes: they don't address the 'root of the problem' which is the whole social and economic structure. John Holt commented on this 'General Staff mentality':

> it is like telling people trying to rescue a drowning man from a lake that their efforts turn us away from the real problem – the need to drain the lake so that no-one could drown in it. Even if true, so what?[27]

The educational radicals of the 1960s and 1970s launched relatively few single-issue campaigns: Teachers Against Racism, the Campaign to Impede Sex Stereotyping in the Young (CISSY), the Children's Rights Workshop campaign on children's books, the Ladbroke School Affair,[28] and STOPP were rare examples. There was a tendency, in fact, for groups to embrace broader and broader objectives as they went along. Thus the Schools Action Union started off with proposals for a limited number of reforms and ended up as a revolutionary party. Within the Rank & File group there was a divisive debate over a proposal that the removal of British troops from Northern Ireland should become one of its major objectives. The thinking in favour of this was that Rank & File was well placed to bring the Irish question to the attention of British teachers as a whole. Opponents of the proposal argued that Rank & File wanted the support of teachers for its trade union and education policies regardless of whether they agreed that British troops should be withdrawn from Northern Ireland. It does seem arithmetically likely that the greater the number of objectives a group has, the smaller the number of people who will agree with all of them. Had radicals been prepared to mount more single-issue campaigns they might have achieved much more than they did.

How much politics?

As we saw in Chapter 5, the school students' movement was invited in 1969 to choose between 'education with a little politics or politics with a little education'. This was a choice which the whole radical movement found difficult. Although, as I suggested in Chapter 2, radicals could be distinguished from progressives by the greater stress they put on politics, the degree of stress varied. There was a

strategic question at issue here: it was possible that a 'purely educational' stand could have a wider appeal than a radical political stand.
This was brought out in an exchange in the columns of *Blackbored*
which is worth quoting in full:

Stoke on Trent, Staffs, 30 Nov 71
Dear Comrades, As socialists in teacher training we were pleased
to find that *Blackbored* existed with the aim of 'stimulating socialist
ideas and practice in the world of teacher training'. Unfortunately,
on reading *Blackbored* 3 we had to conclude that it would not help
to achieve that aim.
' "Socialist" is a loose term', says *Blackbored* 3. Very true. In fact
the oppressive nature of our education system, which *Blackbored*
opposes, has been perpetuated and reinforced by a party which
calls itself socialist, the Labour Party. Anyone who wants to fight
effectively for socialism therefore has to be precise about what he
means by the term. Otherwise he will end up wasting his efforts
on the Labour Party or some other blind alley.
How precise is *Blackbored* about what it means by socialism?
Not very. On page 14 of No 3 we read that 'the Union of Liberal
Students' Executive fully supports the objectives of *Blackbored*'.
Now the Liberal Party is a party openly committed to the preser-
vation of the present system of production for profit. It does not
support the independent action of the working class to overthrow
the system and bring about rational planning of production for
human needs. But this concept of the working class liberating
itself is for us the heart of socialism. The list of basic beliefs on page
2 of *Blackbored* 3 confines itself to condemning a few particular
features of the present educational system. It does not seek to find
the root causes behind those features and point out the basic
outline of how to fight them. This means that *Blackbored* is no
more socialist than the Labour Party or Liberal Party.
We realise that socialists cannot simply ram their ideas down
people's throats and say Take it or leave it. There is nothing wrong
in a socialist magazine including non-socialist articles – so long as
there is a clear socialist editorial line. But with *Blackbored* as it
actually is, the effect is that the issues in education are simply
posed as 'progressives', 'liberals' and 'socialists' on one side versus
'authoritarians' on the other. We believe that much of 'progressive' education is simply a more insidious method of reproducing
the aims of authoritarian education – eg, as Dave Lee (ap-
provingly!) puts it on page 13, to 'push the kids to give of their
best' – to give of their best to the capitalist system.

For us it is a basic principle of socialism not to fear to state what is. That is why we cannot consider *Blackbored* to be a socialist magazine.[29]

This was followed immediately by this reply from one of *Blackbored*'s editors:

It would no doubt have been easy to fill the pages of *Blackbored* with statements like 'only the independent action of the working class can overthrow the present system and bring about rational planning of production for human needs' – which I agree with, though, perhaps unlike the Staffs correspondents, I include teachers in the working class (okay, they haven't got their hands on the machines, but they've got them on the ideology, which is, in a sense, also vulnerable). But what impact would this bald formula have on those many *potential* socialists whose most urgent worries right now are about things like teaching practice, the dictatorship of headmasters, the difficulty of getting across to working class kids in the classroom, the intolerable tensions of school, the petty restrictions and mystifying lectures of college?

What is lacking from the Staffs comrades' position is a sense of imaginative involvement with the particular problems and experiences which preoccupy students and young teachers. Why is it that in college after college *Blackbored* sells scores of copies, frequently 50 or 100, while the resident 'official' socialists can be counted on the fingers of one hand – and frequently say 'Oh, you won't sell many here'? Why is it that many of the most militant people, people who are desperately concerned to understand why they feel dissatisfied with their education or frustrated in their jobs, are not aware of how close they are to socialism, and regard the committed socialists in their own colleges or staff rooms as cranks? Why is it that some of the most committed socialists who find themselves in colleges and schools are 'above' the local issues seething around them – or dormant around them but nonetheless potent – and will settle for nothing less than the Great Struggle of the Industrial Masses? Certainly the industrial struggle is the core of the matter, but it is necessary to re-create socialism from within one's immediate community not merely recognise it somewhere else. Wherever it is we're going, we can only get there through our own experience, however much we seek to widen it to join with others'. If we try to bypass it, we will lose whatever motivation towards socialism we originally had, and become mechanical agents of someone *else*'s ideas, which we will no longer be fit to evaluate.

Many articles in *Blackbored* have drawn a distinction between liberal-progressive and socialist tendencies in education. But this distinction has been *exploratory*. The question of how socialist principles should be applied in education has not by any means been solved yet. I have not come across any hallowed text by Marx on the dialectic of Teaching Practice. The comrades mention but do not grapple with the problem raised by Dave Lee's exhortation to 'push kids to give of their best'. What *is* the socialist answer to the problems of teaching *now*? More permissiveness surely isn't it. Neither can we afford to wait till the workers' revolution delivers us before trying to do anything ourselves.

Contrary to what the Staffs comrades seem to think, the main issue confronting us is not whether *Blackbored* is a socialist magazine; it is what is socialism itself as applied in a particular context and time. One thing it certainly isn't, is a schematic formula brought to people like a gospel instead of arising from their own experience and concerns.[30]

The two sides of this debate are clearly set out here, and there is no need to elaborate them. We might note, however, that this debate foreshadowed the debate within the Labour Party after its election defeats in the 1980s.

A political distinction relevant here is that made by Wini Breines between 'strategic' politics and 'prefigurative' politics.[31] 'Strategic' politics is concerned with 'building organisation in order to achieve power so that structural changes in the political, economic and social orders might be achieved'.[32] 'Prefigurative' politics, by contrast, seeks 'to create and sustain within the live practice of the movement, relationships and political forms that "prefigure" and embody the desired society'.[33] Breines argues that prefigurative politics was characteristic of the new Left in the United States in the 1960s, and that this marked it out from the 'old Left'. In Britain it was variably so. While most of the radical education groups were prefigurative in the sense that they adopted collective (as opposed to hierarchical) forms of organization, some did think in terms of 'winning power' which is a characteristically 'strategic' aim.

This is a more fruitful means of analysing the political differences within the radical movement than the old categories 'Left', 'Right', 'anarchist', 'socialist', and so on. And many of the 'political' differences within the radical movement owed as much to personal and temperamental divergences as to real political distinctions between the positions of the protagonists.[34]

The role of the state

I referred in Chapter 1 to the tension within the progressive movement between the independent progressive schools and progressives
within the state sector. This tension was replicated within the radical
movement: there were those who considered it imperative to work
'within the system' – that is, within state schools – and others who
felt that this was futile. The first view was exemplified by *Teaching
London Kids* or Rank & File, the second by the free schools. The
debate took place on two levels, one practical, the other theoretical.

On a practical level, radicals observed and catalogued the constraints placed upon them in state schools. Some believed that there
was sufficient room for manoeuvre (in some schools at least) for
radicals to operate fruitfully inside state schools, that the much
vaunted autonomy of British schools would permit real latitude. But
others felt that such attempts were too easily blocked, compromised, negated or co-opted. In fact most radicals did work in state
schools, although it is hard to say how successful they were in
offering children significantly different educational experiences. It
was a sense of disillusionment with the possibilities at a practical
level which drove some radicals into freeschooling and other ventures 'outside the system'.

On a theoretical level, there was a debate about whether the
constraints which radicals experienced within state schools were a
necessary concomitant of *state* control of schooling. The simplistic
view that the state somehow controls what goes on in schools with
an iron hand ('The teacher becomes the functionary of state power,
imbuing the children with state-licensed knowledge and ideology')[35]
was countered by an argument that things are more complicated
('educational development is an untidy series of temporary accommodations between conflicting economic and political interests'[36]
and 'though the school system has effectively served the interests of
profit and political stability, it has hardly been a finely tuned
instrument of manipulation in the hands of socially dominant
groups').[37]

The belief that there is an 'iron hand' which blocks radical
developments in state schools required an explanation of the precise
mechanisms by which it operated. As radicals began to develop
theories about such mechanisms (the most promising of which were
theories about knowledge and ideology)[38] it began to seem possible
that these mechanisms would operate quite as much 'outside the
system' (for example, in free schools) as within state schools.

The fate of the radical teachers of William Tyndale school, as well

as of radical headteachers like Robert Mackenzie and Michael Duane,[39] did seem to demonstrate severe limits on the scope for
radicalism in the state sector. But it might be argued that what these
'victims' had in common was a lack of discretion and tactical subtlety
in their dealings with the authorities and other hostile groups.
(Perhaps, for example, they tried to go 'too far, too fast'.) There
were other cases – for example, the successful defence by Countesthorpe College against its critics – which indicated that battles *could*
be won within the state sector.[40]

For Marxists, the issue hinged round their analysis of the state,
with Engels's *The Origins of the Family, Private Property and the State*
and Lenin's *The State and Revolution* often cited. An interesting, if
inconclusive, debate took place in the columns of *Rank & File* about
the interpretation of these texts and their implications for state
schooling.[41] The question which remained unresolved was whether
or not the state is necessarily inimical to forms of education which
advance the independent working-class struggle.

The fact that most radicals chose to work inside the state sector
should not be taken as an indication that they had settled these
theoretical debates in their own minds. It was much more a practical
matter, a matter of money: even radicals have to earn a living. Even
the best-organized ventures found it difficult to raise the money to
work outside the state sector: their existence was precarious and
usually short. But it is worth noting that even the voluntary sector
relies to a considerable extent on state funding (for example, White
Lion Street Free School could not have managed without considerable grants from the London Borough of Islington). As the 1970s
progressed the Left became more convinced that *local* government
did offer scope for radical programmes – hence the influx of left-
wingers onto local councils. Perhaps 'the state' was less monolithic
than some had believed.

Social structure and causality

Radical writings about education can be divided into those which
posit immediate causal relationships between observed phenomena
and those which look for a root (and possibly hidden) cause to which
the observed phenomena may be related. As an example of the
former, consider this statement by John Holt: 'The family even as
most people knew it in this country a hundred years ago has been
almost entirely destroyed, mostly by the automobile and the restless
and rootless society it has helped to create.'[42] Holt points here to two
phenomena – the rise of the automobile and changes in family life

over the past 100 years. He says that the latter was caused ('mostly') by the former. This kind of causal linking of two phenomena is common in Holt's writings. To give another example, he visited many schools and observed bad teaching and children failing to learn effectively. He claimed (at least in his early books) that the former causes the latter.[43]

Now there is an alternative approach to this question of causality. Instead of saying that one factor causes another, we could look for a third factor which is the underlying cause of the other two. In the first example, we might suggest that this underlying cause is the changing nature of industrial production associated with changes in technology. This can be viewed as a historical (and continuing) process which began with the industrial revolution. Development of new technologies led to the development of large factories and required the bringing together of large numbers of people in cities. This had its impact on traditional family and community patterns and created a need for methods of mass transportation (themselves made possible by technological developments).

A good example of the approach which seeks explanations in the social structure is Samuel Bowles and Herbert Gintis's book, *Schooling in Capitalist America*. Bowles and Gintis tried to show how features of schooling are related to the requirements of capitalist production, and how changes in the nature of capitalist production lead to changes in schooling.

Why do so many children fail at school? Holt's answer is that teachers haven't given enough thought to what they are doing. Bowles and Gintis offer a different answer: capitalist production requires a stratified labour force and therefore schools are required to stratify their pupils, labelling some 'successful' and others 'failures'. In the face of this requirement the ordinary teacher is quite powerless. But how does capitalism get teachers, most of whom are benevolent people who would dearly love *all* their pupils to succeed, to collaborate in this process? A social structure explanation would point to mechanisms like the examination system, or to an ideology which fosters the belief that some children are 'able' and others aren't, so that teachers resign themselves reluctantly to the 'fact' that some children will do well and others won't. (This ideology may well include 'scientific' notions of inherited intelligence or sociological notions of cultural deprivation.)

Analyses which relate phenomena to the social structure offer new depth to our understanding. But there are three dangers. The first is that while some phenomena may have a structural explanation, it does not follow that everything does. It was quite common in the

1960s and 1970s in certain left-wing circles to blame virtually *everything* on capitalism. An overemphasis on structural explanations can lead people to forget (or deny) their own responsibility for the consequences of their own actions.

The second danger is that of *determinism*: structural explanations can begin to make things look inevitable. If schools are as they are because capitalism requires them to be so, then it appears that there is nothing we can do about it unless we abolish capitalism. People become merely powerless cogs in the capitalist machine. But the fact that there are significant variations in daily life – some schools have mixed-ability groupings, for example, while others are streamed; some parents bring their children up in a libertarian way, while others don't – suggests that things are far from inevitably determined by hidden structural forces. Structural forces are merely that – forces. But human beings are capable of acting to resist such forces.

Thirdly, there is the problem of *reductionism*, in particular the problem of economic reductionism. Certain Marxists tend to trace the explanation for every phenomenon to *economics*. For example, Rank & File noted in 1977 that there was at that time 'a generalized attack on "progressive" methods', citing the William Tyndale affair and James Callaghan's 'back to the basics' call in his 1976 Ruskin College speech. Rank & File explained that 'The whole thing hinges, as far as the government and ruling class is concerned, upon the need for education cuts' and went on to claim:

> The development of education, in the broadest sense, is determined under the 'economics of scarcity' of the capitalist system, and in a largely negative sense, by 'economics'. So the future shape of education in this country is being determined by the need for cuts . . .[44]

This reduction of educational questions to a question of economics, and, specifically, the perception that the fight against the backlash in education was a matter of 'fighting the cuts', could be found over and over again in the publications of the Rank & File group, the Socialist Teachers Alliance, the Schools Action Union and in *Teachers Action*. It is worth noting that it is unlikely that Marx himself would have gone along with them:

> Marx and Engels repeatedly denied that economic conditions and demands, although 'in the last instance' primary, should be seen as the *only* historical driving forces; they denied that *every* historical movement, *every* political event, *every* philosophical idea must be directly and exclusively ascribed to economic processes.[45]

I agree with Michael Apple, who has written:

> It has become clear that any successful interpretation of how schooling is related to the economic, political and cultural spheres of our society must avoid economic reductionism and will be exceptionally complicated. This relationship cannot be completely caught by any theory that posits a one-to-one correspondence between what happens in schools and the needs of dominant class and gender groups.[46]

Degrees of libertarianism

The division in the radical movement was not between libertarianism and its antithesis (whatever we may call that), for the mood of the times was pervasively anti-authoritarian. All radicals favoured some relaxation of the traditional discipline and authority structures of schools. There was, however, a division between those who believed in maximum freedom for children (with Summerhill as the prototype) and those who, while favouring a relaxed 'open classroom', felt that the teacher must ultimately be in control of the educational process.

Although some might portray this as a division between 'anarchists' and 'socialists', that would not fit the facts. A.S. Neill was not an anarchist and indeed during the 1930s Summerhill had many communist supporters.[47] Of course, much depends upon how one defines 'anarchist' and 'socialist' – matters of incessant debate amongst anarchists and socialists themselves. It is arguable that the distinction between 'libertarian' and 'authoritarian' is primarily a matter of personality and temperament – a psychological matter, although the social formation of personality may well have a political dimension.[48]

The debate within the radical movement was not just about how much libertarianism was desirable in principle (in an 'ideal world') but what was the right practical approach in the present circumstances. All radicals accepted, to a greater or lesser extent, the thesis that schooling induces children to accept the prevailing ideology and 'lived ideology'.[49] The qeustion was, how should radical teachers respond to this? Some held that to give children maximum 'freedom' would be to leave them hopelessly vulnerable to the prevailing ideology; what was needed instead was a systematic attempt to present children with 'the other side of the story':

> I discounted the myth that the teacher must be the objective observer whose political and class allegiances are invisible to the

children . . . Some knowledge has a priority for assimilation: the knowledge of resistance to, and organisation against exploitation and subjection, and contact and empathy with the oppressed of the world, whether in your own street or lands or oceans away.[50]

Others responded that this was to go from the frying pan into the fire: it was merely a new form of indoctrination.[51]

If we leave aside the difficult questions of 'ideology' and 'indoctrination', there is still a dilemma between intervening and not intervening.[52] It is a question of the teacher's role and, more generally, of the relationships between adults and children.[53]

Seeing things from the point of view of the child

According to Leila Berg, 'the main reason why there are two sides in education is not that there are two theories, but that some people follow theories and other people follow children'.[54] In the radical literature there is a *prima-facie* distinction to be made between those writers who write about children (Neill, Holt, Kozol, Dennison, Kohl, Mackenzie, for example) and those who write about teachers or education (Goodman, Postman and Weingartner, Holly, Illich, for example). The former make real efforts to see things 'from the point of view of the child'. They describe children, quote their words and try to articulate the thoughts and feelings which children have about schooling. Their concern is that children should not be acted upon: they should not be thought of as clay to be modelled or plants to be tended. In Neill's opinion ordinary schooling is 'wrong because it is based on an adult conception of what a child should be and of how a child should learn'.[55]

The other set of writers, and almost all writers of educational theory, discuss questions of education from 'an adult perspective', without any necessary reference to the thoughts and feelings of children. Their concern is to develop a proper understanding of the educational process in society. It is not that they don't care about children, but they are, as it were, architects who want to solve problems of design and construction before moving people into the building. As the School of Barbiana students expressed it, with heavy irony: 'A university professor of education doesn't have to look at schoolboys. He knows them by heart, the way we know our multiplication tables.'[56]

Certainly most of the radical literature in Britain was written by teachers preoccupied with the problems of teachers who seemed to assume that what was good for teachers would necessarily be good for children. This was criticized by a correspondent in *Radical Education*:

> you mention the people who *have* to go to school only once . . . You write of 'an increasing militancy among teachers' without relating it at all to the increasing militancy among their students . . . You write of 'the revolt against the educational system of today' without mentioning the school students who are in the vanguard of that revolt . . . it seems possible that you regard the very students who totally reject school (who really are in revolt) as among your adversaries . . .[57]

In fact school students' voices could be heard in this period. Perhaps their most cogently argued statement was the book *Letter to a Teacher* by students of the School of Barbiana in Italy. These students took what I have called the 'quantitist' view in that they accepted the orthodox goals of education but criticized the means, which they found inefficient and unfair. They offered a very different idea of 'what children want' from that presented by the radical writers who claimed to be representing the 'point of view of the child'. For example: 'You say that boys hate school and love play. You never asked us peasants.'[58] They mocked the creed of the free development of the personality[59] and declaimed: 'A student who gives personal opinions on things beyond his reach is an imbecile. He should not be praised for it. One goes to school to listen to the teachers.'[60]

The dichotomy is not, as Leila Berg would have it, between those who follow 'theories' and those who follow 'children', but between theories based upon observation of, and knowledge of, real children, and those which are not. (I say *real* children because I know one Professor of Education who gets his knowledge of children from watching the British television series. *Grange Hill*.) This is why Froebel was such an important pioneer, why the studies of Jean Piaget were so valuable, and why John Holt's first two books, *How Children Fail* and *How Children Learn*, were so perceptive. Of the radical magazines only *Childrens Rights* stand out as drawing on this observation of children. The real argument amoung radicals was how far children *alone* can be allowed to dictate the course of their education, and how far it is possible.

Schoolers and deschoolers

Opposition to compulsory schooling was expressed throughout the 1960s[61] but it was not until Everett Reimer's *School Is Dead* and Ivan

Illich's *Deschooling Society* were published in 1971 that deschooling
became a widely discussed issue. These books called forth a number
of responses[62] but were quite summarily dismissed in radical publications.[63] It is possible to argue that since most active radicals were
teachers, deschooling was against their interests. One might also
wonder whether radical educationists found the prospect of the
abolition of schools unattractive because they would no longer have
anything to grumble about.[64] In my view, the chief effect of the
deschooling proposals was to confuse the radical movement and
thereby sap some of the energy which had previously gone into the
advocacy of school reform.

'Idealism' and 'realism'

In Chapter 2 I referred to the 'idealism' of radicals, defining the word
as a vision of how things ought to be.[65] A number of tensions within
the radical movement arose from this, and a good example is
provided by Rhiannon Evans talking about differences of opinion
which arose at Brighton Free School;

> Only two of us had taught at all. That in itself was a cause of
> factions because constantly you had experience pitted against
> idealism. And some of the stronger personalities were people
> without teaching experience at all. In fact they were from public
> schools: there were two of them, and I think there was a feeling
> they didn't have any understanding of the state system, they didn't
> have any understanding really of how kids have difficulties. They
> were some of the people who were most idealistic about structure
> – they felt it should be completely free, there should be no
> structure at all. They saw us as wishy-washy liberals, as selling out
> the principles and ideals which had arisen collectively but which
> had really come out of fairly minimal experience.[66]

Evans poses the dilemma here as one between 'idealism' and 'experience'. If our idealism tells us what *ought* to be done, our experience
tells us what *can* be done under given circumstances. It seemed to be
common for radical practitioners to experience frustration at the
idealistic advice which non-practitioners offered them and, when
they did not heed the advice, finding themselves accused of 'selling
out' on fundamental principles. The radical movement resembled
football terraces in the high proportion of people who were ready to
shout advice when they didn't have to do the job themselves.

There is a view (and this is related to the philosophical theory of
'idealism') that principles *precede* experience. This view sees one's

principles as fixed, unassailable axioms: what one must do is shape one's practice to conform to the principles. At work here is a characteristically radical desire to establish watertight categories which divide things into 'black' and 'white' and which permit no muddy grey areas which can become the 'thin end of the wedge'. For radicals, to operate in the world as it is (and not as they would wish it to be) is to face conflicts and doubts which are difficult to handle. Whether it is right to make compromises and accommodations, and how far to do so, remains a major radical dilemma.

The place of reason

As Brian Simon points out,[67] an emphasis on rationalism ('an attitude that seeks to solve as many problems as possible by an appeal to reason')[68] has been a characteristic of the radical tradition in British education. It was also a feature of the European libertarian tradition.[69] In the 1960s and 1970s, however, radicals began to depart from this emphasis. First, there was a complaint that schooling was concerned exclusively with the cognitive domain – a complaint A. S. Neill had made in 1945 in his book, *Hearts Not Heads in the School*. Pleas were made for the recognition of the proper place of fantasy and feelings in education.[70]

But there was also a wider view that rationalism was a sort of straightjacket: 'it is part of the process of subjection that our feelings are made to appear untrustworthy and can only be regarded seriously if they are uncontradicted by logic and if they are verified by empirical evidence'.[71] Rationalism, it was suggested, is only one way (and a characteristically Western way) of understanding the world,[72] and it is inadequate on three counts. First, reason is insufficient to comprehend the great cosmic forces – the human soul, the spiritual, the supernatural. Second, rationalism disregards the part that the emotions, and the unconscious, play in human life. Third, rationalism, overlooks the fact that the human being is an *animal* in an environment: rationalism underrates the physical, instinctual and the spontaneous (as opposed to thought-out) forces within us. Those who held this view feared that rationalism – especially its epitome, Western science – was endangering the future of life on this planet, as well as leading away from an understanding of human existence: 'the ever-growing reliance upon objective criteria of thought [has] been paid for by ever deepening ignorance of the real nature of human existence'.[73] And there was a further argument that our conception of 'rationality' is itself a social construction and must therefore be considered as problematic: Michael Young wrote that 'Today it is the commonsense conceptions of the "scientific" and the "rational" that represent the dominant legitimizing categories',[74] and he went on to suggest that questioning these taken-for-granted categories is a necessary preliminary to conceiving of alternatives.

In the broader radical movement of the 1960s and 1970s non-rational modes of expression were abundantly used – music, dance, drama, art, for example – as well as non-rational means of exploring experience – for instance, mysticism or drugs. But it may be a measure of the hold that rationalism has on education that such non-rational modes were rarely found within the radical *education* movement. It is, in fact, hard to see how an appreciation of the non-rational could make inroads into the adult world of education, given that those who inhabit it are selected precisely for their commitment to rationalism.

It is common for non-rational statements, when they are perceived as damaging, to be described as 'mindless'. Thus if a group of children express what they feel about their school by burning it down, their action may be called 'mindless'. Certain sociologists (within the field of deviance) have attempted to explain such actions by showing that they do have a 'rationale'.[75] This approach seems to assume that non-rational expressions can be translated into rational terms.

If there are dangers in ignoring the non-rational dimension of human experience (and I think it is fair to say that the radical movement in education was hardly more conscious of these dangers than 'the world of education' in general), there is equal danger in going to the other extreme of dismissing rationality. Rational thought is also part of human experience. What is needed is a proper acknowledgement of each dimension: a balance, if not a synthesis. It seems probable that the reconciliation of the rational and the non-rational would require great changes in the way we lead our lives and the way we organize our society.[76]

The plea for an acknowledgement of the emotions, of intuition, was the central input into the radical movement of humanistic psychology. This opened up a new set of dilemmas which are more familiar to us than they were in 1971 when Paul Adams, in *Children's Rights*, criticized the revolutionary Left: 'Theirs is a patriarchal and masculine rhetoric that sways only the adult, the male, or the authoritarian (female as well as male) who holds the patriarchal values.'[77] The concept of 'patriarchal values' raises questions not only about the devotion to rationalism of Western educators, but also about several of the other issues raised in this chapter. Are, for example, authoritarianism, revolutionism, confidence in the state, adult perceptions of childhood, or schooling itself, expressions of patriarchy? Indeed, this whole book could be said to be imbued with patriarchal assumptions. It makes a man nervous to put pen to paper.

Hippies and straights

There were few thoroughgoing hippies involved in the radical movement. But there were some in the Free Schools Campaign and in some of the free schools. A particular tension arose within the A.S. Neill Trust:

> The first meetings of the A.S. Neill Trust used to be at conference centres with beds laid on and stuff. And we said 'well there's no need for all that, we'll all bring sleeping bags and cut the price down'. A lot of people actually left the A.S. Neill Trust simply because of that – a lot of people who'd been into it from the Homer Lane, A.S. Neill faction didn't actually like the idea of not having gold-printed invites, rooms reserved for them and stuff. So in a sense it was actually bringing out some people's politics, saying 'are you actually prepared to go as far as the thing is going to go?' It is about urban working-class people and they can't afford to have expensive weekend conferences and if you want children from the free school [to attend the conference] they're probably going to break a few things. So it's not going to be 'nice'. We saw and appreciated that we were taking politics into people's personal lives and not just the abstract thing. Naively to start with we thought that all the Left would support us. In fact the Left didn't want to know.[78]

The Left, in fact, was 'straight'. There are a number of points in this statement we might want to examine, but I will confine myself to the characteristically 'hippy' notion that 'the personal is political'. For hippies, the transformation of society begins with the transformation of individual lifestyles. Those who are unwilling, or unable, to detach themselves from conventionalism (the 'bourgeois lifestyle') in their lives are helping to prop up the system. 'Before you change the world you've got to change yourself' went the slogan. We can see here 'prefigurative' politics taken to its logical conclusion.

Most radical activists within education may have been relatively 'straight', but this did not mean they were unruffled by the hippies' charges. There *is* something anachronistic about middle-class people assembling in a comfortable conference centre to discuss the problems of working-class children, and then getting upset when working-class children come into the conference and disturb the proceedings. It is not easy, however, to say precisely what the nature of this anachronism is (is it something to do with guilt?) or what might be done about it. It is not clear that abandoning your reserved room and sleeping on the floor in a sleeping bag solves the problem (although as a symbolic gesture I suppose it might be worth something).

Paradoxically, if most radicals were regarded by hippies as 'straight', ordinary working-class children may have thought of radicals as hippies. At White Lion Street Free School it was common for the children to call the workers 'hippies', despite the fact that few of the workers fitted that description. Enquiries of the children revealed that hippies, in their eyes, had the following characteristics. First, they were middle-class people who had relinquished certain trappings which the children reckoned were the whole point of being middle-class: posh homes, new cars, smart clothes. Second, they weren't interested in making money. Third, they dressed casually, even scruffily. Fourth, certain tastes could be associated with them: rock music and vegetarian foods, for example. Fifth, they used (albeit occasionally) certain hippy expressions like 'far out', 'too much', 'bread', 'mind-blowing', and so on. Sixth, their lifestyle was unconventional: for example, they lived with partners rather than getting married. Seventh, they weren't prejudiced against homosexuals and blacks like 'normal' people were.

Such perceptions were quite acute: radicals (at least of the free school variety) *had* made changes in their personal lifestyles. But perhaps they didn't go far enough in this direction to contribute to the collapse of bourgeois society which the hippies had in mind.

Conclusion

I have not attempted to cover all the things radicals argued about: they argued about everything. Nor have I tried to suggest the 'right' answer in each of the debates, although it will have been clear in some cases that I am inclined towards one side or the other.

It is tempting to think that if the radical movement could some-how resolve these debates – by intensive study, perhaps, or by examining the evidence, or possibly by just going on debating the issues until a consensus emerges – it would gain a sense of unity and coherence which could make it a potentially much more powerful force than it was in the 1960s and 1970s. I think that might be a very good thing. On the other hand, it may be a characteristic of the radicalism that, underlying the superficial bravado of its assertions, there was a deeper ambivalence. It was, perhaps, incompatible with that kind of *certainty* which steamrollers everything before it: the certainty of the *Black Papers*, for example, or of Margaret Thatcher's style of government. In this respect, those sections of the radical movement which did express certainties – the Rank & File group or the Schools Action Union, for example – were atypical.

But to be uncertain is, in the world of politics, to be vulnerable. All too often uncertainty is taken as weakness. In 1978 I received a telephone call from the BBC asking me to take part in a studio debate with Rhodes Boyson: 'Dr Boyson will be saying that standards in schools have fallen; we want someone to say that standards are rising.' 'Well', I replied, 'I'm not too sure that standards *are* rising, though I don't agree with Dr Boyson that they are falling'. 'Sorry for bothering you', came the response, 'we'll find someone else who is willing to say that standards are rising'. And they did.

Uncertainty is difficult to live with, but my own feeling is that the field of education is a field in which uncertainty ought to prevail, because we have no means of finally settling educational debates. That is why educational arguments have a way of recurring periodically – often every 30 or 40 years, and why so many of Plato's ideas about education (for example) remain matters of debate today. I will return to this 'periodicity' in the next chapter, where I will suggest that it offers opportunities to radicals which were missed in the 1960s and 1970s.

CHAPTER 11

The present moment
in education

The radical movement of the 1960s and 1970s looked for enormous and fundamental changes in education: in the way that education was conceived of, in the way it was organized, in its aims and methods, and in the way we view children and arrange their learning. Moreover, radicals saw these changes taking place within equally drastic changes in the wider economic and social structures.

It is hardly necessary to point out that these sweeping changes did not occur. It might seem, then, that we could declare the radical movement a failure. Certainly those 1960s radicals who expected the world to be transformed within a few years were disappointed. But the desire for 'instant success' was a feature of the 1960s; experience has taught us that the road will be long and hard. Has any progress been made along that road?

Progressive developments

Despite the backlash of the 1980s a number of progressive developments were sustained. We might point, for example, to the relative security of comprehensive schooling (at least until 1987) in the face of concerted opposition; the continuance of mixed-ability groupings; the continued existence of progressive primary schools in many areas; the advent of a single exam at 16-plus; progressive curriculum developments such as Peace Studies, World Development Studies, and anti-racist and anti-sexist initiatives; and the abolition of corporal punishment in maintained schools. While some radicals would consider such things as mere 'tinkering', others would consider them steps, however small, in the right direction.

Some of these developments would have occurred even if the radical movement had not existed; indeed, it is arguable that the radicals hindered such changes by tarring them with the brush of 'extremism'. Conversely, one might suggest that radicalism, in its 'extremism', made progressivism look decidely moderate by comparison and thus helped to make progressivism more widely acceptable. Whichever is the case, there are at least a few changes which can be said to have originated in the radical movement. Much of the credit for the abolition of corporal punishment must go to the Society of Teachers Opposed to Physical Punishment (STOPP). The enormous improvements in the content of children's books over the past decades began in the radical movement (see page 79). The growing interest in the education of children outside of schools, associated with Education Otherwise, can be traced to the radical disaffection with schooling in the early 1970s. The 1985 Swann Report on multi-cultural education acknowledged that its antecedents lay in the thinking of the late 1960s.[1] And there can be little doubt that contemporary attempts to eliminate sexism from schooling owe their impetus to the renaissance of the women's movement in the 1960s. At a local level there have been some developments first suggested by radicals, such as the practice, now established in some LEAs, of having secondary school pupils (and in some areas, primary school pupils) on the governing bodies of schools.

Theoretical developments

There have been, too, a number of developments at the level of *ideas* for which the radical movement can be credited. If few of the 1960s and 1970s ideas were new, the radical movement brought these ideas back for theoretical scrutiny – opening up territory that had previously been neglected. The first such developments came in the early 1970s with the renewed interest in the sociology of knowledge[2] and in the history of working-class self-education.[3] There followed lines of enquiry within sociology and history which had an explicitly radical outlook.[4] Then there was extensive theoretical work on race and gender.[5]

What all these theoretical developments have in common is that they have abandoned the pretence of political 'neutrality' which characterized most educational theory prior to 1970. (Needless to say, this brought forth objections from right-wing critics who pointed to 'Marxist subversion' and so forth.)[6] Thus they made a start on building what *Radical Education* in the editorial of its first issue called the 'socialist theory of education' which it considered to be at that time (1974) non-existent.

One of the most difficult tasks which radicals always face is to challenge conceptions which have become embedded in ordinary language. An example was given in *Lib Ed* magazine: 'It is an aspect of the dominant ideology that education and schooling are synonymous: it is the job of libertarians to break with this false identification.'[7] To some extent this break has been achieved: not fully, to be sure, but it has become fairly common for people to draw a distinction between 'schooling' (which is what goes on in schools) and 'education' (which happens to everyone from the cradle to the grave and which may, or may not, be improved by the experience of schooling).

Similarly, the concept of 'equality of opportunity' which was at one time considered to be something *everyone* was in favour of has, thanks to the radical movement, been called into question.[8]

Adult education

The radical thinking of the 1960s and 1970s had much more impact on adult education than on schools.[9] In particular, adult education has put into practice, in many instances, the integration of education and social action referred to in Chapters 7 and 9.

The probable reasons for this are that adult education is not statutory, and there are fewer constraints on radical experimentation. Since adults are presumed to understand 'what they are letting themselves in for' it is harder to level charges of 'indoctrination' against voluntary adult courses. Radical teachers who felt frustrated by the constraints on schools often found more scope for their ideas by working with adults. Furthermore, notions such as 'self-directed learning' and 'equal relationships between learner and teacher' are more easily realized with motivated adults attending courses of their own choosing than with the reluctant conscripts of the schoolroom.

Setting a radical agenda

If the radical movement achieved nothing else, its abundant literature succeeded in setting out an agenda of issues to be debated. However bleak the outlook for radical ideas at the moment, their time will come again. I hope that the experience and thinking of the 1960s and 1970s can be built upon. Harking back to the distinction used in Chapter 3, I propose developments within the radical tradition, rather than expressions of spontaneous radicalism.

Practical experience

In assessing the radical movement, we should acknowledge its effect on the people taking part. That old Olympic motto 'the important thing is not to have won, but to have taken part' reminds us that even if radicals did not succeed in changing the world, they gained something from their attempt to do so. Of particular importance is the practical experience gained from working for radical change. This includes experience in schools, in campaigning groups and publications, and in educational alternatives such as free schools.

Unfortunately, there is a tendency for such experience to be lost, as the people involved move on to other things, retire and, eventually die. For example, the experiences of the experimental schools which mushroomed in the 1920s and 1930s were, with few exceptions, inadequately recorded and are probably now lost. Often, the documentary records which are available to us are defensive and polemical: we cannot learn from the *mistakes* of those experiments if the mistakes were not documented.

Learning the lessons

I want now to make some general remarks about the radical movement, the purpose of which is to highlight areas in which the performance of the movement could have been improved upon.

Organization

Almost every group within the radical movement was handicapped by lack of resources – in terms both of money and of people willing to take on a workload. Ways of raising finance were insufficiently explored. Some methods of raising funds may seem to go against principles cherished by radicals, or require some compromise of those principles, and then a dilemma is faced: is it better to make some compromises and continue, or stick fast to your principles and 'go under'? An example of this dilemma was provided by free schools which might have survived longer had they been prepared to charge fees. Similarly, some radical magazines might have survived longer if they had sought a wider circulation by popularizing their content, accepting advertisements and so on.

While many of the people in the radical movement did have incomes which allowed them a comfortable lifestyle (meals in restaurants, holidays abroad, nicely furnished homes, and so on), they were reluctant to commit a large part of their own resources to the campaigns they participated in. This raises an interesting question of how desperately such radicals *needed* their campaigns to succeed. This is not a jibe: there is a serious question of whether middle-class radicals really have a material interest in far-reaching social changes, and of what deprivations they are prepared to suffer to achieve them. There is, perhaps, an element of 'bet hedging' – just in case there *isn't* a revolution we'd better hold on to what we've got.

If radicals were not willing to give all their *money* to the causes they espoused, they often did give virtually all their *time* to them. Hyperactivity was common – meetings every evening; hours at the typewriter into the night; pasting up journals; attending demonstrations or conferences every weekend. It was probably inevitable that such effort could not be sustained in the long run.

Another area of difficulty was the internal organization of radical groups. In some there was a problem of structurelessness – the Libertarian Teachers' Association was a prime example. In others there were excessive rigidities which led to constant in-fighting. Most groups favoured collective forms of organization, but one wonders how far this detracted from efficiency and effectiveness. For example, most radical magazines spurned any division of labour and had an editorial collective which shared decision-making, writing, editing, sub-editing, layout and artwork and distribution. (Printing, however, required equipment and expertise beyond their reach.) Such an arrangement was thought to be beneficial, providing an equal sense of involvement and valuation, and opportunities to share and learn skills. But against these benefits had to be set costs; indifferent editing, messy presentation and, very often, a failure to make a favourable impression on the reader.

With the benefit of hindsight, one of the most surprising weaknesses of the radical movement was the lack of link-ups between different radical groupings both within the field of education and beyond it. There was no radical equivalent of the New Education Fellowship which for many years served as an umbrella organization for the progressive movement. The 1969 National Convention of the Left, which had an education section, was not successful in its aim of bringing together all the strands of the Left; perhaps it set its sights too high. A very different venture, the Community Levy for Alternative Projects (CLAP), sought in the early 1970s to establish a funding pool for projects which saw themselves as 'counter-cultural', but it was not notably successful.

Such link-ups as did exist between radical groupings occurred where their activists belonged to the same political sect. But this kind of link-up had its drawbacks, most especially sectarianism. It is hard for those who were not involved in the radical movement to appreciate the extent and ferocity of the sectarian squabbles which took place both within groups and between them. The school students' movement was particularly badly affected by this, and there were few corners of the radical movement which were untouched. Given the depth of the antagonisms, it is difficult to imagine how such a movement could ever have hoped to improve the world.

The means of communication preferred by the radicals were books, magazines and meetings. Very little attention was given to gaining access to the means of mass communication – especially radio and television.[10] Activists within the movement were sometimes offered the opportunity to participate in broadcasts – usually studio discussions – but very rarely on their own terms, in ways in which they could determine the message put across. Sometimes, in fact, the programmes had the effect – whether by accident or design – of making radicals look foolish. It seems fairly obvious that a movement which has something to say to large sections of the population – parents, for example – must necessarily find ways of getting access to the airwaves: not an easy task, but not impossible either. Similarly, radicals in education made few attempts to explore the possibilities of film and video: a notable exception was Pat Holland's film *What Are Schools For?*[11] which, unfortunately, wasn't finished until 1980 and now rarely gets a showing.

In retrospect it is easy to see the limitations of the magazines which radicals produced. With some exceptions, they were unattractive to look at, didactic in tone and poorly planned. Insufficient thought was given to making them appeal to a wider readership – they often look like the 'house journals' of an inward-looking clique. Some magazines tried to set up readers' groups around the country which served two functions: to provide feedback to the editorial group and to help with the distribution of the journal. Distribution was a constant headache: commercial distributors were not interested in small-circulation magazines which offered them a margin of only a few pence per copy. The gap was filled in the mid-1970s when a radical distributor, the Publications Distribution Co-operative, was set up, but this was rather too late for most of the magazines mentioned in this book. In any case, the Publications Distribution Co-operative soon discovered for itself the financial burdens of distributing small magazines. An important outlet was the network of radical booksellers and bookstalls which mushroomed in the early 1970s. Although better than nothing, they had a habit of disappearing overnight leaving unpaid bills; and they tended to serve a specific

clientele: people who were already sympathetic to the radical movement. There was no substitute for going out and selling a magazine.
It was possible, for example, to visit a College of Education and sell
perhaps 100 copies in an afternoon. What was lacking was people
prepared to do this kind of chore.

Strategy

The radical movement set itself two tasks: to identify and explain the
wrongs of schooling; and to set about remedying these wrongs. But
the movement was far from clear about how to set about this second
task.

As we have seen, many radicals considered that they were representing the interests of the working class, ethnic minorities, and
women, who were seen as the chief victims of contemporary
schooling. Strategy required, therefore, winning support from these
groups for radical programmes. While radicals made some headway
among women (at least among those active in the women's movement) it was conspicuously unsuccessful in winning any significant
support among the working class or the ethnic minorities. This
failure of radicals to gain the support of the constituency which it
chose for itself is a specific instance of the problem which has become
very clear to the Left generally in the 1980s. Perhaps the central
question which needs to be asked is this: in what way do the
educational changes proposed by radicals relate to the interests of
working-class and ethnic minority people *as those people themselves
perceive their own interests at the present moment*?

An example of this problem is supplied by the title of an article by
the founders of White Lion Street Free School. The article is called
'Abolishing the Curriculum and Learning Without Exams'.[12] But to
those people – most people – who conceive of a good education as
consisting of ingesting a curriculum and then passing exams, the idea
of a school which 'abolishes the curriculum' and does away with
exams must seem absurd.

To some extent, the difficulty here is one of communication:
perhaps it *is* possible to win people's support for radical ideas, but
only if there is an opportunity to explain fully those ideas to them. As
I have suggested, the radicals did give insufficient attention to
putting their ideas across to the generality of people. Although there
were exceptions – the books of John Holt and R.F. Mackenzie were
good attempts at popularizing radical ideas; and *Children's Rights*
magazine attempted to attract a wide readership – most radical
publications were not addressed to ordinary people.

But it would be a mistake to think that the problem was only one of communication. The plain fact is that working-class and ethnic minority people just did not see the ideas of the radical educationists as being in their interests. Some radicals would explain this in terms of 'false consciousness' or 'bourgeois indoctrination'.[13] There may well be a grain of truth in that: but to accept it as a complete explanation is to avoid asking two central questions; first, are the programmes proposed by radicals *really* what the people want; and second, what is the point of going on insisting that it is the 'working class' who ought to want them most? My own feeling is that a strategy which depends upon winning mass working-class support for a programme of radical educational change is a doomed strategy.

I am not, of course, arguing that the educational ideas put forward by radicals are in *no one's* interest. I believe that there is a body of people, which will grow in size over the next decade or two, which will be attracted to the radical banner. Radicals face the challenge of identifying and addressing that body of people: but their efforts to do so will be hampered by the unexamined presumption that it can be defined as 'the working class'.

Another way of looking at radical strategy is in terms of *power base*. By a power base I mean any section of the population which is collectively able to exert social, political or economic influence. Of the groups surveyed in earlier chapters, only a few tried to locate a power base for themselves. The Rank & File group, for example, sought a base in the NUT, the Schools Action Union and the National Union of School Students among school students – certainly a numerically large section of the population. The rest appealed in a vague way to radicals in general, and radical teachers in particular. While the NUT probably had a certain amount of influence, it is difficult to see what power 'radicals' as a group had. There was a notion of being a 'vanguard' (or avant-garde) – leading the way in the hope that others would follow. But it was unclear what would happen if others did not follow.

In matters of strategy, *timing* is critical. It has become clear from this study that the radical movement was overtaken by events. A product of the 1960s, it did not reach its peak until well into the 1970s, by which time the climate had changed decisively. Thus, for example, *Radical Education* set out in 1974 to 'give voice to the revolt against the educational system of today' but very soon found itself defending that same system against the growing tide of reaction. And the sophisticated theory which the radicals required only began to come together in the 1970s – ten years after it was needed.

It is not easy to pinpoint the exact moment when the tide began to turn. The first *Black Paper* in 1969 was a warning shot. The Conservative victory of 1970 suggested that the electorate had had enough of the 'swinging sixties'. The 1973 Yom Kippur war – with the subsequent vast rise in oil prices and world economic recession – undermined the expansion which had, arguably, provided the economic basis for the radicalism of the 1960s. The closure of Penguin Education in 1974 was a significant setback. In that same year the Labour Party returned to government – but the appointment of Reginald Prentice (soon to defect to the Conservative Party) as its first Education Secretary indicated that it would give little succour to radicals. The dispute at William Tyndale School in 1975 – and especially the hounding of its teachers by the press – showed clearly that the progressive consensus had ended and that the 'back to the basics' (the codewords, along with 'standards', for wholesale reaction) era had arrived. It remained only for Prime Minister Callaghan, in his October 1976 speech at Ruskin College, Oxford, to put the official imprimatur on the new orthodoxy. There followed Shirley Williams's 'Great Debate' which was, as far as radicals were concerned, no debate at all. The parameters of the debate had in fact been set down in advance: the week *before* Callaghan's speech it was announced that 'a multi-million pound emergency programme to monitor standards [note the codeword] in primary and secondary schools has been started by the DES'.[14] The hand-picked participants in the 'Great Debate' included no representation whatsoever of the radical viewpoint.

Radicals had missed their time. Their time was the 1960s, but they were not able to take the opportunities which presented themselves in that decade. It is part of the argument of this book that radicals need to prepare themselves if they are to take full advantage of the opportunities which arise.

The present predicament

There seems to be an educational equivalent of Newton's Third Law of Motion: to every action there is an equal and opposite reaction. The first *Black Paper*, it may be remembered, was a response to the 'student revolt', in 1967 and 1968: it was predominantly concerned with higher education. It was only the later *Black Papers* which focused on schooling. What motivated the *Black Paper* editors' crusade was their perception that 'progressive ideas are now in the ascendant'.[15] Five *Black Papers* were published between 1969 and 1977, and they were followed by a steady stream of books and pamphlets produced by a small clique of determined right-wingers – Anthony Flew, C.B. Cox, Caroline Cox, John Marks and Roger Scruton were the most prominent.[16] Rhodes Boyson may have been the 'spiritual father' of this group but, holding government office, he was unable to play quite such an active role as formerly.

Radicals – and others – have frequently made the mistake of ignoring right-wing writings on education, perhaps because they regard them as unworthy of serious attention. This is a mistake for two reasons. It is necessary to demonstrate, in closely argued detail, the fallacies these writings contain. If this is not done, there is a real likelihood that the fallacies will be accepted into popular mythology.[17] But also, these right-wing critics often have a clearer perception of educational realities than their political opponents. In particular, they were quite right to perceive that there was a widespread unease among parents – and especially the parents of children in inner-city secondary schools – about the quality of schooling. Far from assuaging such parental anxieties, radical offers to 'abolish the curriculum' or do away with exams merely exacerbated them. In the absence of any left-wing proposals for meeting parental anxieties, it was easy for the right-wing to move in and win the support of parents for backward-looking proposals.

Labour governments of the 1960s and 1970s pushed through comprehensive schooling, announcing a new era of opportunity for every child. It was explicitly claimed that this would mean that many more children would achieve examination passes: a 'grammar school education for all'. It did not turn out that way: although there has been a steady growth in the proportion of children passing examinations, this cannot be ascribed to the coming of comprehensive schooling.[18] There was, therefore, a growing scepticism through the 1970s about the wisdom of 'going comprehensive'.[19] The radical Left (in contrast to Prime Minister Callaghan, who saw which way the wind was blowing), responded to this only by reasserting its commitment to comprehensive schooling. Failing to recognize that doubts about comprehensive schools were more than just a right-wing conspiracy, it offered no response to growing popular concern, and left the door open to the right-wing clamour for 'back to the basics' and the subsequent major right-wing offensive.

In the late 1980s radicals faced the bleakest of outlooks. The Conservative government had pushed through a series of reforms which were the very antithesis of what radicals stood for: a narrow curriculum imposed by law on all schools, reminiscent in many ways of the Revised Code of 1862; compulsory testing of all children at the ages of 7, 11 and 14, reopening the door to all the psychologi-

cally damaging effects of the old 11-plus; a greater orientation of
schools towards the 'needs of the economy', negating all those
progressive aspirations for an education which unlocks the imagination and enables children to examine society critically; a drift back
towards selective schooling; the attack on LEAs which had tried to
force the pace of educational change in their schools; and arrangements which raised the spectre of fee-paying, separate schools for the
rich and the poor, racially segregated schools, and schools account-
able to no public interest except 'market forces'.[Under such circumstances it might seem that the heady ideas of the radicals are mightily
irrelevant. Clearly the primary need is for an alliance of all progressives and liberals – and this will include some in the Conservative
Party – to defend schools from any further encroachments by the
New Right. That may well be accepted as the immediate task.)But I
want to consider the position a little further, and to do so I will refer
to the analysis made by Ken Jones in his interesting book, *Beyond
Progressive Education*. We can summarise Jones's thesis in this way:
schooling in Britain was dominated between 1930 and 1979 by a
consensus based on the twin planks of 'progressive reform' and
'equality of opportunity'. In the 1970s this consensus started to break
up, as the New Right detached itself and went off on an independent
route.[20] Once this had happened the planks of the consensus turned
out to be hollow and were insufficient for the labour movement to
mount a counter attack. Jones goes on to argue that the New Right
cannot be defeated merely by renewed appeals for progressive
reform or more equality of opportunity. Instead he urges that the
labour movement must be won over to a programme of radical
education, thus moving 'beyond progressive education'.

[It is difficult to quarrel with Jones's contention that the slogan
'let's get back to the good old 1950s and 1960s' – which is what the
'progressive consensus' response to the New Right amounts to – is
hardly likely to arouse mass popular enthusiasm.] Rightly or
wrongly, the leading lights of the 'progressive consensus' (or post-
war settlement as it is sometimes called) – from Butler through
Boyle to Shirley Williams – are not remembered as people who had
the answers.

The predicament can therefore be stated in this way: if we are to
oppose the present programmes of the New Right, what are we
proposing to put in their place? Jones answers 'radical programmes',
although he does not spell out what these might consist of.

My own starting point is the firm conviction that the educational
reforms of Mrs Thatcher's third term in office (the 'Baker reforms')
will not work. That is, they will not achieve their aims; even less will

they allay popular anxiety about schooling. My reason for this conviction may be summed up in the proverb 'you can take a horse to water but you can't make it drink'. In Chapter 8 I argued that the key factor determining whether children learn or not is *motivation*, and I argued that this must be understood as a *social* phenomenon, not an individual characteristic. [No educational programme which ignores the three-way relationships between children, content of learning, and society has any future.]

In this light, let us look at the 'Baker reforms'. First, they were predicated upon the continuance of the social, political and economic structures which Mrs Thatcher diligently erected in the 1980s. It is my contention that these structures, in relation to education, impose contradictory demands upon children. Children are at once offered a *motivation* which is essentially competitive and, at the same time, asked to learn a curriculum which is essentially based upon notions of 'national interest' (or, more specifically, the 'needs of industry'). The contradiction lies in the two messages: 'you're on your own: get up, get on, to hell with everyone else' and 'knuckle down: do your duty; serve your country by fitting in and acquiescing'.

[To prescribe a 'national curriculum' is one thing; to get childen to learn it is quite another. In my opinion, children will *not* learn it. To add insult to injury, the government is testing all children at the ages of 7, 11 and 14 to see how well they have learned the government curriculum. We can predict that the majority of children will fail these tests because there is little in contemporary society to motivate them to pass them.] The Revised Code of 1862 established a national curriculum, and it was the duty of the inspectorate to visit schools and test all children to see whether they had learned the set curriculum. Worse, the system of 'payment by results' meant that the grants given to schools (and hence the salaries of teachers) were determined by the proportion of children who passed the tests.

Now the crucial historical fact about the Revised Code was that it *did not work*. And it did not work even though desperate teachers often thrashed children mercilessly in their attempt to get children to learn. Only about 25 per cent of children passed the tests and the Cross Commission in the 1880s [21] found abundant evidence that the Revised Code was actually causing a decline in standards. Furthermore, everything else was forced out of the school curriculum as teachers concentrated on coaching children for the narrow subject matter of the tests. [22] The proposal to return to the Revised Code was first made by *Black Paper* writer Stuart Froome in 1978. [23] Froome made this proposal in apparent ignorance of the disastrous effects of the code (which was abolished in the 1890s, having been universally discredited) and it does seem extraordinary that this ill-informed proposal should have been taken up by a modern government (among whose advisers there must surely be *one* who has read a history textbook) albeit in a rather different guise.

The history of education may be viewed as the history of policies which failed to achieve their aims. Once it has become apparent that they have not succeeded, a reaction sets in and policies are proposed which to some extent return to earlier orthodoxy.[24] The 1890s, the 1920s and the 1960s were favourable decades for radicals: in these periods their views were listened to. In the intervening periods reaction was in the ascendant. If history repeats itself (and we should never forget that history is made by people) we can expect, in the 1990s, new opportunities to arise for radical educational ideas. It may well be that this will coincide with the public realization that the 'Baker reforms' did not work. Radicals will then have the chance to explain why they did not work. For a start, it was the radicals who insisted that educational planners must take children into their calculations.

Preparing for the future

I want to urge that radicals *prepare* themselves for the opportunities which will assuredly arise in the future. I wish to suggest several areas in which such preparatory work might be undertaken.

Theory

Theoretical work is important. Even the daftest theories can find *some* adherents, but it surely must be likely that the sounder the theory, the more adherents it will gain in the long run. Developing a profound and credible theory is, therefore, one thing radicals can do as part of a long-term programme to gain support. Radicals need to put forward practical proposals with confidence that they will work, and so they need to establish a sound theory on which their proposals can be based. Unsound theory leads to unsound practice.

Every educational practice is premised on a theory, even if the practitioner cannot articulate what that theory is.[25] When I started teaching, an 'untrained graduate' with no knowledge whatsoever of educational theory, I asked a fellow probationary teacher, just out of teacher training college, what philosophy underpinned her class-room practice. She replied by bringing me a copy of *Ethics and Education* by R.S. Peters. I asked her what it said, to which she answered: 'Oh, I don't know, I haven't read it. But it's all in there.'

Practitioners may be comforted in their adherence to convention by the belief that someone 'up there' in the universities has thought it all out and given the go-ahead. Radicals need to confront such beliefs.

Running through the radical movement is a tenacious anti-thereotical, or anti-intellectual, current. It is surprising how often Marx is quoted in this connection: 'The philosophers have only *interpreted* the world, in various ways; the point, however, is to *change* it'.[26] This statement is sometimes taken to mean 'enough of all this philosophizing – let's have some action'. But this was very far from Marx's meaning: he would hardly have spent all those years in the reading room of the British Museum if he thought that theory was a waste of time. On the contrary, Marx often criticized those whose attempts to change the world were based on an inadeqaute understanding of it.[27]

My plea, then, is for more, radical, theorizing. It might be retorted that the shelves of libraries are already sagging under the weight of books on educational theory. Why can't radicals just take the theory that's already in existence?

Certainly radicals need to engage with mainstream educational theory. This will involve studying it and criticizing it: producing a thoroughgoing critique of it. Such a task can be a stimulating way of generating new ideas. And there may well be a good deal of existing theory on which radicals can draw; but there are a number of reasons why radicals must ultimately construct their own theories.

First, radical theory will differ from much mainstream theory in that it will be based on a *practice–theory–practice* model. That is, theoretical analysis starts from, and ends with, our practical experience in the day-to-day world. The questions which radical theory asks are not abstract questions, but questions which arise from real problems we have encountered. And the answers which such theory offers must be answers which have implications for practice in the day-to-day world. Ideally, radical theory is generated by people who have been practitioners and intend to go on being practitioners. This contrasts with the tendency for theorists – academics – to form a separate caste of full-time, life-long theorists. On the other hand, theorizing does require peace, time and space and I think it is unrealistic to imagine that practitioners – whether teachers, parents or others – can do proper theoretical work in their spare moments. Ways must be found of making extended periods available for full-time concentration on this type of work. And here is a real difficulty: while millions of pounds are spent annually on educational research, we cannot assume that funding bodies will be keen to finance research which asks radical questions and proposes radical answers. There is an analogy here with the contrast, often remarked upon, between the enormous resources poured into research into nuclear energy and the paltry sums offered for research into alternative energy sources. Radicals will have to find ways around this difficulty.

Second, radical theory must begin from axioms of its own choosing. Part of a critique of mainstream theory will involve demonstrating how it starts from presuppositions which radicals do not share. For example, Geoffrey Bantock's *Freedom and Authority in Education* tackles questions which are of great interest to radicals, but he starts from the presumption that society must always be hierarchically ordered. An example of an axiom which radicals may want to take as their own is that of taking 'the community' as their starting point rather than the individual 'bare human being'.[28]

Third, radical theory will be *interdisciplinary*. It will oppose the tendency, which has become pronounced since the 1950s, to split the study of education into specialist subjects – history, psychology, philosophy and sociology, in particular. While it is possible to confine abstract theorizing within one or other of these specialisms, it is a matter of common experience that if we start from practical questions which have arisen in the real world (and that is what the practice–theory–practice model requires us to do) we find that they raise issues which involve all the disciplines. As Brian Jackson and Dennis Marsden pointed out: 'More and more human knowledge is divided into separate disciplines. Yet the richest land may fall betwixt and between.'[29]

There is a problem which advocates of interdisciplinary theory have not always faced up to. This is the sheer difficulty of mastering even one specialism, let alone four or five. Interdisciplinary theory (and this book includes examples of it) runs the risk of being bad history, bad sociology, bad philosophy and bad psychology. I believe that there is a necessary place for specialists who have a thorough grasp of their own field, and I suggest that the way out of our difficulty lies in having *teams* of specialists who collaborate together to do theoretical work.[30] Each team member can put in her or his own specialist knowledge, but the final product does justice to the essential indivisibility of human experience. The future of radical theorizing lies in collaborative teams, which should be balanced not only in terms of specialisms but also in terms of including men and women, different ethnic groups, and so on.

There are a number of other comments I wish to make about theory. One concerns the question of difficulty. Radicals have often been uneasy about theory because it can become extremely difficult to understand. The more difficult it is, the fewer people there are who are willing to follow it. Theorizing can therefore become an esoteric and exclusive pursuit. Certainly something can be done by way of presenting theory clearly and simply, and avoiding jargon, erudite references and complicated language. But there is a limit to how far this can go. Some ideas will remain necessarily difficult, however well they are expressed. Indeed, the attempt to express a theory in simple language can result in misunderstanding of key points of the theory. I confess that I see no easy way out of this problem. In the early nineteenth century the independent working-class education movements set themselves the task of studying in order to be able to understand complex ideas.[31] Perhaps this is something which contemporary radicals could revive.

Next, I am in favour of taking account of empirical evidence. In the 1970s 'empiricism' was a rude word for radicals.[32] Certainly there are all kinds of dangers in a simplistic concept of 'facts',[33] but we might observe that radicals have not been unwilling to cite empirical evidence in support of their case when it suits them. I am thinking here of the results of research such as that of Rosenthal and Jacobson which purported to show that if teachers were persuaded that certain children were clever, those children would be more successful than other children who, their teachers had been persuaded, were not clever.[34] Another piece of research, seized upon gleefully by libertarians, was that of Stanley Milgram, who demonstrated just how conditioned some people are to do what they are told even under absurd circumstances.[35] Now there is, of course, a vast body of empirical evidence relating to education, and, in my view, radicals ought to take note of it. But at the same time, they ought to discriminate between good research and bad research – and there are plenty of examples of the latter. 'Bad' research includes research which leaves conventional taken-for-granted assumptions unquestioned – for example, Neville Bennett's much vaunted 1976 study, *Teaching Styles and Pupil Progress*, which attempted to assess children's 'creativity' by setting them an essay to be writen in 30 minutes – surely the very antithesis of what radicals would understand by creativity.

Urging that we pay attention to the empirical evidence is *not* the same thing as saying that disagreements about education can always be settled by establishing 'the facts'. Education is not a science and many disagreements stem, not from ignorance of the facts, but from a divergence of philosophy, values or ideology. Given that radical views are premised upon (by definition) unorthodox philosophy, values and ideology, radicals should never expect to be able to *prove* their case by pointing to the empirical evidence alone.

Next, there is a pressing need for conceptual clarity. The radical literature is full of talk about 'freedom', 'nature', 'spontaneity', 'needs', 'wants', 'interests', 'relevance', 'ideology', 'culture', 'authority', 'equality'. All of these are difficult concepts and they are too readily deployed by radicals without sufficient care.

My final comment on radical theory is this. Theory involves honest thinking about things: we have to be prepared for the possibility that the outcome of hard thinking could be that some cherished radical beliefs are shown to be false. It is even possible that we could arrive at the conclusion that radicals have been completely mistaken about education. As I suggested in Chapter 2, radicals tend to make statements which are not open to the possibility of refutation. There is often an insistence that we *must* be right and our opponents *must* be wrong. This seems to me to be deeply arrogant. In my opinion, radicals ought to specify what kind of evidence – if it were available – could demonstrate that they are wrong. For one thing, they would then be in the moral position to make a similar requirement of their opponents. More importantly, they cannot expect people to take seriously their claim that they are right if there are no circumstances under which they could be shown to be wrong. It is the utter non-admissibility of counter-argument which makes, for many people, religious sects like the Jehovah's Witnesses so tiresome. Radicals shouldn't be like that. They should live dangerously.

To summarize, then, the theoretical work radicals need to undertake: it will comprise:

(a) A critique of existing school practice. This is largely in place, built up over the years, but it must be constantly updated.
(b) An exposition of the theory which underpins that practice, and a critique of it.
(c) A critique of existing theory. This is not the same as (b) because the gap betwen (orthodox) theory and (orthodox) practice has often been noted.[36]
(d) A vision of how things *could* be. This vision must, however, be tempered with realism – for example, the vision of a rural utopia is surely a thing of the past.
(e) Inspired by (d), a theory of ideal education, that is, the theory which would underpin (d).
(f) The formulation of short- and medium-term reforms which would take us towards (d) and be *feasible* in the short and medium

term. These may well involve single-issue campaigns.

(g) A strategy of how educational change may be achieved, taking into account the forces which might realistically be mobilized.

Strategies for change

How do we change schools? Different sectors of the radical movement had different ideas about this. We can identify at least nine possible strategies:

(a) Persuading teachers to support a programme of radical change.

(b) A process of militant *struggle*, by school students or teachers or both, and with or without parents, both inside and outside schools.

(c) Advancing radical practice 'in the interstices' – that is, wherever an opportunity, however small, presents itself. This might be done by individual departments within particular schools, or even by individual teachers on their own, or individual groups of school students.

(d) Curriculum reform at school, local authority or national level; and the development of new learning resources, methods, books or schemes.

(e) Single-issue campaigns, such as the STOPP campaign against physical punishment, or the Campaign on Racism, IQ and the Class Society (CRIQCS) which campaigned against IQ testing.

(f) Mobilizing parents in support of radical change.

(g) Establishing alternative schools, or other projects, which serve as models for a new kind of schooling.

(h) Getting a major political party to accept a radical programme and, when the party wins power, at local or national level, implementing the programme.

(i) Transforming society – by whatever means – in the belief that schools are a mirror of society and schooling cannot be significantly reformed until society is transformed.

These strategies are not, of course, mutually exclusive. The possibilities of each need to be analysed if radicals are to become clearer about what they are aiming to achieve and how they intend to achieve it. It is unlikely that there will be only *one* correct strategy. Different strategies will appeal to different individuals or groups according to what they feel they can do best in the circumstances they find themselves in. It is constructive to *debate* strategy, to try to show the strengths or weaknesses of particular strategies; but it becomes destructive when the debate turns into condemnation, and groups start attacking each other for having the 'wrong' strategy. In 1973 the Rank & File group held a public meeting to discuss the topic 'Changing our schools: the way forward.' Attendance at the meeting surpassed the organizers' expectations: some 400 people packed into London's Conway Hall. But the evident enthusiasm of the meeting was dissipated, and then transformed into bitter frustration, by a series of long-winded speakers from one particular left-wing sect who insisted that those who tried to reform schools were wasting their time and the only thing to do was to build 'the revolutionary party'. If I had to pick out the least savoury aspect of the radicalism of the 1960s and 1970s, it would be such insensitive dogmatism.

There is an urgent need for an umbrella organization to co-ordinate and foster the movement for radical reform of schooling. Such an organization would have the following tasks:

(a) to encourage research and development of radical ideas and theory, and the publication of this;
(b) to disseminate information about radical ideas and radical practice;
(c) to support and encourage radical groups to achieve the ends they set themselves;
(d) to increase public awareness of the faults of contemporary schools and to suggest remedies;
(e) to mediate in disputes between radical groups;
(f) to co-ordinate the preparation of a radical blue-print in readiness for the time when it becomes appropriate to put it before the general public; and
(g) to explore the use of contemporary media in publicizing radical views on education.

Why radical?

Having spent so much of this book criticizing radicalism, the reader may well by now be wondering why I remain committed to the radical cause. I want to end this book by explaining why.

I remain deeply unhappy with contemporary schooling, for moral and functional reasons. On the moral level, schooling attempts to do things to children against their wills – things which few adults would permit themselves to be subjected to. The fact that coercion is found to be a necessary part of the educational process proves that something is profoundly wrong. On the functional level, schooling fails to unlock the human potential of the majority of children. It's as simple as that.

Right-wing critics of schooling have never shared such moral qualms about the process of schooling. And, while sensing the failure of schooling to be effective, they can think of this only in terms of *falling standards*, as if there was some golden age in the past when schooling was successful. This is so demonstrably false that one wouldn't give it a moment's thought if it weren't that so many people evidently find it believable.

My belief is that only a radical socialism can offer a solution to the moral and functional problems of schooling; that only socialism offers the possibility of an integrated theory and practice of education. The key proposition is that it is *society* which is the dominant educative force, and, that, therefore, only by radical reform of society, to create that 'worthwhile world' of which Paul Goodman wrote, can we create an environment in which children will happily and willingly involve themselves in a process which unlocks their potential and which permits them to commit *themselves* to the social purpose and the education they need to serve that purpose. Our aim will be to eliminate the conflict between the needs of the individual and the needs of society. And that means eliminating the conditions which give rise to such a conflict.

The point I want to make here is so important that I want to explain it a little further. When I say that society is the dominant educative force, I mean that young people learn from what happens in society – in the 'real world' – regardless of what they are taught in schools. For example, I imagine that many schools try to teach children to be non-violent. But we live in a society which glorifies violence and most children, faced with a conflict between what they're taught in school and what they see in the street and on the television screen, adopt the values of the street and the television rather than of the school. Similarly, the legal requirement on schools to teach religion is more than negated by the fact that we live in a non-religious society. And again, I do not believe that the society we live in requires people to fulfil their human potential – rather the reverse.

The radical movement of the 1960s and 1970s threw up an array of insights and suggestions all of which seem to me to hover around these central questions. We were bees who knew there was a pot of honey somewhere but couldn't find it. On the track of something important, we groped our way, as if blindfolded, constantly taking wrong turnings and backtracking into old cul-de-sacs. I see nothing to be ashamed of in this, because the questions we are dealing with are enormously complicated and may well require decades more work before we make what I called in the introduction the decisive breakthrough.

And I see no reason to be pessimistic about the long-term prospects. Presently substantial resources are being poured into the search for a cure for AIDS. Slow as progress is, few people doubt that it is within human capability eventually to discover that cure. By contrast, pitifully few resources are put into the search for the radical solution to the problem of education. I wish to urge that more resources are put into that quest, in a spirit of optimism that one day the solution will be found.

What lingers in the minds of those who lived through the 1960s and early 1970s is that sense of excitement and confidence that the world could be changed for the better. We need to rekindle that sense; and we need to remember the 1960s and 1970s, not in any vain attempt to recreate the past, but to learn from the mistakes we made. This book has been my contribution to that learning.

APPENDIX

A note on 'class'

In the radical literature – as elsewhere – there is considerable confusion in the use of the terms 'working class' and 'middle class'. We can discern at least three distinct usages.

Usage 1.
An ordinary language usage. As Harold Entwistle suggests: a common assumption would be that class is defined by a richer complex of factors than power, income, wealth and property. Education, artistic taste, religion, speech, manners, dress, geographical location and size of residence, ownership of property and source of income all seem to mesh into that web of factors which define one's social class.[1]

Such ordinary language usage, being multi-dimensional, is somewhat loose and has a significant element of subjectivity: people's ideas of which class they belong to may not tally with the class to which others would ascribe them; and the criteria by which such judgements are made vary from person to person.

Usage 2.
Stricter definitions of class made by sociologists, the most widely used in education being definitions based on the Registrar General's categories of occupational group.[2]

Usage 3.
The Marxian distinction between 'proletariat' and 'bourgeoisie', the former defined as those who must sell their labour power in order to live, the latter as the owners of the means of production. Socialists commonly equate 'proletariat' with 'working class' and 'bourgeoisie' with 'middle class'.

As Raymond Williams pointed out,[3] the confusion of usages is historical in origin. Different meanings have emerged in different epochs, with no clarification of terms ever having taken place.

Some Marxist writers on education have urged radicals to cut through the difficulties by adhering to the Marxian definitions.[4] But for several reasons this advice is not easy to follow. First, the words 'proletariat' and 'bourgeoisie' have never fully established themselves in the English language, nor have they found satisfactory English translations. Their English usage has tended to remain curiously 'alien' and peripheral – sometimes used as terms of abuse, sometimes easily ridiculed as the jargon of naive slogan-mongers, sometimes with humorous connotations. Although Marxists may know what they mean when they say 'proletariat', the trouble is that most other people don't. But if they say 'working class' instead, they are likely to be taken to mean either usage 1 or usage 2 above.

Second, the categories 'proletariat' and 'bourgeoisie' don't seem to connect very well with the accumulated sociological evidence. For example, the evidence on the relationships between schooling and class suggests, for radicals at any rate, that schooling systematically discriminates against working-class children (usage 2) rather than against the proletariat; the latter would include many middle-class (usage 2) children attending selective schools. If, as some Marxists argued,[5] private schooling is in the main for children of the bourgeoisie, and state provision for the children of the proletariat, it is not clear that this offers the bourgeoisie any *educational* advantage (although it may offer them *social* advantage) because, in terms of traditional criteria such as examination passes, the old direct grant schools (which were open to the proletariat, though not much to the working class (usage 2)) far outstripped private schooling, and grammar schools were on a par with private schools.[6] Nor is it clear that the advent of comprehensive schooling has greatly changed this situation.[7]

It is true that sociologists have, generally, collected their evidence on the basis of usage 2 rather than usage 3. And so it is arguable that, had sociologists started their investigations using usage 3, they might have uncovered significant differences relating to proletarian and bourgeois schooling. But this remains to be demonstated.

Third, a number of developments not envisioned by Marx – such as the extension of share ownership, both private and institutional – have tended to obfuscate the Marxian distinction between bourgeois and proletarian. While Marxists have sought to accommodate these developments into their economic and political analyses (for example, by pointing out that the extension of share ownership has done little to alter the power relationships of capitalism), it is not at all clear what the educational implications might be.

It is for these reasons that almost all Marxist discourse on education has readily lapsed into acceptance of the category 'working class' as defined in usages 1 or 2. But this has produced confusion. For example, in Chapter 8 I examined the radical notion of education for working-class struggle. This required a Marxist conception of the proletariat engaged in a historical struggle for liberation. But the notion also hinged on the concept of 'working-class culture', which was not taken to mean proletarian culture, but rather the culture of the working class as defined in usages 1 or 2. There is an intermediate class of people who are neither working-class (usage 1 or 2) nor bourgeois (usage 3). These are people who are ordinarily termed 'middle-class' but who have no significant income from capital or rent. Teachers are a typical example. Marxists tried to have it both ways when they claimed that teachers are proletarian (by Marx's definition) and yet were trying to impose their 'middle-class culture' on working-class children.

One way out of this difficulty proposed by certain radicals[8] was that such intermediate classes could choose for themselves whether they would align themselves with the proletariat or bourgeoisie. This introduces an element of subjectivity into the categorization: it is consistent with the element of *consciousness* which Marx sometimes recognized as a component of class.

In this study I have used the terms 'working class' and 'middle class' in the sense of usage 2 unless otherwise stated.

Notes

Introduction

1. See Nigel Wright, 'The White Lion Free School Experiment'.
2. For example, Centre for Contemporary Cultural Studies, *Unpopular Education*, whose aim was 'to understand the ways in which educational politics have been constructed in England . . . during the post-second world war period' makes only the slightest references to the radical movement, even though its authors' perspectives were avowedly radical. Similarly, an Open University course unit entitled *Liberal and Radical Alternatives* (E202, Block VI, Unit 31) mentions, of all the radical groups and publications, only the deschoolers. And, to give one final example, Ken Jones in his study *Beyond Progressive Education* refers only to *Radical Education*, Rank & File, the Socialist Teachers Alliance and *Teaching London Kids*.
3. John Lawson and Harold Silver, *A Social History of Education in England*, pp. 154–7.

Chapter 1   The background

1. The publications of these groups included *Radical Philosophy; History Workshop Journal; Red Rat* and *Humpty Dumpty* (both journals of radical psychologists); *Copeman* and *Heavy Daze* (both concerned with the interests of mental patients); *Issues in Radical Therapy; Red Scientist; Radical Science; Science for People; Cultural Studies; Needle* (radicals in the health service); *Arse* (radical architects); *Real Time* (radicals in computers); *Open Secret* (radical journalists); *Towards Socialist Child Care; Case-Con* (radical social workers); *Conference of Socialist Economists; Critique of Anthropology; Camerawork; Radical Statistics; ASS* (radical lawyers); *Radical Alternatives to Prison; Shrew* and *Red Rag* (feminists); *Gay News; Black Voice; Race Today*.
2. Leslie Halliwell, *Film Guide*, p. 1033.
3. George Melly, *Revolt into Style*, pp. 79–80.

4. The significance of the Soviet invasion of Czechoslovakia perhaps needs explaining; it did for the 1960s generation what Hungary had done for the previous generation; convince them that Soviet socialism was not the kind of model they were looking for. It caused the 1960s generation to write books with titles like *Obsolete Communism; The Left-Wing Alternative* (Daniel and Gabriel Cohn-Bendit).

5. Brian Simon, *The Radical Tradition in Education in Britain*; W.A.C. Stewart, *Progressives and Radicals in English Education 1750–1970*; W.A.C. Stewart and W.P. McCann, *The Educational Innovators 1750–1880*; W.A.C. Stewart, *The Educational Innovators*, Vol. 2; Harold Silver, *English Education and the Radicals 1780–1850*.

6. Simon Maccoby, *The English Radical Tradition 1763–1914*; Christopher Hampton (ed.), *A Radical Reader*.

7. See Fred Inglis, *Radical Earnestness*.

8. Simon, *The Radical Tradition*. Simon refers in his title to 'Britain' rather than England because he includes Robert Owen and his son Robert Dale Owen in the tradition; they were, of course, Welsh. I am persisting in talking about the *English* tradition, not out of disregard for Scotland and Wales, but out of respect for their independent traditions which I am not qualified to discuss. None the less, I have taken liberties throughout this study: R.F. Mackenzie is Scottish, as was A.S. Neill.

9. Liam Hudson, *The Cult of the Fact*, p. 92.

10. Douglas Holly, *Society, Schools and Humanity*, p. 23.

11. This idea comes from Helvétius, *De L'Esprit*, p. 494–5, which reminds us that there is nothing peculiarly English about the ideas we are discussing here.

12. Raymond Williams, *The Long Revolution*; Paul Goodman, *Growing Up Absurd*.

13. For example, in the debate about whether particular religious groups should be allowed to set up separate schools.

14. See, for example, Richard Johnson, 'Really Useful Knowledge'.

15. Paolo Freire, *Pedagogy of the Oppressed*.

16. See Ken Worpole, 'The School and the Community' in Douglas Holly (ed.), *Education or Domination*.

17. See Appendix, page 191.

18. E.P. Thompson, *The Making of the English Working Class*; Brian Simon, *Education and the Labour Movement 1870–1920*; Harold Silver, *The Concept of Popular Education*; J.F.C. Harrison, *Learning and Living 1790–1960*.

19. A.H. Halsey, Jean Floud and C. Arnold Anderson (eds), *Education, Economy and Society*; Brian Jackson and Dennis Marsden, *Education and the Working Class*; J.W.B. Douglas, *Home and School*.

20. G.D.H. Cole, 'Education and Politics: A Socialist View', p. 46.

21. Ken Jones, *Beyond Progressive Education*.

22. See Worpole, 'School and Community', p. 196; and Chris Searle, *This New Season*, pp. 8–9.

23. Samuel Bowles and Herbert Gintis, *Schooling in Capitalist America*.

24. Colin Ward, 'A Modest Proposal for the Repeal of the Education Act'.

25. See Ian Wright, 'And Now for A Bit of Theory'.
26. W. Boyd and W. Rawson, *The Story of the New Education*; R.J.W. Selleck, *The New Education 1870–1914*; R.J.W. Selleck, *English Primary Education and the Progressives 1914–1939*. Again, there is significance in the fact that these books were published in the 1960s.
27. See Trevor Blewitt (ed.), *The Modern Schools Handbook*; and H.A.T. Child (ed.), *The Independent Progressive School*. To my knowledge there has never even been a list of these schools published, so it may be worth listing them here, with their dates of foundation. This list may, however, be incomplete; advertisements in *The New Era* throughout the 1920s and 1930s indicate that a number of other schools felt close enough to the progressive movement to advertise in that magazine. The schools are (in order of year of foundation): Abbotsholme (1889); Bedales (1893); King Alfred's (1897); St Christopher's (1915); The Garden School (1917); Summerhill (1921); Greater Felcourt (?); The Malting House (1924); Frensham Heights (1925); Tiptree Hall (1926); Dartington Hall (1926); Beacon Hill (1927); Kingmoor (1927); Forest School (1932); Priory Gate (?); Burgess Hill (1936); St Mary Town and Country (1937); Wennington (1940); Monkton Wyld (1940); Kilkquahanity (1940); Kirkdale (1965); Durdham Park (1971). To this list we might add four public schools which had certain progressive features: Leighton Park (1890); Bembridge (1919); Rendcomb College (1920) and Bryanston (1928). In some respects certain religious schools might also be included such as Friends School, Saffron Walden (1702), the Steiner Schools and Brockwood Park Krishnamurti Educational Centre. Finally we ought to add progressive schools which specialized in 'problem' children such as Clayesmore (1896), The Little Commonwealth (1913), The Farmhouse School (1917), Finchden Manor (1930), Red Hill (1934), Barns School (1940) and Epping House (1958).
28. Findlay Johnson's Sompting Village School was immortalized in Edmond Holmes, *What Is and What Might Be*: E.F. O'Neill's Prestolee Village School is described in Gerard Holmes, *The Idiot Teacher*; Alex Bloom's St George's In the East School, Cable Street, East London, has to my knowledge never been written up although it was a source of inspiration to many in the decade after 1945 – see Stewart, *Progressives and Radicals*, p. 479 and *The Times*, 24 September 1955; Braehead is described by headteacher R.F. Mackenzie in *A Question of Living* and *Escape from the Classroom*; and Risinghill in Leila Berg, *Risinghill: Death of a Comprehensive School*.
29. See Nigel Wright, *Progress in Education*, p. 47, footnote 8.
30. Maurice Ash, *Who Are the Progressives Now?*, p. ix.
31. Stewart, *Progressives and Radicals*, Chapter 24.
32. For example in Jonathan Kozol, *Death at an Early Age*.
33. Martin Carnoy, *Education as Cultural Imperialism*.
34. See John Rowan, *Ordinary Ecstasy: Humanistic Psychology in Action*.
35. See especially Carl Rogers, *On Becoming a Person*; and Carl Rogers, *Freedom to Learn*.
36. See Paul Adams *et al.*, *Children's Rights*.

37. For example David Hargreaves, *Interpersonal Relations and Education*, Chapter 6.
38. Jeff Nuttall, *Bomb Culture*; Melly, *Revolt into Style*; Frank Musgrove, *Ecstasy and Holiness*; Theodore Roszak, *The Making of a Counter Culture*; the literature is enormous. For a recent re-evaluation, see Robert Hewison, *Too Much: Art and Society in the Sixties*. An interesting collection of documents from the period may be found in Peter Stansill and David Zane Marowitz, *Bamn: Outlaw Manifestos and Ephemera 1965–1970*.
39. Raphael Samuel 'Breaking Up is Very Hard to Do'.
40. For example Alan Watts, *The Book on the Taboo Against Knowing Who You Are*; Carlos Castaneda *Tales of Power*. For an examination of the numerous points of contact between eastern mysticism and alternative education, see Vinoba Bhave, 'Education or Manipulation?'.
41. John Lawson and Harold Silver, *A Social History of Education in England*, p. 234.
42. *Oz* 28, May 1970.
43. Jonathan Croall (ed.), *All the Best, Neill: Letters from Summerhill*, p. 91.
44. See Adams, *et al.*, *Children's Rights*.
45. I have not, in this study, made more than passing reference to films, but the role of film in changing and forming attitudes is clearly a major one. See, for example, Peter Biskind, *Seeing is Believing*.
46. See especially Jules Henry, *Culture Against Man*, and Jules Henry, *Essays on Education*.
47. For example, John Holt, *How Children Fail*, p. 130.

Chapter 2   Identifying the radicals

1. Robin Barrow, *Radical Education*, p. 1.
2. Raymond Williams, *Keywords*.
3. 'It is doubtful if RSSF would have had the term "revolutionary" included in its name if it had been set up prior to May (1968)' – Revolutionary Socialist Students' Federation, *The Political Theory of the Student Movement*, p. 27.
4. The position of the Communist Party of Great Britain during this period was interesting. CP policy on education was determined by a group of veteran communists – of whom Max Morris was the best known – who were implacably hostile to the radical movement: see their journal *Education Today and Tomorrow* throughout this period. Individual members of the CP – especially the younger ones – found this hard to accept and commonly left the CP if they wanted to be involved in the organizations of the radical education movement.
5. See bibliography for reference to their work.
6. See Chapter 11, note 5.
7. Graham Murdock, 'The Politics of Culture', p. 99.
8. See Ken Jones, *Beyond Progressive Education*, and Ted Benton, 'Education and Politics'.

9. For example, Douglas Holly, *Beyond Curriculum*, p. 11; and Colin Ball and Mog Ball, *Education for a Change*.

10. David Gorbutt, 'The New Sociology of Education'.

11. Michael F.D. Young (ed.), *Knowledge and Control*.

12. Ball and Ball, *Education for a Change*, p. 7.

13. For example Mike Smith, *The Underground and Education*.

14. Harry Ree, 'The Lost Generation'.

15. See Leila Berg, *Risinghill: Death of a Comprehensive School*; and R.F. Mackenzie, *The Unbowed Head*.

16. E.P. Thompson 'The Peculiarities of the English' in Thompson, *The Poverty of Theory and Other Essays*, p. 67.

17. This was the argument of Herbert Marcuse in *One Dimensional Man*.

18. John Holt, *Freedom and Beyond*, p. 11.

19. Brian Simon, *The Radical Tradition in Education in Britain*, p. 9. A similar perception was claimed for the American radicals – see Ronald Gross and Beatrice Gross, *Radical School Reform*, p. 17.

20. Michael P. Smith, *The Libertarians and Education*, p. 16.

21. Big Flame, *The Crisis in Education*, p. 11.

22. Brian Simon 'Streaming and Unstreaming in the Secondary School' in David Rubinstein and Colin Stoneman (eds), *Education For Democracy*, p. 149.

23. Douglas Holly, *Society, Schools and Humanity*, p. 10.

24. For some Marxists, the fact that progressivism gained Conservative support was proof that there must be something wrong with it. Thus it was argued (for example by Big Flame, *Crisis in Education*) that progressivism was merely an attempt to update the education service in order better to meet the needs of modern capitalism.

25. Barrow, *Radical Education*, p. 4.

26. Quoted in W.A.C. Stewart, *Progressives and Radicals in English Education 1750–1970*, p. 35.

27. See Tyrell Burgess (ed.), *Dear Lord James: A Critique of Teacher Training*.

28. 'Compromise is always a lie' – A.S. Neill, *A Dominie's Log*, p. 64.

29. This was the idea expressed by Ernst Zander, 'The Great Utopia'.

30. Edmond Holmes, *What Is and What Might Be*, p. 177.

31. Judy Palfreman in *Rank & File*, no. 7, p. 22.

32. An exception was the submission made by School Without Walls to the Taylor Committee on the management and government of schools. See School Without Walls, *Learning not Schooling*.

33. The specialist in such allegations was Tory MP John Stokes.

34. See for example John Holt, *The Underachieving School*, p. 13. See also White Lion Street Free School's definition of learning quoted on page 139.

35. Nigel Wright, *Progress in Education*.

Chapter 3   Radical teachers: *Libertarian Teacher* and Rank & File

1. A good example, which foreshadowed things to come, was Martin Daniel, 'A Charter for the Unfree Child'.

2. Interview with Peter Ford, 9 July 1986.
3. *Libertarian Teacher*, no. 3, July 1967, p. 3.
4. See reports in *The Teacher*, 11 October 1968; and *Freedom*, 17 August 1968.
5. See Joreen Freeman, *The Tyranny of Structurelessness*.
6. This was the fate of four anarchist ventures: the Anarchist-Syndicalist Alliance Teachers' Network in the early 1970s; the Libertarian Education News Service in 1973; the Blackburn-based Schools Anarchy Propagation Action Group in 1973; and the Wolverhampton-based Libertarian Education Network in 1974.
7. The first four issues were called *Bulletin of the Libertarian Teachers Association*.
8. Michael P. Smith, *The Libertarians and Education*, p. 114.
9. John Holt, *Instead of Education*.
10. Smith *The Libertarians and Education*, p. 132. *Libertarian Education*'s first response to deschooling came with a critique of Illich by Nicholas Walter in *Libertarian Education*, no. 16, September 1974.
11. Janet Gooch, 'Community Schools', *Libertarian Teacher*, no. 8, p. 4.
12. Editorial, *Libertarian Education*, no. 11.
13. Val Hennessy, letter, *Libertarian Education*, no. 19.
14. This interest in sexuality was nothing new: as Karl Teschitz, *Sex-Pol Essays*, had noted in 1937: 'it has always been the anarchists who of all the groups put most emphasis on the liberation and revolutionising of personal life – and who therefore were quick to take up the problem of sexual liberation'.
15. For another view of *Libertarian Education*, see Mike Smith, *The Underground and Education*.
16. The International Socialism group, which changed its name to the Socialist Workers' Party in the mid-1970s, was one of a number of descendants of the Trotskyist Revolutionary Communist Party which was active in the post-1945 period. Others were the Socialist Labour League (now the Workers' Revolutionary Party), the Revolutionary Socialist League (related to the Militant Tendency) and the International Marxist Group.
17. *Rank & File*, no. 1, p. 2.
18. See Vincent Burke, *Teachers in Turmoil*.
19. Judith Weymont, letter, *Rank & File*, no. 4, p. 5.
20. David Spencer, letter, *Rank & File*, no. 4, p. 6.
21. The 'Moscow gold' theory, for all its improbability, is continually revived by people who know nothing about radical groups. A recent example can be found in Len Deighton, *Mexico Set*.
22. Judy Palfreman, 'Black Paper 2 – and its Liberal Critics'; Martin Hoyles, 'Conflict Theory and Educational Institutions'; Chanie Rosenberg, 'School Self-Government: The Russian Experiment'.
23. Rank & File, *A Teachers' Charter*, p. 2.
24. See *Freedom*, vol. 29, no. 20, 29 June 1968.
25. Rank & File, *Democracy in Schools*, p. 23.
26. See *Rank & File*, no. 17, pp. 6–8.

27. This switch to the 'agitational paper' is discussed by Ken Jones, *Beyond Progressive Education*, p. 116.
28. *The Fight for Education: Rank & File Occasional Journal*, no. 1, Spring 1977, p. 28.
29. This 'vanguardism' was attacked by the *Teachers Action* group – see page 53.
30. See, for example, Chanie Rosenberg, *Education and Society*. Marx's concept of 'base and superstructure' was elaborated in his *Preface to the Critique of Political Economy*, but it was far from simplistic.
31. Ken Worpole, 'Towards a Socialist Critique of Secondary Education'.

Chapter 4   More radical teachers

1. *Teaching London Kids*, no. 2, p. 1.
2. Gerald Grace, 'Facing the Contradictions', p. 10.
3. Gabriel Chanan, 'Gabriel Replies', p. 20.
4. For example Douglas Barnes, James Britton and Harold Rosen, *Language, the Learner and the School*; Carol Burgess *et al.*, *Understanding Children's Writing*.
5. See Gerald Grace, *Education and the City*.
6. Editorial, *Teaching London Kids*, no. 3, p. 2.
7. John Holt was also going through a (temporary) phase of new realism: his book *What Do I Do Monday*? was published in Britain in 1971.
8. For example, John Clossick, 'Teaching London Kids or Improving Your Lot'; and *Teachers Action*, no. 8, p. 18.
9. Centre for Contemporary Cultural Studies, *Unpopular Education*, p. 13.
10. Edward Blishen, *A Nest of Teachers*, p. 43.
11. For further discussion of the content of *Hard Cheese*, see Mike Smith, *The Underground and Education*.
12. *Radical Education* preliminary broadsheet *Why Radical Education*?
13. Editorial, *Radical Education*, no. 1, p. 2.
14. Sue Symons, letter, *Radical Education*, no. 7, p. 8.
15. Howard Walter, letter, *Radical Education*, no. 8, p. 19.
16. Teachers Action Collective, *Teachers and the Economy*, p. 7.
17. Wilhelm Reich, *What is Class Consciousness*?, p. 25.
18. Keith Paton, *The Great Brain Robbery*, p. 59.
19. This point had been made a few years earlier in Søren Hansen and Jesper Jensen, *The Little Red Schoolbook*, p. 13.
20. Douglas Holly, *Society, Schools and Humanity*, p. 29. The point is elaborated by Ted Benton, 'Education and Politics', p. 15.
21. Contrast Julia McNeal and Margaret Rogers (eds), *The Multi-Racial School*.
22. Baron Swann (chmn), *Education for All, The Report of the Committee of Inquiry into the Education of Children from Ethnic Minority Groups* (The Swann Report) p. vii.
23. Right to Learn Group, *School Does Matter*, p. 34.
24. G.H. Bantock, 'Towards a Theory of Popular Education'.
25. Right to Learn Group, *School Does Matter*, p. 36.

26. Right to Learn Group, *The Right to Learn*, p. 2.
27. Roy Nash, *Teacher Expectations and Pupil Learning*, explores the possibilities of this emphasis.
28. Peter Newsam, 'The Good Old Days'.
29. See Leila Berg, *Risinghill: Death of a Comprehensive School*.
30. Resources Programme for Change in Education, final newsletter, 8 July 1974.
31. *Socialist Teacher Bulletin*, June 1976, p. 2.
32. *Socialist Teacher*, no. 1, p. 16.
33. *Ibid*.
34. See *Case Con*, passim.

Chapter 5   The school students' movement

1. Students and Staff of Hornsey College of Art, *The Hornsey Affair*, p. 9.
2. *Partisans* (Paris), no. 49, September–October 1969, provides a full documentation of the *lycée* movement.
3. *Libertarian Education*, no. 16.
4. From Schools Action Union report on the conference.
5. Roger Sadiev, 'The Free Schools Campaign', p. 11.
6. *Democratic Schools*, Third National Conference Issue, p. 2.
7. As the theoretical journal, *Democratic Schools*, clearly shows.
8. See also Martin Hoyles (ed.), *Changing Childhood*, part 4, on this question.
9. Frank Musgrove, *Ecstasy and Holiness*, p. 19.
10. Some examples of this mail are given in Nigel Wright, 'Radicals in English Education 1960–1980', PhD thesis, Open University, 1988.
11. A specific case is described in ibid., p. 139.
12. For details, see ibid., pp. 139–40.
13. *Times Educational Supplement*, 25 July 1969.
14. See *Vanguard*, no. 8, p. 3.
15. *Rank & File*. no. 21, p. 6.
16. Schools Action Union, *Revolution in the Schools*, paragraph 10.
17. Schools Action Union, *Schools Charter*, presented to 1970 conference of the SAU.
18. *Vanguard*, no. 9, pp. 2–3.
19. See Ray Chatwin, 'An Experiment in Democracy'.
20. *Rebel*, no. 4, p. 9.
21. For an example of this, see Frances Morrell in *Times Educational Supplement*, 21 February 1969.
22. See Wright, 'Radicals', pp. 144–6.
23. See, for example, Dave Marson, *Children's Strikes in 1911*.
24. *Vanguard*, no. 7, p. 1.
25. The International Socialism group changed its name to Socialist Workers' Party in 1977.
26. Examples were *Ashes and Grapes* (Cardiff), *Brain Damage* (Oxford), *Compulsory Miseducation* (Manchester), *Enigma* (Portsmouth), *Fang* (Yorkshire), *Hackney Miscarriage* (East London), *HOD* (Leeds), *Kids Review* (West London), *Kraken* (Islington, North London), *Little*

Digger (Brighton), *Pigeon* (Slough), *Rustle* (Essex), *SAM* (Plymouth) and *Troll* (Canterbury). These were not school magazines mixing reports on football matches with jokes about teachers. They were overtly radical, with the characteristics of radicalism I described in Chapter 1. At various times political sects also produced magazines for school students, such as the Young Communist League's *Format* (1969) and the Socialist Workers' Party's *Rebel* (late 1970s).

Chapter 6   Children's rights and alternative education

1. Quoted in Brian Jackson and Dennis Marsden, *Education and the Working Class*, pp. 260–1.
2. Jonathan Croall, *Neill of Summerhill*, p. 302.
3. Paul Adams *et al.*, *Children's Rights*.
4. Nan Berger, 'The Child, the Law and the State', p. 179.
5. See Bronislaw Malinowski, *The Sexual Life of Savages in North estern Melanesia*.
6. Robert Ollendorf 'The Rights of Adolescents' in Paul Adams *et al.*, *Children's Rights*, p. 114.
7. See *Times Edcational Supplement*, 23 April 1971.
8. Robert Ollendorf 'Sex and the Teenager' in *Children's Rights*, no. 1, p. 19.
9. *Children's Rights*, no. 1, p. 10.
10. *Children's Rights*, no. 5, p. 16.
11. See Jonathan Croall (ed.), *All the Best, Neill: Letters from Summerhill*, p. 91.
12. First in the field was Bob Dixon's two-volume analysis of sex, race, class and political prejudice in children's books, *Catching Them Young*.
13. See M.D.A. Freeman, *The Rights and Wrongs of Children*; and C.A. Wringe, *Children's Rights: A Philosophical Study*.
14. See Bob Franklin (ed.), *The Rights of Children*.
15. *Radical Education*, no. 1, p. 17.
16. School Without Walls, *Lunatic Ideas* (edited by Pat Holland).
17. Tom Taylor (chmn), *A New Partnership for our Schools* (The Taylor Report). The Schools Without Walls submission to the Taylor Committee was reprinted in SWW, *Learning Not Schooling*.
18. *Radical Education*, no. 1, p. 16.
19. Brian Simon, *Intelligence Testing and the Comprehensive School*.
20. Arthur Jensen, 'How Much Can We Boost IQ and Scholastic Achievement?'; Hans Eysenck, *Race, Intelligence and Education*.
21. See, for example, *Times Educational Supplement*, 27 September 1974.
22. Questions asked by, for example, Leon Kamin, *The Science and Politics of IQ*; and Liam Hudson, *The Cult of the Fact*, Chapter 8.
23. A.S. Neill Trust appeal letter, undated.
24. In 1975, for example, grants totalling £865 were paid to *Little Digger* magazine, Leeds Free School, North Kensington Free School, Kirkby House Project, Bermondsey Lamp Post, Delta Free School, Moorland

Village Project, Basement Writers Project, Brixton Literacy Project and Tyndale School Project.

25. Interview with Phil Collins, 9 September 1986. I will discuss this further in Chapter 10.
26. See, for example, Joy Baker, *Children In Chancery*.
27. The social class composition of members of Education Otherwise is considered by Roland Meighan, 'Home-Based Educators and Education Authorities: The Attempt to Maintain a Mythology', p. 279.
28. Hudson, *The Cult of the Fact*, p. 74.
29. Editorial, *Humpty Dumpty*, no. 2, p. 2.
30. See Ivan Illich, *Disabling Professions*.
31. See also Nigel Armistead (ed), *Reconstructing Social Psychology*; and Bill Gilham (ed.), *Reconstructing Educational Psychology*.
32. Advertisement for *Radical Philosophy*, in *Radical Education*, no. 4, p. 32.
33. *Needle*, no. 6.
34. Principally Ivan Illich, *Deschooling Society*; Everett Reimer, *School is Dead*; John Holt, *Instead of Education*; and Ian Lister (ed.), *Deschooling*.
35. *Libertarian Education*, no. 10, p. 16.
36. See, for example, the annual reports of Community Projects Foundation.
37. See *WEBNEWS: The Newsletter of World Education Berkshire*.
38. Angus Maude, 'Biased Penguins', p. 605.
39. See, for example, *The Spectator*, 30 September 1972; and Anthony Flew, *Sociology, Equality and Education*.
40. See Martin Lightfoot, 'A Publisher Remembers'.
41. See Gerard Holmes, *The Idiot Teacher*, on E.F. O'Neill; Leila Berg, *Risinghill: Death of a Comprehensive School*, on Michael Duane; R.F. Mackenzie, *The Unbowed Head*; John Watts, *The Countesthorpe Experience*, on Tim MacMullen; and Philip Toogood, *The Head's Tale*.
42. Bruno Bettelheim in Nathan W. Ackerman *et al., Summerhill: For and Against*. I'm aware of Ray Hemmings' comment in *Fifty Years of Freedom*, p. 22; 'Neill has always embarrassed the more intellectually, as well as the more spiritually, inclined of the radicals'.

Chapter 7   Free schools

1. See Michael P. Smith, *The Libertarians and Education*.
2. See L.B. Pekin, *Progressive Schools*, pp. 34–7.
3. See Chapter 1.
4. See W.A.C. Stewart, *Progressives and Radicals in English Education 1750–1970*, p. 113.
5. See Smith, *The Libertarians and Education*, pp. 60ff.
6. See Bertram Edwards, *The Burston School Strike*.
7. G.D.H. Cole, 'Education and Politics: A Socialist View'; and Ken Jones, *Beyond Progressive Education*.
8. Maurice Ash, *Who Are the Progressives Now?*
9. Eric Midwinter, 'Stick with the System'.

10. See Smith, *The Libertarians and Education*.
11. Peter Jenner, 'The London Free School'.
12. They were described in *Anarchy*, no. 103, September 1969.
13. Kirkdale School in South London, which opened in 1965, has a claim to being the first British free school; but it did not call itself a 'free school' when it first started, and did not at that time come within the criteria of free schools I have listed – it was fee-paying and had two principals (albeit nominal). The founders of Kirkdale saw it as part of the independent progressive tradition. However, in the 1970s Kirkdale began to call itself Kirkdale Free School.
14. *New Era*, vol. 10, no. 37, January 1929.
15. Children's Rights Workshop, *Newsletter*, no. 1, December 1974, p. 3.
16. *Guardian*, 22 June 1971.
17. *Libertarian Teacher*, no. 8, Spring 1972, claimed that there were 'at least 30 Free School Projects'. This claim is repeated in *Lib Ed*, vol. 2, no. 4, Spring 1987.
18. Allen Graubard, *Free the Children*, pp. 40–1.
19. Samuel Bowles and Herbert Gintis, *Schooling in Capitalist America*, p. 7.
20. For example, Rob Grunsell, *Born to Be Invisible*; and Roger White, *Absent With Cause*.
21. Her Majesty's Inspectorate of Schools, *Behavioural Units: A Survey of Special Units for Pupils with Behavioural Problems*.
22. Graubard, *Free the Children*, p. 42.
23. Which was not the case in America, as Jonathan Kozol angrily points out in *Free Schools*.
24. See Lucia Backett, 'Street School'.
25. Nigel Wright 'Lesson for the People'.
26. Bowles and Gintis, *Schooling in Capitalist America*, p. 252. Bowles and Gintis go on to analyse this problem.
27. Interview with Phil Collins, 9 September 1986.
28. Only four showed consistent and active support for free schools – the A.S. Neill Trust, the Children's Rights Workshop, London Educational Alternatives Programme and School Without Walls. All were small organizations representing no great sector of public opinion. In the late 1970s the Advisory Centre for Education championed free schools after one of White Lion Street Free School's founders went to work there. In 1979 the Campaign for State Supported Alternative Schools took up the cause of freeschooling (see note 32 below).
29. Michael Young, 'Hackney Survey: Support for Alternatives'.
30. Nick Peacey, 'Could it Happen Here?'.
31. The Campaign for State Supported Alternative Schools (CSSAS) arose out of a day conference organized by the Advisory Centre for Education in December 1978 on the subject of 'State Supported Alternatives in School-Age Education'. CSSAS published a policy document, *A Case For Alternative Schools within the Maintained System*, and a series of ten newsletters until 1984. An account of the thinking of CSSAS can be found in Laura Diamond, 'State Supported Alternative Schools'.

32. 'The Delta Free and Community School' in A.S. Neill Trust *Newsletter*, no. 3, Christmas 1974.

33. See David Head (ed.), *Free Way to Learning*, pp.75, 139.

34. The choice of independent status by free schools damned them in the eyes of many left-wingers since the independent sector is often associated with private schooling and privilege. In practice there was no alternative legal status for a school with five or more children. As White Lion Street Free School put it: 'We do not relish this status, but it is the only legal status available to us until the Authority [i.e. the ILEA] agrees to fund the school. Ideally we would like to be an integral part of the maintained system. We will de-register as an independent school as soon as a viable alternative status can be arranged' (White Lion Street Free School, *Why ILEA Should Not Fund the Free School (And Why It should)* page 3). White Lion did de-register in 1982.

35. For further details on this see Alison Truefitt, *How to set up a Free School*.

36. Jonathan Croall, *Neill of Summerhill*, pp. 338–41.

37. Interview with John Ord, 24 September 1986. See also Backett, 'Street School'.

38. It was the same in American free schools: see John Holt, *Freedom and Beyond*, pp. 78–80.

39. Barrowfield Community School, *Progress Report*.

40. From preliminary brochure of the Leeds Free School and Community Trust. Between the draft and the printed version of this statement, a fourth section entitled 'A New Society' was omitted. It said that free schools would point the way to 'a totally new society'.

41. Scotland Road Free School, *An Alternative School for Liverpool*.

42. Backett, 'Street School'; W. Kenneth Richmond, *The Free School*; Maurice Punch 'Tyrannies of the free school' in the *Guardian*, 8 May 1973; for examples from North America see Graubard, *Free the Children*; and Anne Long, 'The New School – Vancouver'.

43. This distinction between 'them' and 'us' was explored by Richard Hoggart, *The Uses of Literacy*, Chapter 3.

44. See Colin Ball and Mog Ball, *Education for a Change*, pp. 12ff. Colin and Mog Ball talk of 'delegated functions' when the community delegates all its caring functions to professionals and institutions, (see ibid., pp. 44, 61).

45. Scotland Road Free School, *An Alternative School for Liverpool*, p. 2.

46. As exemplified by Preston R. Wilcox, 'The Community Centred School'.

47. See Gastone Tassinari, 'The "Scuola and Quartiere" Movement: a Case Study'.

48. Paolo Freire, *Pedagogy of the Oppressed*; Chris Searle, *This New Season*.

49. Ball and Ball, *Education for a Change*; Stephen Kemmis, Peter Cole and Dahle Suggett, *Towards the Socially Critical School*; Wyn Williams and John Rennie, 'Social Education'; and Douglas Barnes, *From Communication to Curriculum*.

50. Margaret Mead, 'Our Educational Emphases in Primitive Perspective', p. 639.
51. 'Nothing is more detrimental to the regular progress of the school than visitors' – Leo Tolstoy, *Tolstoy on Education*, p. 228.
52. White Lion Street Free School, *Bulletin*, no. 3, p. 6.
53. Benson R. Snyder, *The Hidden Curriculum*.
54. White Lion Street Free School, 'What Goes on at the Free School', 1982 (not published).
55. Smith, *The Libertarians and Education*, p. 15.
56. It is still common to find courses in education divided into 'curriculum' and 'pedagogy'. Another component, 'organization', is relegated to a marginal status, as if it were a matter of mechanics that can be left to the administrators and the technically-minded. But mixed-ability grouping gives us an example of an 'organizational' question which has crucial implications for learning. Groupings are just one example of the structures which free schools were concerned with.
57. Ray Hemmings, *Fifty Years of Freedom*, p. 173. Contrast Raymond Williams's viewpoint: 'I agree, in principle, that a society has a right to make demands on its educational system' (Raymond Williams 'The Teaching Relationship: Both Sides of the Wall', p. 220).
58. Jules Townshend, 'A.S. Neill: A Critical Appreciation'.
59. C.B. Cox and Rhodes Boyson, *Black Paper 1975*, p. 1.
60. Cole, 'Education and Politics', p. 57.
61. The gradually expanding co-operative sector of the economy, fostered by organizations like the Industrial Common Ownership Movement, suggests one possible sector to which free schools might constructively have orientated themselves. Unfortunately this sector was minuscule in the early 1970s, leaving aside the Co-op (Cooperative Wholesale Societies and Cooperative Retail Societies) which, in the opinion of many radicals, had lost touch with its radical origins.
62. Bowles and Gintis, *Schooling in Capitalist America*, pp. 246, 351.
63. Guy Neave, 'The "Free Schoolers" ', p. 242.
64. White Lion Street Free School, internal documents, 1972.
65. Leeds Alternative Society, *A Free School in Leeds*, a leaflet published *c.* 1972.
66. See n. 45 above.
67. This style of politics has been called 'prefigurative; see p. 156.
68. The exceptions were Bowles and Gintis, *Schooling in Capitalist America*; and the writings of Jules Henry.
69. Carl Rogers, *Freedom to Learn*, pp. 5 and 9.
70. Holt, *Freedom and Beyond*, Chapters 9 and 10.

Chapter 8   Radical perspectives on learning

1. R.S. Peters dates this from the early 1960s – see Paul Hirst (ed.), *Educational Theory and its Foundation Disciplines*, p. 40.
2. Douglas Holly, *Society, Schools and Humanity*, p. 26.
3. Learning is not the only purpose of schools. There is also, for example, a

child-minding function. And schools are subject to pressures to fulfil other functions as well, such as social stratification: see Samuel Bowles and Herbert Gintis, *Schooling in Capitalist America*, Part 2.

4. J.H. Pestalozzi, *Leonard and Gertrude*, p. 152.
5. Note the title of the 1972 UNESCO Report: *Learning to Be*.
6. George Dennison, *The Lives of Children*, p. 11. Carl Rogers makes a similar opposition in *Freedom to Learn*, p. 39.
7. Quoted in Jonathan Croall, *Neill of Summerhill*, p. 306.
8. A.S. Neill, *Summerhill: A Radical Approach to Education*, p. 25.
9. Ibid., p. 27.
10. R.H. Quick, *Essays on Educational Reformers*, p. 411.
11. See Ray Hemmings *Fifty Years of Freedom*, pp. 38–41.
12. White Lion Street Free School, *Bulletin*, no. 2, p. 6. A very similar statement can be found in John Holt, *The Underachieving School*, p. 13. Compare also John Dewey's definition of education: 'That reconstruction or reorganisation of experience which adds to the meaning of experience, and which increases the ability to direct the course of subsequent experience' (*The School and Society*, pp. 89–90).
13. Quoted in Karl Popper, *The Open Society and Its Enemies, Volume 2* , p. 214.
14. Cited in Quick, *Essays on Educational Reformers*, p. 403.
15. Dennison, *The Lives of Children*, p. 11.
16. Earl Kelley, quoted in Neil Postman and Charles Weingartner, *Teaching as a Subversive Activity*, p. 94. See also Raymond Williams, *The Long Revolution*, p. 32.
17. Postman and Weingartner, *Teaching as a Subversive Activity*, p. 94.
18. See Basil Bernstein, 'Education Cannot Compensate for Society', p. 116.
19. See Kevin Harris, *Education and Knowledge*.
20. Dennison, *The Lives of Children*, p. 67.
21. Holly, *Society, Schools and Humanity*, p. 60.
22. Not only knowing *that* and knowing *how*, but also knowing in the familiar sense. It is interesting that this third 'familiarity' category of knowledge is undervalued by conventional schooling, with the exception of the public schools which are well aware of the uses of the 'old boy network'.
23. Paolo Freire, *Pedagogy of the Oppressed*, p. 27.
24. In case anyone should think that only reactionary authoritarians would advocate such learning, I draw attention to the story told by A.S. Neill, *Summerhill: A Radical Approach to Education*, p. 167.
25. Quoted in David Gribble, *Considering Children*, p. 38.
26. Quoted in Richard Johnson, 'Really Useful Knowledge', *Radical Education*, 7, p. 20.
27. Michael P. Smith, *The Libertarians and Education*, p. 43.
28. Douglas Holly, *Beyond Curriculum*, pp. 143–5.
29. John Holt, *How Children Learn*, p. 118.
30. See, for example, Holly, *Beyond Curriculum*, Chapter 9.
31. Ajoy S. Ghose, 'Fun With Learning: A Supplementary Programme', p. 122.

32. Holly, *Beyond Curriculum*; Gabriel Chanan and Linda Gilchrist, *What School Is For*; Postman and Weingartner, *Teaching as a Subversive Activity*.

33. For example, Michael Armstrong, *Closely Observed Children*; and Stephen Rowland, *The Enquiring Classroom*.

34. Colin Ball and Mog Ball, *Education for a Change*, p. 126.

35. See Dennison, *The Lives of Children*, p. 62; Paul Goodman, *Compulsory Miseducation*, p. 27; John Holt, *The Underachieving School*, p. 23.

36. Holt, *How Children Learn*, p. 57.

37. Edmond Holmes, *What Is and What Might Be*, p. 216.

38. H. Lane, *The Wild Boy of Aveyron*.

39. Margaret Mead, 'Our Educational Emphases in Primitive Perspective', p. 637.

40. Holt, *How Chldren Learn*, pp. 171–3. Compare this quotation from Charles Hoole, *A New Discovery of the Old Art of Teaching Schoole* (1660): 'it is Tully's observation of old, and Erasmus his assertion of later years, that it is as natural for a child to learn, as it is for a beast to go, a bird to fly, or a fish to swim'. It is worth remembering, too, William Godwin: 'Liberty is the school of understanding. This is not enough adverted to. Every boy learns more in his hours of play, than in his hours of labour. In school he lays in the materials of his thinking; but in his sport he actually thinks: he whets his faculties, and he opens his eyes. The child from the moment of his birth is an experimental philosopher.' (*Fleetwood*, pp. 247–9.)

41. John Holt, *Freedom and Beyond*, p. 68. But Holt seems to contradict himself in an earlier book when he says 'At a certain age, and particularly with a little encouragement from parents and teachers, they may become very interested in where words come from' (*The Underachieving School*, p. 73). I cannot see any distinction between 'motivation' (in the sense in which Holt is using it) and 'a little encouragement'.

42. This is an example Holt himself uses in *How Children Learn*, pp. 109ff.

43. R.S. Peters, *Ethics and Education*, p. 39.

44. John Holt, *What Do I Do Monday?*, p. 41.

45. Ibid.

46. Cited in Hemmings, *Fifty Years of Freedom*, p. 48 (emphasis added).

47. This is the view found, for example, in D.M. Pinn, 'What Kind of Primary School?', p. 103.

48. Herbert Kohl, *The Open Classroom*, p. 77. See also Jonathan Kozol, *Death at an Early Age*, p. 57 for a discussion of this point.

49. This is no accidental oversight on Holt's part. He belongs to a tradition of thought described by Raymond Williams: 'In England from Hobbes to the Utilitarians, a variety of systems share a common starting point: man as a bare human being, 'the individual', is the logical starting point of psychology, ethics and politics . . . It is rare, in this tradition, to start from the fact that man is born into relationships. The abstraction of the bare human being, as a separate substance, is ordinarily taken for granted. In other systems of thinking, the community would be the

axiom, and individual man the derivative' (*The Long Revolution*, p. 94). English as this tradition may be, it is more clearly visible in the work of American radical writers on education than in most of their British counterparts.

50. For example, Goodman, *Compulsory Miseducation*, p. 27; Everett Reimer, *School Is Dead*, p. 32.

51. For an opposing view to the one I am arguing here, see Paul Goodman, *Growing Up Absurd*, pp. 3–16.

52. Michael Duane 'Freedom and the State System of Education', p. 187. It is worth noting here the point made by J. Goody and I. Watt, 'The Consequences of Literacy', that 'literacy skills form one of the major axes of differentiation in industrial societies'. They also argue that since reading and writing are essentially individual activities, a literate culture is characterized by increasing individualization. See Michael F.D. Young (ed.) *Knowledge and Control*, pp. 19–46, for a discussion of this. See also Martin Hoyles (ed.), *The Politics of Literacy*.

53. See Jules Henry, *Essays on Education*.

54. But Henry claims (ibid., p. 177) that no culture in the world, at any time, has assumed a natural impulse to learn. 'This does not mean that children are not everywhere naturally investigative, but there is no evidence that children will not lose interest in learning when it requires work.'

55. Ibid, pp. 122ff.

56. William Van der Eyken and Barry Turner, *Adventures in Education*, and Greta Brooks, 'The Creed of Cuthbert Rutter'.

57. Goodman, *Growing Up Absurd*, pp. 34–5.

58. Dennison, *The Lives of Children*, p. 150.

Chapter 9   Learning in society

1. Peter A. de Villiers and Jill G. de Villiers, *Early Language*, p. 61.

2. John Holt, *Freedom and Beyond*, p. 75.

3. Holt in fact acknowledges this later in the same book. See his discussion of 'the discipline of culture' in ibid., Chapter 7.

4. This is argued by David Head, *Free Way to Learning*, p. 10. But a decidedly less glamorous picture of the static society is offered by Jules Henry, *Culture Against Man*, p. 234.

5. Paolo Freire, *Cultural Action for Freedom*, p. 21.

6. A.S. Neill, *Summerhill: A Radical Approach to Education*, p. 102.

7. Jules Henry, *Culture Against Man*, p. 234.

8. Edgar Stones, *An Introduction to Educational Psycholog*, p. 108.

9. Sir Fred Clarke, *Freedom in the Educative Society*, p. 29.

10. Douglas Holly discusses this in *Beyond Curriculum*, Chapter 8. Holly tries to distinguish between the 'common human heritage' (acceptable) and the 'class-related human heritage' (unacceptable) (p. 33). Rejecting the libertarian view that it can be left to children to decide, on their own, which are the 'acceptable parts' and which are the 'unacceptable parts' of the culture, Holly eventually falls back on a 'neutrality' argument: 'If concepts . . . are developed systematically . . . it is possible to have

independent structures of learning relatively free from ideological control' (p. 139). But in *Society, Schools and Humanity* Holly had been concerned to expose 'neutrality' as an illusion (p. 10).

11. See Holly, *Beyond Curriculum*, pp. 21–2.
12. See Graham Vulliamy, 'What Counts As School Music?'.
13. See Ken Worpole, 'The School and the Community'.
14. Interview with Susie Powlesland, 30 August 1986.
15. See Students of Bishop's College, *Writing from Carriacou*.
16. For an example of how this works in a contemporary utopian fantasy see Marge Piercy, *Woman on the Edge of Time*.
17. Chris Searle, *This New Season*, pp. 8–9.
18. Chris Searle (compiler), *Classrooms of Resistance*, p. 11.
19. Such 'escape-ism', espoused by the *Black Papers*, has been fiercely opposed by radicals for over 200 years. Consider Pestalozzi's fable of the fish and the pike (cited in R.H. Quick, *Essays on Educational Reformers*, pp. 292–3): 'The fishes in a pond brought an accusation against the pike who were making great ravages among them. The judge, an old pike, said that their complaint was well founded, and that the defendants, to make amends, should allow two ordinary fish every year to become pike.' R.H. Tawney, *Equality*, pp. 108–9, uses the same idea in his fable of the tadpoles and the frogs. For further discussion of this question see Richard Hoggart, *The Uses of Literacy*, p. 102; and Ken Jones, *Beyond Progressive Education*, pp. 52, 167.
20. Gabriel Chanan and Linda Gilchrist, *What School Is For*, p. 77.
21. Paolo Freire, *Cultural Action for Freedom*, p. 78.
22. Hoggart, *The Uses of Literacy*; and Raymond Williams, *The Long Revolution*.
23. Chris Searle (ed.), *Stepney Words*, 1 and 2; Searle, *Classrooms of Resistance*.
24. For example, Geoffrey Summerfield, 'Brainwashed Replicators', p. 23.
25. Gastone Tassinari, 'The Scuola and Quartiere Movement: A Case Study', p. 120. See also Paolo Freire's warning on this matter in *Pedagogy of the Oppressed*, p. 59.
26. For a discussion of this question, see Chanan and Gilchrist, *What School Is For*.
27. George Dennison, *The Lives of Children*, p. 232.
28. Annie Davidson, cited in Centre for Contemporary Cultural Studies, *Unpopular Education*, p. 39.
29. John Holt, *How Children Learn*, p. 104.
30. Samuel Butler, *Notebooks*, quoted in Jonathan Croall, *Neill of Summerhill*, p. 391.
31. Peter Newell and Alison Truefitt, 'Abolishing the Curriculum and Learning Without Exams', p. 78. (Note the prescriptive definition). Carl Rogers, *Freedom to Learn*, p. 52, makes a similar statement: 'the student learns by making independent choices of goals and means, making these choices in terms of what will be valuable to him, and taking the initiative in implementing these choices'.

32. Samuel Bowles and Herbert Gintis, *Schooling in Capitalist America*, p. 272.
33. I have taken the information in this paragraph from Holly, *Beyond Curriculum*, pp. 115ff.
34. L.S. Vygotsky, *Thought and Language*, p. 104.
35. White Lion Street Free School, 'A Free School "Curriculum" ', pp. 181–2.
36. A similar argument to the one presented here can be found in Willard Waller, *The Sociology of Teaching*, p. 448.
37. See Ray Hemmings, *Fifty Years of Freedom*, p. 173.
38. Holly, *Beyond Curriculum*, p. 137.
39. Editorial in *Socialist Teacher*, no. 23.
40. Dennison, *The Lives of Children*, p. 198.
41. As, for example, Sir Fred Clarke, quoted on page 130.
42. See Nigel Wright, 'The White Lion Free School Experiment'.
43. See Jacques Barzun, 'To Give an Education', p. 29.
44. Ken Jones, *Beyond Progressive Education*, pp. 160–1.
45. Consider Douglas Barnes's concept of 'action knowledge' in *From Communciation to Curriculum*. See also the quote from *Teaching London Kids* on page 46.
46. A feature of some American free schools — see Allen Graubard, *Free the Children*.
47. Jules Henry, *Essays on Education*, p. 168.
48. Bowles and Gintis, *Schooling in Capitalist America*, pp. 235–41.
49. Big Flame, *The Crisis in Education*, p. 11.
50. Paul Goodman, *Compulsory Miseducation*, p. 55.
51. Ken Coates 'Education as a lifelong experience', p. 29. The same point is made by Bowles and Gintis, *Schooling in Capitalist America*, p. 252, when they say: 'If schools are to assume a more humane form, so too must jobs.'
52. For the mathematically minded, this may be likened to an equation with three variables, x, y and z. The more possible solutions for x we rule out, the fewer possible solutions there will be for y and z.
53. See Wright, 'Radicals in English Education'.

Chapter 10   Radical dilemmas

1. From an unpublished manuscript, 'The Radical Rift', kindly lent by Gabriel Chanan.
2. David Rubinstein and Colin Stoneman (eds), *Education for Democracy*, 2nd edition, 'Introduction', p. 11.
3. Brian Jackson and Dennis Marsden, *Education and the Working Class*, p. 16.
4. David Ransom in *Rank & File Occasional Journal*, no. 1, Spring 1977, p. 2.
5. This was also what the right-wing understood by the crisis in education: see Rhodes Boyson, *The Crisis in Education*.
6. Paul Goodman, *Compulsory Miseducation*, p. 51.

7. R.F. Mackenzie, *Escape from the Classroom*, p. 87.
8. Keith Paton, *The Great Brain Robbery*, p. 3.
9. R.F. Mackenzie, *A Question of Living*, p. 28.
10. This is discussed by Douglas Holly, *Beyond Curriculum*, pp. 38ff. For example: 'The argument is that any confusion or slackness in teaching aims is bound to disadvantage the working-class pupil by comparison with his middle-class contemporaries, who are less dependent on schools for their education' (p. 40).
11. Ian Lister, *Deschooling*, p. 4.
12. Chanie Rosenberg, *Education and Society*, p. 10, claims that it would because 'In any rational society by far the biggest spender will be education'. However, socialists whose chief interest is in other fields – health, industry or overseas development, for example – might disagree.
13. See, for example, Chris Searle, *This New Season*. This view can also be found in the pages of *Rank & File, Socialist Teacher* and *Vanguard*.
14. Gabriel Chanan and Linda Gilchrist, *What School Is For*, p. 49.
15. Edward Blishen, *The School That I'd Like*, was a compilation of responses to an invitation in the *Observer* to school students to send in their views of school.
16. Such as the books of A.S. Neill; Gerard Holmes, *The Idiot Teacher*; the books of W. David Wills; Michael Burn, *Mr. Lyward's Answer*; Michael Croft, *Spare the Rod*; Paul Goodman, *Growing Up Absurd*; and Mackenzie, *A Question of Living*. By 1965, however, Mackenzie had taken up the question of class (see *Escape from the Classroom*, pp. 173ff.)
17. See Chapter 1, notes 18 and 19.
18. Mackenzie, *A Question of Living*, p. 96.
19. Colin Ball and Mog Ball, *Education for a Change*, p. 11.
20. By 'revolutionists' I mean those who advocate revolution – as opposed to revolutionaries, who actually make revolutions.
21. A.E. Jenning, *The Struggle in Education*, p. 28.
22. Ibid., p. 33.
23. C.A. Helvétius, *De L'Esprit*, p. 489.
24. Jenning, *The Struggle in Education*.
25. Ibid., p. 40.
26. This view was argued by Goodman, *Growing Up Absurd*, Chapter XI.
27. John Holt, *The Underachieving School*, p. 129.
28. See Campaign Against Repression of Pupils at Ladbroke School, *Ladbroke School: Situation and Struggle*. The campaign, in 1972 and 1973, was mounted largely against the headteacher of Ladbroke School who, it was claimed, was contemptuous of black and working-class students.
29. Martin Thomas and Paul Wimpeney, letter in *Blackbored*, no. 4, pp. 13–14.
30. John Cox (a pseudonym for Gabriel Chanan) in *Blackbored*, no, 4, pp. 14–15.
31. Wini Breines, 'Community and Organisation: The New Left and Michel's "Iron Law" '.
32. Ibid., p. 422.

33. Ibid., p. 421. The case for 'prefigurative' politics had been made in 1950 by Ernst Zander, 'The Great Utopia', p. 15: 'The party must incorporate and anticipate the organisation of the future society in all its essentials, that is, it must manifest the outlines in skeletal form'.
34. Nigel Wright, 'One Disaster After Another.'
35. Searle, *This New Season*, p. 7. But, despite this view, Searle did believe that there was room for manoeuvre in state schools.
36. Douglas Holly, *Society, Schools and Humanity*, p. 25.
37. Samuel Bowles and Herbert Gintis, *Schooling in Capitalist America*, p. 8. For similar viewpoints, see Chanan and Gilchrist, *What School Is For*, p. 10; and Ken Jones, *Beyond Progressive Education*, p. 19.
38. See, for example, Kevin Harris, *Education and Knowledge*.
39. See Colin Fletcher, Maxine Caron and Wyn Williams, *Schools on Trial*.
40. See John Watts, *The Countesthorpe Experience*. However, it has been argued that in the long run the Countesthorpe experiment was defeated: see (anon.) 'The Death of a Progressive School', *Lib Ed*, vol. 2, no. 6, Winter 1987, p. 18.
41. See *Rank & File*, nos 19–25, *passim*.
42. John Holt, *Escape from Childhood*, p. 37.
43. See Holt, *The Underachieving School*, p. 37.
44. *Rank & File Occasional Journal*, no. 1, 1977, p. 2.
45. Ernst Fischer, *Marx in his Own Words*, pp. 90–1, (emphasis in original).
46. Michael W. Apple, 'Series Editor's Introduction' in William J. Reese, *Power and the Promise of School Reform*.
47. Ray Hemmings, *Fifty Years of Freedom*, Chapter 8.
48. See, for example, Wilhelm Reich, *The Mass Psychology of Fascism*.
49. See Harris, *Education and Knowledge*, pp. 140ff.
50. Chris Searle (compiler), *Classrooms of Resistance*, pp. 8–9.
51. Geoffrey Summerfield, 'Brainwashed Replicators'. See also George Dennison, *The Lives of Children*, p. 232.
52. See Martyn Hammersley *Teacher Perspectives*, Units 9 and 10 of Open University course *Schooling and Society* (E202).
53. This is explored, for example, by Stephen Rowland, *The Enquiring Classroom*.
54. Leila Berg in Paul Adams *et al.*, *Children's Rights*, pp. 42–3.
55. A.S. Neill, *Summerhill*, p. 4.
56. School of Barbiana, *Letter to a Teacher*, p. 19.
57. Jeremy Mulford, letter in *Radical Education*, no. 1, p. 5.
58. School of Barbiana, *Letter to a Teacher*, p. 20.
59. Ibid., p. 93.
60. Ibid., pp. 105–6.
61. In 1962 by Goodman, *Compulsory Miseducation*; in 1965 by Colin Ward 'A Modest Proposal for the Repeal of the 1944 Education Act'; in 1969 by School Without Walls (see page 80 above); and also in 1969 by Holt, *The Underachieving School*, p.32.
62. Notably Harry Judge, *School is Not Yet Dead*; and Chanan and Gilchrist, *What School Is For*.
63. For example Nigel Wright 'A Black and Red Herring'; Holly, *Beyond Curriculum*, Chapter 9; Nicholas Walter 'Tool of Conviviality'.

64. The serious hypothesis is that the 'oppositional' mentality referred to in Chapter 2 could create a dependency on the part of radicals on the things they oppose. If a large part of one's sense of identity is built around being part of a political campaign, then the success of that campaign – which would make it redundant – could be deeply threatening to that sense of identity.
65. I am not using 'idealism' in the philosophical sense of a theory of the origin of ideas. But this philosophical sense does have a relevance to my discussion, as do the competing theories of materialism and dialectical materialism.
66. Interview with Rhiannon Evans, 26 August 1986.
67. Brian Simon (ed.), *The Radical Tradition in Education in Britain*.
68. Karl Popper, *The Open Society and Its Enemies, Volume 2: Hegel and Marx*, p. 224.
69. Michael P. Smith, *The Libertarians and Education*.
70. R.M. Jones, *Fantasy and Feeling in Education*.
71. Hemmings, *Fifty Years of Freedom*, p. 178.
72. Lynn White, 'The changing canons of our culture'.
73. Karl Jaspers, cited by Philip Mairet in his introduction to Jean-Paul Sartre, *Existentialism and Humanism*, p. 11.
74. Michael F.D. Young (ed.), *Knowledge and Control*, p. 3.
75. For example, Paul Willis, *Learning to Labour*.
76. This is the viewpoint represented, for example, by the magazine *Resurgence*.
77. Paul Adams, 'The Infant, the Family and Society' in Paul Adams *et al.*, *Children's Rights*, p. 53.
78. Interview with Phil Collins, 9 September 1986.

Chapter 11   The present moment in education

1. Baron Swann (chmn), *Education For All*, p. vii.
2. For example, Michael F.D. Young (ed.), *Knowledge and Control*; Nell Keddie (ed.), *Tinker, Tailor . . . The Myth of Cultural Deprivation*; R.K. Brown (ed.), *Knowledge, Education and Cultural Change.*
3. For example, Richard Johnson, 'Really Useful Knowledge'.
4. The literature is quite large. The following is a random list which gives the flavour: Michael Flude and John Ahier (eds), *Educability, Schools and Ideology*; Rachel Sharp and Anthony Green, *Education and Social Control*; Paul Corrigan, *Schooling the Smash Street Kids*; Madan Sarup, *Marxism, Structuralism and Education*; Ted Tapper and Brian Salter, *Education and the Political Order*; Centre for Contemporary Cultural Studies, *Unpopular Education*; Paul Willis, *Learning to Labour*; and the Open University course *School and Society* (E282). A journal which kept track of these developments more fully than any other was *Schooling and Culture*, published by the Cultural Studies department of London's Cockpit Theatre.
5. See Mica Nava, 'Gender and Education'; Madeleine Arnot and Gaby Weiner (eds), *Gender Under Scrutiny*; Rosemary Deem *Women and Schooling*. For a review of the literature on race and education, see

Educational Review, vol. 37, no. 2 (1985), special issue on ethnic minorities.

6. Julius Gould, *The Attack on Higher Education: Marxist and Radical Penetration*.

7. Editorial in *Lib Ed*, no. 27, p. 18.

8. See Ted Benton, 'Education and Politics'.

9. See, for example, Stephen Brookfield, *Adult Learning, Adult Education and the Community*; Jim Cosgrove and Mike Stevenson, 'The Work of the Leith Community Education Project'.

10. There were exceptions – for example, an *Open Door* programme made by STOPP; and a programme broadcast on London's Capital Radio, made by the Local Radio Workshop and *Radical Education*.

11. This film is distributed by The Other Cinema.

12. Peter Newell and Alison Truefitt, 'Abolishing the Curriculum and Learning Without Exams'.

13. See Kevin Harris, *Education and Knowledge*, Chapter 4.

14. *Guardian*, 14 October 1976.

15. C.B. Cox and A.E. Dyson, *Fight for Education: A Black Paper*, p. 6.

16. I will list these at some length because it is interesting to note how diligent the New Right have been at proselytizing their ideas: C.B. Cox and others, *The Accountability of Schools*; C.B. Cox, *Education: The Next Decade*; Caroline Cox and John Marks, *Education and Freedom: The Roots of Diversity*; Caroline Cox and Roger Scruton, *Peace Studies, A Critical Survey*; Caroline Cox and John Marks, *Real Concern: An Appraisal of the NCB's Report on Progress in Secondary Schools*; Caroline Cox and John Marks (eds), *The Right to Learn*; Caroline Cox and John Marks, *Sixth Forms in ILEA Comprehensives: A Cruel Confidence Trick?*; Caroline Cox, John Marks and Maciej Pomian-Srzednicki, *Standards in English Schools*; Caroline Cox and others, *Whose Schools? A Radical Manifesto*; Anthony Flew and others, *The Pied Pipers of Education*; Anthony Flew, *Education, Race and Revolution*; Anthony Flew, *Sociology, Equality and Education*; John Marks, *London's Schools: When Even the Communist Party Gives Up*; John Marks, *Peace Studies in Our Schools: Propaganda for Defencelessness*; Roger Scruton, *World Studies: Education or Indoctrination?*; Roger Scruton, Angela Ellis-Jones and Dennis O'Keefe, *Education and Indoctrination*; Dennis O'Keefe, *The Wayward Curriculum*.

17. Examples of such popular mythology are considered in Robert Bell and Nigel Grant, *A Mythology of British Education*.

18. See Nigel Wright, *Progress in Education*, Chapter 4.

19. This scepticism was not confined to right-wingers: see Colin McCabe, 'Blueprint for Democratic Schools'.

20. It was an explicit claim of the *Black Paper* editors that they had succeeded in destroying the 'damaging consensus' which had prevailed up until 1969. See Wright, *Progress in Education*, p. 173.

21. Reports of the Cross Inquiry Commission 1886–9 (5 volumes).

22. See Nigel Wright, 'Standards and the Black Papers'.

23. Stuart Froome, 'It's Time Our Teachers Went Back to the Old Values'.

24. Sir John Adams, *Modern Developments in Educational Practice*, p. 11.

25. See S.J. Curtis, *Introduction to the Philosophy of Education*, Chapter 2.

26. 'Theses on Feuerbach' in Karl Marx and Frederick Engels, *Selected Works in One Volume*, p. 30.
27. I discuss this question further in 'In Need of Theory', p. 19.
28. See note 49 to Chapter 8.
29. Brian Jackson and Dennis Marsden, *Education and the Working Class*, p. 17.
30. A pioneering example of this was the work of the Farmington Trust on moral education; a more recent example is the Centre for Contemporary Cultural Studies volume, *Unpopular Education*.
31. See Johnson, 'Really Useful Knowledge'.
32. This seemed to originate with Perry Anderson, 'Origins of the Present Crisis'.
33. See Harris, *Education and Knowledge*, Chapter 1.
34. R. Rosenthal and L. Jacobson, *Pygmalion in the Classroom*.
35. Stanley Milgram, *Obedience to Authority*.
36. See Mary Warnock, *Schools of Thought*.

Appendix   A note on 'class'

1. Harold Entwistle, *Class Culture and Education*, p. 35.
2. See A.H. Halsey, A.F. Heath and J.M. Ridge, *Origins and Destinations*.
3. Raymond Williams, *Keywords*, pp. 51–9.
4. For example, Douglas Holly, 'The Invisible Ruling Class', p. 108.
5. For example, Chanie Rosenberg, *Education and Society*.
6. Nigel Wright, *Progress in Education*, p. 76.
7. See Jane Steedman, *Progress in Secondary Schools*.
8. See Chapter 1, p. 7.

Bibliography

The radical literature on schooling, 1960–1980

(Note: this section of the bibliography contains all the radical books, pamphlets and periodicals on the subject of schooling published in Britain in this period. Radical literature published prior to 1960 or after 1980, or published elsewhere but not in Britain, may be found in the main bibliography which follows. Radical literature on further and higher education is not included here.

To be included in this section of the bibliography the work must have been explicitly radical and propagandist in tone. Certain works which were radical but conformed to academic proprieties – such as Raymond Williams, *The Long Revolution*, Brian Jackson and Dennis Marsden, *Education and the Working Class*, or Douglas Holly, *Beyond Curriculum* and *Society, Schools and Humanity* are placed in the main bibliography.)

Books

Adams, Paul *et al.*, *Children's Rights* (Elek Books 1971).
Ball, Colin and Ball, Mog, *Education for a Change* (Penguin 1973).
Barbiana, School of, *Letter to a Teacher* (Penguin 1970; first published in Italy 1969).
Berg, Leila, *Risinghill: Death of a Comprehensive School* (Penguin 1968).
Blishen, Edward (ed.), *The School That I'd Like* (Penguin 1969).
Bowles, Samuel and Gintis, Herbert, *Schooling in Capitalist America* (Routledge and Kegan Paul 1976).
Buckman, Peter (ed.), *Education Without Schools* (Souvenir Press 1973).
Chanan, Gabriel and Gilchrist, Linda, *What School Is For* (Methuen 1974).
Dennison, George, *The Lives of Children* (Penguin 1972; first published in the USA 1969).
Dixon, Bob, *Catching Them Young 1: Sex, Race and Class in Children's Fiction* (Pluto Press 1977).
Dixon, Bob, *Catching Them Young 2: Political Ideas in Children's Fiction* (Pluto Press 1977).

Freire, Paolo, *Cultural Action for Freedom* (Penguin 1972; first published in the USA 1970).

Freire, Paolo, *Education for Critical Consciousness* (Sheed and Ward 1974).

Freire, Paolo, *Education, the Practice of Freedom* (Writers and Readers 1976; first published in Brazil 1967).

Freire, Paolo, *Pedagogy of the Oppressed* (Penguin 1972; first published in the USA 1970).

Freire, Paolo, *Pedagogy in Progress* (Writers and Readers 1978).

Gilchrist, Linda, *see* Chanan, Gabriel.

Gintis, Herbert, *see* Bowles, Samuel.

Goodman, Paul, *Compulsory Miseducation* (Penguin 1971; first published in the USA 1962).

Goodman, Paul, *Growing Up Absurd* (Gollancz 1961; first published in the USA 1960).

Gross, Ronald and Gross, Beatrice, *Radical School Reform* (Gollancz 1971; first published in the USA, 1969).

Hansen, Søren and Jensen, Jasper, *The Little Red Schoolbook* (Stage 1, 1971; first published in Denmark in 1969).

Head, David (ed.), *Free Way to Learning* (Penguin 1974).

Hemmings, Ray, *Fifty Years of Freedom* (George Allen & Unwin 1972).

Henry, Jules, *Culture Against Man* (Penguin 1972; first published in the USA 1963).

Henry, Jules, *Essays on Education* (Penguin 1971).

Herndon, James, *The Way It Spozed to Be* (Pitman 1970).

Holly, Douglas (ed.), *Education or Domination* (Arrow 1974).

Holt, John, *Escape from Childhood* (Penguin 1975).

Holt, John, *Freedom and Beyond* (Penguin 1973; first published in the USA 1972).

Holt, John, *How Children Fail* (Pitman 1965; first published in the USA 1964).

Holt, John, *How Children Learn* (Penguin 1970; first published in the USA 1967).

Holt, John, *Instead of Education* (Penguin 1977).

Holt, John, *The Underachieving School* (Penguin 1971; first published in the USA 1970).

Holt, John, *What Do I Do Monday?* (Pitman 1971; first published in the USA 1970).

Hoyles, Martin (ed.), *Changing Childhood* (Writers and Readers 1979).

Hoyles, Martin (ed.), *The Politics of Literacy* (Writers and Readers 1977).

Illich, Ivan, *Deschooling Society* (Calder and Boyars 1971).

Illich, Ivan and Verne, Etienne, *Imprisoned in the Global Classroom* (Writers and Readers 1976).

Jensen, Jasper, *see* Hansen, Søren.

Keddie, Nell (ed.), *Tinker, Tailor . . . The Myth of Cultural Deprivation* (Penguin 1973).

Kohl, Herbert, *36 Children* (Gollancz 1968; Open University Press 1988; first published in the USA 1967).

Kohl, Herbert, *The Open Classroom* (Methuen 1970; first published in the USA 1969).

Kozol, Jonathan, *Death at an Early Age* (Penguin 1968; first published in the USA 1967).

Lister, Ian, *Deschooling* (Cambridge University Press 1974).

Mackenzie, R.F., *Escape from the Classroom* (Collins 1965).

Mackenzie, R.F., *A Question of Living* (Collins 1963).

Mackenzie, R.F., *The Sins of the Children* (Collins 1967).

Mackenzie, R.F., *State School* (Penguin 1970).

Mackenzie, R.F., *The Unbowed Head* (Edinburgh University Student Publications Board 1977).

Neill, A.S., *Summerhill* (Penguin 1968).

Neill, A.S., *Summerhill: A Radical Approach to Education* (Gollancz 1962).

Neill, A.S., *Talking of Summerhill* (Gollancz 1967).

Otty, Nicholas, *Learner Teacher* (Penguin 1972).

Paton, Keith, *The Great Brain Robbery* (Keith Paton 1971).

Postman, Neil and Weingartner, Charles, *Teaching as a Subversive Activity* (Penguin 1971; first published in the USA 1969).

Reimer, Everett, *School Is Dead* (Penguin 1971).

Rogers, Carl, *Freedom to Learn* (Columbus, Ohio; Merrill 1969).

Rubinstein, David and Stoneman, Colin (eds), *Education for Democracy* (1st edn: Penguin 1970; 2nd edn: Penguin 1972).

School Without Walls, *Lunatic Ideas* (Schools Without Walls/Corner House Bookshop 1978).

Searle, Chris (compiler), *Classrooms of Resistance* (Writers and Readers 1975).

Searle, Chris (compiler), *The World in a Classroom* (Writers and Readers 1977).

Searle, Chris (ed.), *Stepney Words* (Reality Press 1971).

Searle, Chris (ed.), *Stepney Words 2* (Reality Press 1971).

Searle, Chris, *This New Season* (Calder and Boyars 1973).

Stoneman, Colin *see* Rubinstein, David.

Verne, Etienne *see* Illich, Ivan.

Weingartner, Charles *see* Postman, Neil.

Whitty, Geoff and Young, Michael (eds), *Explorations in the Politics of School Knowledge* (Nafferton Books 1976).

Pamphlets, etc.

Adelstein, David, *The Wisdom and Wit of R.S. Peters* (University of London Institute of Education Students' Union 1971).

Allen, Chris *et al.*, *Sexism in Schools* (Sheffield Women and Education 1978).

Antistudent Pamphlet Collective, *Antistudent* (1972).

Barrowfield Community School, *Progress Report* (Aberdeen Peoples' Press 1975).

Berger, Nan, *The Rights of Children and Young Persons* (NCCL 1967).

Big Flame, *The Crisis in Education* (Big Flame Teachers Commission 1977).

Bootstrap Union, *Bootstrappers' Charter* (*c.*1973).

Brantingham, Tony, *In Place of School* (1973).

Campaign Against Repression of Pupils at Ladbroke School, *Ladbroke School: Situation and Struggle* (1973).

Campaign for State Supported Alternative Schools, *A Case for Alternative Schools within the Maintained System* (Advisory Centre for Education 1980).

Campaign to Impede Sex Stereotyping in the Young, *CISSY Talks to Publishers* (1974).

Coard, Bernard, *How The West Indian Child is Made Educationally Subnormal in the British School System* (New Beacon Books 1971).

Collins, Phil *et al., The Only Interruption in My Education was When I Went to School* (Oadby, Leics: The A.S. Neill Trust 1978).

Gregory, R.G., *Ring Your Own Bloody Bell* (Market Drayton: R.G. Gregory 1972).

Illich, Ivan, *The Alternative to Schooling* (Student Christian Movement 1972 or 1973).

Illich, Ivan, *After Deschooling, What?* (Writers and Readers 1974).

Illich, Ivan, *Learning Webs* (Student Christian Movement undated).

Illich, Ivan, *Why We Must Abolish Schooling* (Reprinted from *New York Review of Books*, 2 July 1970).

Jenning, A.E., *The Struggle in Education* (International Marxist Group/ Red Books 1973).

Language and Class Workshop, *Language and Class* (no. 1, February 1974; no. 2, November 1974).

National Council for Civil Liberties, *Children Have Rights*: a series of six pamphlets: 1, *Children in Schools*; 2, *Handicapped Children*; 3, *Children in Residential Care*; 4, *Children at Home*; 5, *Legal*; 6, *Compulsory School Attendance* (NCCL 1970–1).

National Council for Civil Liberties, *Rights of Children* (NCCL 1972).

Progressive Labor Party, *Racism IQ and the Class Society* (American Progressive Labor Party; reprinted by Campaign on Racism, IQ and the Class Society and *Humpty Dumpty* 1974).

Rank & File, *Democracy in Schools* (1971).

Rank & File, *The Fight for Education* (*Rank & File Occasional Journal*, no. 1, Spring 1977).

Rank & File, *Fighting Sexism in Schools* (no date).

Rank & File, *A Teachers Charter* (1969).

Rank & File, *Teachers Salaries: The Fight for a Single Scale* (1974).

Rat, Myth and Magic (Published by a collective: Nigel Armistead and others: 1972).

Right to Learn, *The Right to Learn* (1973).

Right to Learn, *School Does Matter* (1974).

Rosen, Harold, *Language and Class* (Falling Wall Press 1972).

Rosenberg, Chanie, *Education and Revolution* (Rank & File 1974).

Rosenberg, Chanie, *Education and Society* (Rank & File 1973).

SCANUS (Student Community Action of the National Union of Students), *Action Education Kit* (NUS 1974).

Schools Action Union, *Revolution in the Schools* (1970).

Schools Action Union, *Schools Charter* (1970).

School Without Walls, *Learning not Schooling* (Pack: 1st edn 1976).

Scotland Road Community Trust, *Our Lives in Our Hands* (July 1973).

Scotland Road Free School, *An Alternative School for Liverpool* (1971).

Socialist Child Care Collective, *Towards Socialist Child Care* (1975).

Socialists in Art Education, *In Pursuit of Change in Education and Society* (undated).

Student Christian Movement, *Education, Liberation and the Church* (undated).

Teachers Action Collective, *Teachers and the Economy* (1975).

Truefitt, Alison, *How to Set Up a Free School* (White Lion Street Free School 1973; 2nd edn 1974).

White Lion Street Free School, *Why ILEA Should Not Fund The Free School (And Why It Should)* (White Lion Street Free School 1981).

Periodicals

Ashes and Grapes (Cardiff School Students; extant 1968).

A.S. Neill Trust Newsletter (no. 1, 1974; ceased publication *c.*1981).

Blackbored (no. 1, 1970; ceased publication with no. 4, January 1972).

Blazer (Oxford school students; at least three issues published *c.*1974).

Blot (National Union of School Students; no. 1, October 1978; ceased publication with no. 4, September 1980).

Brain Damage ('Journal of School Revolt', Oxford, *c.*1972).

Children's Rights (no. 1, December 1971; after no. 6, July 1972, name changed to *Kids*).

Children's Rights Workshop Newsletter (no. 1, December 1974).

Compulsory Miseducation (magazine produced by Manchester Secondary Schools Union, *c.*1968).

Democratic Schools (Theoretical Journal of the Schools Action Union: no. 1, 1971; ceased publication with no. 5, 1974).

Educat (Brighton: no. 1, 1974; ceased publication with no. 2).

Enigma (produced by a school-student collective in Portsmouth: no. 1, 1975 or 1976).

Format (Young Communist League's schools magazine: extant 1969).

Free Schools Educational Supplement (Free Schools Campaign: no. 1, 1968; ceased publication with no. 4, June 1969).

Hard Cheese (no. 1, January 1973; ceased publication with no. 4/5, November 1975).

HOD (Handful of Dust, a magazine dedicated to pupil power: Leeds, 1969).

Humpty Dumpty (no. 1, November 1972; ceased publication with no. 6/7, 1975).

ID (Journal of the Summerhill Society).

Kids (formerly Children's Rights; no. 7, 1972; ceased publication in 1973).

Lib Ed (formerly *Libertarian Education*: no. 25, Autumn 1978; ceased publication with no. 30, 1981; resumed publication as *Lib Ed*, Second Series, vol. 2, no. 1, 1986; continues).

Libertarian Education Network Bulletin (no. 1, January 1973; ceased publication with no. 5, June 1973).

Libertarian Education (formerly *Libertarian Teacher*; no. 10, February 1973; name changed to *Lib Ed* from no. 25).

Libertarian Teacher (no. 1, April 1966; named changed to *Libertarian Education* from no. 10).

Militant Teacher (extant 1969).

Pied Paper (Exeter: no. 1, 1975; ceased publication with no. 4, 1976).

Radical Education (no. 1, 1974; ceased publication with no. 13, 1979).

Rank & File (no. 1, April 1968; ceased publication with no. 81, February–March 1982).

Rebel (London Region of Schools Action Union: no. 1, October 1969; ceased publication with no. 4, June 1970).

Red Rat (no. 1, Summer 1970; ceased publication with no. 6, 1974).

Rustle ('Inter Schools Mag': Essex, *c*.1970).

SAM (Schools Alternative Mag: Plymouth, *c*.1970).

Socialist Teacher (no. 1, Spring 1977; continues).

Teaching London Kids (no. 1, 1973; ceased publication with no. 25, March 1987).

Teachers Against Racism (no. 1, February 1972; ceased publication with no. 4, 1973).

Teachers Action (no. 1, 1974; ceased publication with no. 14, 1981).

This Magazine is About Education (Scotland: no. 1, 1974(?)).

Vanguard (Schools Action Union: no. 1, January 1969; ceased publication with no. 13, 1972).

White Lion Street Free School Bulletin (no. 1, 1972; last issue no. 5, December 1980).

Women and Education (no. 1, October 1973; ceased publication with no. 24, Winter 1982(?)).

Y-Front (no. 1, 1972; ceased publication with no. 4, 1973).

Main bibliography

Books and pamphlets

Ackerman, Nathan W. *et al.*, *Summerhill: For and Against* (New York: Hart 1970).

Adams, Sir John, *Modern Developments in Educational Practice* (2nd edn: University of London Press 1928).

Ahier, John *see* Flude, Michael.

Anderson, C.A. *see* Halsey, A.H.

Armistead, Nigel (ed.), *Reconstructing Social Psychology* (Penguin 1974).

Armstrong, Michael, *Closely Observed Children* (Writers and Readers 1980).

Arnot, Madeline and Weiner, Gaby (eds), *Gender Under Scrutiny* (Hutchinson Education 1987).

Ash, Maurice, *Who Are the Progressives Now?* (RKP 1969).

Auld, Robin, *William Tyndale Junior and Infants School Public Enquiry: A Report to the Inner London Education Authority* (ILEA 1976).

Baker, Joy, *Children in Chancery* (Hutchinson 1964).

Bantock, Geoffrey, *Freedom and Authority in Education* (Faber 1965).

Barnes, Douglas, *From Communication to Curriculum* (Penguin 1976).

Barnes, Douglas, Britton, James and Rosen, Harold, *Language, the Learner and the School* (Penguin 1971).

Barrow, Robin, *Radical Education: A Critique of Freeschooling and De-schooling* (Martin Robertson 1978).

Barton, Len and Walker Stephen, *Schools, Teachers and Teaching* (Lewes: Falmer Press 1981).

Bazely, E.T., *Homer Lane and the Little Commonwealth* (George Allen & Unwin 1928).

Bell, Robert and Grant, Nigel, *A Mythology of British Education* (Panther 1974).

Bennett, Neville, *Teaching Styles and Pupil Progress* (Open Books 1976).

Berlak, Ann and Berlak, Harold, *The Dilemmas of Schooling* (Methuen 1981).

Bernstein, Basil, *Class, Codes and Control, Vol 2* (RKP 1973).

Biskind, Peter, *Seeing is Believing* (Pluto Press 1984).

Blewitt, Trevor (ed.), *The Modern Schools Handbook* (Gollancz 1934).

Blishen, Edward, *A Nest of Teachers* (Allison and Busby 1985).

Boyd, W. and Rawson, W., *The Story of the New Education* (Heinemann 1965).

Boyson, Rhodes, *The Crisis in Education* (Woburn Press 1975).

Britton, James *see* Barnes, Douglas.

Brookfield, Stephen, *Adult Learners, Adult Education and the Community* (Open University Press 1983).

Brown, R.K. (ed.), *Knowledge, Education and Cultural Change* (Tavistock 1973).

Bruner, Jerome, *Towards a Theory of Instruction* (Cambridge, Mass.: Harvard University Press 1966).

Burgess, Carol *et al.*, *Understanding Children Writing* (Penguin 1973).

Burgess, Tyrell (ed.), *Dear Lord James: A Critique of Teacher Training* (Penguin 1971).

Burke, Vincent, *Teachers in Turmoil* (Penguin 1971).

Burn, Michael, *Mr. Lyward's Answer* (Hamish Hamilton 1956).

Carnoy, Martin, *Education as Cultural Imperialism* (New York: McKay 1964).

Caron, Maxine *see* Fletcher, Colin.

Castaneda, Carlos, *Tales of Power* (Hodder and Stoughton 1974).

Castaneda, Carlos, *Teachings of Don Juan* (Penguin 1970).

Centre for Contemporary Cultural Studies, *Unpopular Education* (Hutchinson 1981).

Child, H.A.T. (ed.), *The Independent Progressive School* (Hutchinson 1962).

Clarke, Sir Fred, *Freedom in the Educative Society* (University of London Press 1948).

Cohn-Bendit, Daniel and Cohn-Bendit, Gabriel, *Obsolete Communism: The Left-Wing Alternative* (André Deutsch 1968).

Cole, Peter *see* Kemmis, Stephen.

Corrigan, Paul, *Schooling the Smash Street Kids* (Macmillan 1979).

Cox, C.B. and Boyson, Rhodes (eds), *Black Paper 1975* (J.M. Dent 1975).

Cox, C.B. and Dyson, A.E. (eds), *Fight for Education: A Black Paper* (Critical Quarterly Society 1969).

Cox, C.B. and Dyson, A.E. (eds), *Black Paper Two: The Crisis in Education* (Critical Quarterly Society 1969).

Croall, Jonathan (ed.), *All the Best, Neill: Letters from Summerhill* (André Deutsch 1983).

Croall, Jonathan, *Neill of Summerhill* (RKP 1983).

Croft, Michael, *Spare the Rod* (Longman 1954).

Cross Inquiry Commission 1886–9, *Report* (5 volumes).

Curtis, S.J., *History of Education in Great Britain* (University Tutorial Press 1948).

Curtis, S.J., *Introduction to the Philosophy of Education* (University Tutorial Press 1958).

Dale, Roger, *Liberal and Radical Alternatives* (Open University course *Schooling and Society* (E202), Block VI, Unit 31; Open University Press 1977).

Davis, Angela, *Women, Race and Class* (The Women's Press 1981).

Deighton, Len, *Mexico Set* (Panther 1985).

Deem, Rosemary, *Women and Schooling* (RKP 1978).

de Villiers, Peter A. and de Villiers, Jill G., *Early Language* (Fontana/Open Books 1979).

Dewey, John, *Experience and Education* [1938] (Collier Macmillan 1963).

Dewey, John, *The School and Society* [1915] (revised edn: Chicago: University of Chicago Press 1943).

Douglas, J.W.B., *The Home and the School* (MacGibbon and Kee 1964).

Doyle, James F. (ed.), *Educational Judgements* (RKP 1973).

Edwards, Bertram, *The Burston School Strike* (Lawrence and Wishart 1974).

Egan, Kieran *see* Strike, Kenneth A.

Ellis, Terry *et al.*, *William Tyndale: The Teachers' Story* (Writers and Readers 1976).

Engels, Frederick *The Origins of the Family, Private Property and the State* [1884] (Lawrence and Wishart 1972).

Entwistle, Harold, *Class, Culture and Education* (Methuen 1978).

Eysenck, H.J., *Race, Intelligence and Education* (Temple Smith 1971).

Eysenck, H.J., *Check Your Own IQ* (Penguin 1966).

Fauré, Edgar *et al.*, *Learning to Be* (Harrap, for UNESCO, 1972).

Fischer, Ernst, *Marx in His Own Words* (Penguin 1973).

Fletcher, Colin, Caron, Maxine and Williams, Wyn, *Schools on Trial* (Open University Press 1985).

Flew, Anthony, *Sociology, Equality and Education* (Macmillan 1976).

Floud, J. *see* Halsey, A.H.

Flude, Michael and Ahier, John (eds), *Educability, Schools and Ideology* (Croom Helm 1974).

Franklin, Bob (ed.), *The Rights of Children* (Basil Blackwell 1986).

Freeman, M.D.A., *The Rights and Wrongs of Children* (Frances Pinter 1983).

Giddens, Anthony, *Positivism and Sociology* (Heinemann 1974).

Gilham, Bill, *Reconstructing Educational Psychology* (Croom Helm 1978).

Godwin, William, *The Enquirer: Reflections on Education, Manners and Literature* [1797] (facsimile edn: New York: Augustus M. Kelley 1964).

Godwin, William, *Fleetwood: or, The New Man of Feeling* (London 1805).

Gould, Julius, *The Attack on Higher Education: Marxist and Radical Penetration* (Institute for the Study of Conflict 1977).

Grace, Gerald, *Education and the City* (RKP 1984).

Grant, Nigel *see* Bell, Robert.

Graubard, Allen, *Free the Children* (New York: Vintage Books 1974).

Green, Anthony *see* Sharp, Rachel.

Gretton, John and Jackson, Mark, *William Tyndale: Collapse of a School — or a System?* (Allen & Unwin 1976).

Gribble, David, *Considering Children* (Dorling Kindersley 1985).

Grunsell, Rob, *Born to Be Invisible* (Macmillan 1978).

Haddow, Brian *see* Ellis, Terry.

Halliwell, Leslie, *Film Guide* (Paladin 1979).

Halsey, A.H., Floud, J. and Anderson, C.A. (eds), *Education, Economy and Society* (Glencoe, Illinois: The Free Press 1961).

Halsey, A.H., Heath, A.F. and Ridge, J.M., *Origins and Destinations* (Oxford: Clarendon Press 1980).

Hammersley, Martyn, *Teacher Perspectives* (Open University course *Schooling and Society* (E202), Block II, Units 9 and 10; Open University Press 1977).

Hammersley, Martyn and Woods, Peter (eds), *The Process of Schooling* (Open Univesity Press 1976).

Hampton, Christopher, *A Radical Reader: The Struggle for Change in England 1381–1914* (Penguin 1984).

Harber, Clive, Meighan, Roland and Roberts, Brian (eds), *Alternative Educational Futures* (Holt, Rinehart and Winston 1984).

Hargreaves, David, *Interpersonal Relations and Education* (RKP 1972).

Harris, Kevin, *Education and Knowledge* (RKP 1979).

Harrison, J.F.C., *Learning and Living 1790–1960* (RKP 1961).

Heath, A.F. *see* Halsey, A.H.

Heidegger, Martin, *Being and Time* [1927] (Oxford: Basil Blackwell 1962).

Helvétius, C.A., *De l'Esprit* [1758] or *Essays on the Mind* translated by William Midford (M. Jones 1807).

Her Majesty's Inspectorate of Schools, *Behavioural Units: A Survey of Special Units for Pupils With Behavioural Problems* (DES 1978).

Hewison, Robert, *Too Much: Art and Society in the Sixties* (Methuen 1986).

Hill, Matthew Davenport, *Plans for the Government and Liberal Instruction of Boys in Large Numbers Drawn from Experience* (London: G & W.B. Whittaker 1822).

Hirst, Paul H. (ed.), *Educational Theory and Its Foundation Disciplines* (RKP 1983).

Hoggart, Richard, *The Uses of Literacy* (Chatto and Windus 1957).

Holbrook, David, *English for the Rejected* (Cambridge University Press 1964).

Holly, Douglas, *Beyond Curriculum* (Hart-Davis MacGibbon 1973).

Holly, Douglas, *Society, Schools and Humanity* (MacGibbon and Kee 1971).

Holmes, Edmond, *The Tragedy of Education* (Constable 1913).

Holmes, Edmond, *What Is and What Might Be* (Constable 1911).

Holmes, Gerard, *The Idiot Teacher* (Faber 1952).

Hoole, Charles, *A New Discovery in the Old Art of Teaching Schoole* [1660] (Liverpool University Press 1913).

Hooper, R. (ed.), *The Curriculum: Context, Design and Development* (Oliver and Boyd 1971).

Hornsey College of Art, Staff and Students of, *The Hornsey Affair* (Penguin 1969).

Hudson, Liam, *Contrary Imaginations* (Methuen 1966).

Hudson, Liam, *The Cult of the Fact* (Jonathan Cape 1972).

Illich, Ivan *et al., Disabling Professions* (Marion Boyars 1977).

Inglis, Fred, *Radical Earnestness* (Martin Robertson 1982).

Isaacs, Susan, *Social Development in Young Children* (Routledge 1933).

Jackson, Brian and Marsden, Dennis *Education and the Working Class* [1962] (Penguin 1966).

Jackson, Mark *see* Gretton, John.

Jacobson, L. *see* Rosenthal R.

Jones, Ken, *Beyond Progressive Education* (Macmillan 1983).

Jones, Richard M., *Fantasy and Feeling in Education* (Penguin 1972).

Judge, Harry, *School is Not Yet Dead* (Longman 1974).

Kamin, Leon, *The Science and Politics of IQ* (Penguin 1977).

Kemmis, Stephen, Cole, Peter and Suggett, Dahle, *Towards the Socially Critical School* (Victoria Institute of Secondary Education 1983).

Kozol, Jonathan, *Free Schools* (Boston: Houghton Mifflin 1972).

Krishnamurti, *Beginnings of Learning* (Gollancz 1975).

Lane, H., *The Wild Boy of Aveyron* (Cambridge, Mass.: Harvard University Press 1976).

Lawson, John and Silver, Harold, *A Social History of Education in England* (Methuen 1973).

Leavis, F.R. and Thompson, Denys, *Culture and Environment: The Training of Critical Awareness* (Chatto and Windus 1933).

Lenin, V.I., *The State and Revolution* [1917] (Central Books 1972).

Locke, John, *Two Treatises on Government* [1690] (Cambridge University Press 1967).

McCann, W.P. *see* Stewart, W.A.C.

Maccoby, Simon, *The English Radical Tradition 1763–1914* (Kaye 1952).

McNeal, Julia and Rogers, Margaret (eds), *The Multi-Racial School* (Penguin 1971).

Makarenko, Anton, *Road to Life* (Stanley Nott 1936).

Malinowski, Bronislaw, *The Sexual Life of Savages in North Western Melanesia* (3rd edn: RKP 1932).

Marcuse, Herbert, *One Dimensional Man* (RKP 1964).

Marowitz, D.Z. *see* Stansill, Peter.

Marsden, Dennis *see* Jackson, Brian.

Marson, Dave, *Children's Strikes in 1911* (History Workshop 1973).

Marx, Karl and Engels, Frederick, *Selected Works in One Volume* (Lawrence and Wishart 1968).

Meighan, Roland *see* Harber, Clive.

Melly, George, *Revolt into Style* (Penguin 1970).

Milgram, Stanley, *Obedience to Authority* (Tavistock 1974).

Miliband, Ralph, *The State in Capitalist Society* (Weidenfeld and Nicolson 1969).

Morris, William, *News from Nowhere*[1890] (RKP 1970).

Musgrove, Frank, *Ecstasy and Holiness* (Methuen 1974).

Nash, Roy, *Teacher Expectations and Pupil Learning*(RKP 1976).

Neill, A.S., *A Dominie's Log* (Herbert Jenkins 1917).

Neill, A.S., *Hearts Not Heads in the School* (Herbert Jenkins 1945).

Nunn, T. Percy, *Education: Its Data and First Principles* (Edward Arnold 1926).

Nuttall, Jeff, *Bomb Culture* (MacGibbon and Kee 1968).

Nyberg, David (ed.), *The Philosophy of Open Education* (RKP 1975).

Paul, Leslie, *The Republic of Children* (Allen & Unwin 1938).

Pekin, L.B., *Progressive Schools* (Hogarth Press 1934).

Pestalozzi, J.H., *Leonard and Gertrude* [1787] (Boston: D.C. Heath and Co. 1898).

Peters, R.S., *Ethics and Education* (George Allen & Unwin 1966).

Piercy, Marge, *Woman on the Edge of Time* (The Women's Press 1976).

Pluckrose, Henry and Wilby, Peter (eds), *The Condition of English Schooling* (Penguin 1979).

Popper, Karl, *The Open Society and Its Enemies, Volume 2: Hegel and Marx* (RKP 1945).

Quick, R.H., *Essays on Educational Reformers* (Longman 1910).

Radical Therapist-Rough Times Collective (eds), *The Radical Therapist* (Penguin 1975).

Rawson, W. *see* Boyd, W.

Read, Herbert, *Education through Art* [1943] (Faber 1961).

Reese, William J., *Power and the Promise of School Reform* (RKP 1986).

Reich, Wilhelm, *The Mass Psychology of Fascism* [1932] (Penguin 1975).

Reich, Wilhelm, *What is Class Consciousness?* [1933] (Socialist Reproduction 1971).

Reissman Frank, *The Culturally Deprived Child* (Harper and Row 1962).

Revolutionary Socialist Students' Federation *The Political Theory of the Student Movement* (RSSF 1969).

Richmond, W. Kenneth, *The Free School* (Methuen 1973).

Ridge, J.M. *see* Halsey, A.H.

Roberts, Brian *see* Harber, Clive.

Rogers, Carl, *On Becoming a Person* (Boston: Houghton Mifflin 1961).

Rogers, Margaret *see* McNeal, Julia.

Rosen, Harold *see* Barnes, Douglas.

Rosenthal, R. and Jacobson, L., *Pygmalion in the Classroom* (Holt, Rinehart and Winston 1968).

Roszak, Theodore, *The Making of a Counter Culture* (Faber 1970).

Rowan, John, *Ordinary Ecstasy: Humanistic Psychology in Action* (RKP 1976).

Rowland, Stephen, *The Enquiring Classroom* (Falmer Press 1984).

Salter, Brian *see* Tapper, Ted.

Sartre, Jean-Paul, *Existentialism and Humanism* (Methuen 1948).

Sarup, Madan, *Marxism, Structuralism and Education* (Falmer 1983).

Selleck, R.J.W., *English Primary Education and the Progressives 1914–1939* (RKP 1972).

Selleck, R.J.W., *The New Education 1870–1914* (Pitman 1968).

Sharp, Rachel and Green, Anthony, *Education and Social Control* (RKP 1975).

Silberman, Charles, *Crisis in the Classroom* (New York: Vintage Books 1971).

Silver, Harold, *The Concept of Popular Education* (MacGibbon and Kee 1965).

Silver, Harold, *English Education and the Radicals 1780–1850* (RKP 1975).

Silver, Harold, *see* Lawson, John.

Simon, Brian, *Education and the Labour Movement 1870–1920* (Lawrence and Wishart 1965).

Simon, Brian, *Intelligence Testing and the Comprehensive School* (Lawrence and Wishart 1953).

Simon, Brian (ed.), *The Radical Tradition in Education in Britain* (Lawrence and Wishart 1972).

Smith, Michael P., *The Libertarians and Education* (George Allen & Unwin 1983).

Smith, Mike, *The Underground and Education* (Methuen 1977).

Snyder, Benson R., *The Hidden Curriculum* (New York: Knopf 1971).

Spock, Benjamin, *The Common Sense Book of Baby and Child Care* [1946] (J. Lane 1955).

Stansill, Peter and Marowitz, David Zane, *Bamn: Outlaw Manifestos and Ephemera 1965–70* (Penguin 1971).

Steedman, Jane *Progress in Secondary Schools* (National Children's Bureau 1980).

Stewart, W.A.C., *Progressives and Radicals in English Education 1750–1970* (Macmillan 1972).

Stewart, W.A.C., *The Educational Innovators, Volume 2: Progressive Schools 1881–1967* (Macmillan 1968).

Stewart, W.A.C. and McCann, W.P., *The Educational Innovators 1750–1880* (Macmillan 1967).

Stones, Edgar, *An Introduction to Educational Psychology* (Methuen 1966).

Strike, Kenneth A, and Egan, Kieran (eds), *Ethics and Educational Policy* (RKP 1978).

Students of Bishop's College, *Stories from Carriacou* (Britain Grenada Friendship Society 1983).

Suggett, Dahle *see* Kemmis, Stephen.

Swann, Baron, (chmn) , *Education for All: The Report of the Committee of Inquiry into the Education of Children from Ethnic Minority Groups* (HMSO 1985).

Tapper, Ted and Salter, Brian *Education and the Political Order* (Macmillan 1978).

Tawney, R.H., *Equality* (George Allen & Unwin 1931).

Taylor, Tom (chmn), *A New Partnership for our Schools* (HMSO 1977).

Teschitz, Karl, *Sex-Pol Essays* [1934–7] (Socialist Reproduction 1973).

Thompson, Denys *see* Leavis, R.F.

Thompson, E.P. *The Making of the English Working Class* (Gollancz 1963).

Thompson, E.P., *The Poverty of Theory and Other Essays* (Merlin Press 1978).

Tolstoy, Leo, *Tolstoy on Education* (Chicago: University of Chicago Press 1967).

Toogood, Philip, *The Head's Tale* (Dialogue 1984).

Van der Eyken, William and Turner, Barry, *Adventures in Education* (Penguin 1975).

Vygotsky, L.S., *Thought and Language* [1934] (Massachusetts Institute of Technology Press/John Wiley 1962).

Waller, Willard, *The Sociology of Teaching* [1933] (New York: John Wiley 1965).

Warnock, Mary, *Schools of Thought* (Faber 1977).

Watts, Alan, *The Book on the Taboo Against Knowing Who You Are* (Jonathan Cape 1969).

Watts, John (ed.), *The Countesthorpe Experience* (George Allen & Unwin 1977).

Weiner, Gaby *see* Arnot, Madeleine.

White, Lynn (ed.), *Frontiers of Knowledge in the Study of Man* (Harper Brothers 1956).

White, Roger, *Absent With Cause* (RKP 1980).

Wilby, Peter *see* Pluckrose, Henry.

Williams, Raymond, *Culture and Society 1780–1950* (Chatto and Windus 1958).

Williams, Raymond, *Keywords* (Fontana 1976).

Williams, Raymond, *The Long Revolution* (Chatto and Windus 1961).

Williams, Wyn *see* Fletcher, Colin.

Willis, Paul, *Learning to Labour* (Saxon House 1977).

Wills, W. David, *The Barns Experiment* (George Allen & Unwin 1945).

Wills, W. David, *Homer Lane: A Biography* (George Allen & Unwin 1964).

Wilson, P.S., *Interest and Discipline in Education* (RKP 1971).

Wollstonecraft, Mary, *Vindication of the Rights of Women* [1792] (Penguin 1975).

Woods, Peter, *The Divided School* (RKP 1979).

Woods, Peter *see* Hammersley, Martyn.

Wright, Nigel, 'The White Lion Free School Experiment' (*Lib Ed* 1989).

Wright, Nigel, *Progress in Education* (Croom Helm 1977).

Wringe, C.A., *Children's Rights: A Philosophical Study* (RKP 1981).

Young, Michael F.D. (ed.), *Knowledge and Control* (Collier Macmillan 1971).

Zamoyska, Betka, *The Burston Rebellion* (BBC Publications 1985).

Articles

Anderson, Perry, 'Origins of the Present Crisis', *New Left Review*, 23, January–February 1964, pp.26–54.

Backett, Lucia, 'Street School', in David Head (ed.), *Free Way to Learning*.

Bantock, G.H., 'Towards a Theory of Popular Education', in R. Hooper (ed.), *The Curriculum: Context, Design and Development*.

Barzun, Jacques, 'To Give an Education', in C.B. Cox and A.E. Dyson (eds), *The Fight for Education: A Black Paper* (Critical Quarterly Society 1969).

Benton, Ted, 'Education and Politics', in Douglas Holly (ed.), *Education or Domination*, pp. 9–37.

Berger, Nan, 'The Child, the Law and the State', in Paul Adams *et al.*, *Children's Rights*.

Bernstein, Basil, 'Education Cannot Compensate for Society', in David Rubinstein and Colin Stoneman (eds), *Education for Democracy*, pp. 104–16.

Bettelheim, Bruno, untitled article in Nathan W. Ackerman *et al.*, *Summerhill: For and Against*, pp. 98–119.

Bhave, Vinoba, 'Education or Manipulation?', *Resurgence*, vol. 4, no. 6, January–February 1974, pp. 11–18.

Blundell, Colin, 'Notes Towards a Libertarian Philosophy of Education', in *Libertarian Teacher*, no. 5, April 1969, pp. 13–18.

Breines, Wini, 'Community and Organisation: The New Left and Michel's "Iron Law" ', *Social Problems*, vol. 27, no. 4, April 1980, pp. 419–29.

Brooks, Greta, 'The Creed of Cuthbert Rutter', *Forest School Camps Magazine*, no. 3, 1968, pp. 6–8.

Callaghan, James, 'Towards a National Debate', *Education*, 22 October 1976, pp. 332–3.

Chanan, Gabriel, 'Gabriel Replies', *Radical Education*, no. 5, Winter 1976, pp. 20–1.

Chatwin, Ray, 'An Experiment in Democracy', *Radical Education*, no. 1, Autumn 1974, pp. 10–11.

Clossick, John, 'Teaching London Kids or Improving Your Lot', *Rank & File*, no. 30, February–March 1974, p. 7.

Coates, Ken, 'Education as a lifelong experience', in Peter Buckman (ed.), *Education Without Schools*.

Cole, G.D.H., 'Education and Politics: A Socialist View' in *Year Book of Education 1952* (Evans Brothers 1952), pp. 42–63.

Cosgrove, Jim and Stevenson, Mike, 'The Work of the Leith Community Education Project', *Liberal Education*, no. 53, pp. 20–2.

Daniel, Martin, 'A Charter for the Unfree Child', *Anarchy*, no. 21, 1962.

Davidson, Clive, 'Alternative Ways', *Resurgence*, no. 118, September–October 1986, p. 17.

Diamond, Laura, 'State Supported Alternative Schools', in Clive Harber *et al.* (eds), *Alternative Educational Futures*.

Duane, Michael, 'Freedom and the State System of Education' in Paul Adams *et al., Children's Rights*, pp. 180–240.

Feinberg, Joel, 'The Idea of a Free Man', in James F. Doyle (ed.), *Educational Judgements*.

Freeman, Joreen, *The Tyranny of Structurelessness*, origin uncertain, reprinted as a pamphlet by Dark Star, undated.

Froome, Stuart, 'It's Time Our Teachers Went Back to the Old Values', *Sunday Express*, 9 April 1978.

Ghose, Ajoy S., 'Fun With Learning: A Supplementary Programme' in David Head (ed.), *Free Way to Learning*.

Goldberg, Steven and Griffiths, Peter, 'Double Talk', *Teaching London Kids*, no. 9, 1977, pp. 5–6.

Gooch, Janet, 'Community Schools', in *Libertarian Teacher*, no. 8, p. 4.

Goody, J. and Watt, I., 'The Consequences of Literacy', *Comparative Studies in History and Society*, vol. V, no. 3, 1962.

Gorbutt, David, 'The New Sociology of Education', *Education for Teaching*, no. 89, Autumn 1972, pp. 3–11.

Grace, Gerald, 'Facing the Contradictions', *Teaching London Kids*, no. 15, 1980, p. 10.

Griffiths, Peter *see* Goldberg, Steven.

Hamilton, Ian, 'Agitate Educate Organise', *Radical Education*, no. 1, Autumn 1974, pp. 6–8.

Holly, Douglas, 'The Invisible Ruling Class' in Douglas Holly (ed.), *Education or Domination*.

Hoyles, Martin, 'Conflict Theory and Educational Institutions', *Rank & File*, no. 11, Autumn 1970, pp. 10–12.

Humphrey, Di and Humphrey, Arthur, 'Schools – State, Free, None?', *Libertarian Education*, no. 10, February 1973, p. 7.

Jefferys, Deena, 'How Psychology Fails the Teacher', *British Journal of Teacher Education*, vol. 1, no. 1, January 1975, pp. 63–9.

Jenner, Peter, 'The London Free School', *Anarchy*, no. 73, March 1967.

Jensen, Arthur, 'How Much Can We Boost IQ and Scholastic Achievement?', *Harvard Educational Review*, Winter 1969.

Johnson, Richard, 'Really Useful Knowledge', *Radical Education*, no. 7, Winter 1976, pp. 20–3; and *Radical Education*, no. 8, Spring 1977, p. 22–4.

Jones, Ken, 'Progressive Education and the Working Class', *Radical Education*, no. 6, Summer 1976, pp. 6–9.

Lightfoot, Martin, 'A Publisher Remembers', *Times Educational Supplement*, 14 June 1974, p. 40.

Long, Anne, 'The New School — Vancouver' in Ronald Gross and Beatrice Gross, *Radical School Reform*, p. 260–82.

Mairet, Philip, 'Introduction', in Jean-Paul Sartre, *Existentialism and Humanism*.

Maude, Angus, 'Biased Penguins', *The Spectator*, 14 November 1970, p. 605.

McCabe, Colin, 'Blueprint for Democratic Schools', *New Statesman*, 9 September 1983, pp. 12–14.

McNiff, Ann, 'Delta Free School', *New Era*, vol. 59, no. 1, February 1978, p. 199.

Mead, Margaret, 'Our Educational Emphases in Primitive Perspective', *American Journal of Sociology*, vol. 48, 1942–3, pp. 633–9.

Meighan, Roland, 'Home-Based Educators and Education Authorities. The Attempt to Maintain a Mythology', *Educational Studies*, vol. 10, no. 3, 1984.

Midwinter, Eric, 'Stick With the System', *Times Educational Supplement*, 19 November 1971, p. 2.

Murdock, Graham, 'The Politics of Culture', in Douglas Holly (ed.), *Education or Domination*.

Nava, Mica, 'Gender and Education', *Feminist Review*, no. 5, p. 70.

Neave, Guy, 'The "Free Schoolers" ' in Douglas Holly (ed.), *Education or Domination*.

Newell, Peter and Truefitt, Alison, 'Abolishing the Curriculum and Learning Without Exams', in Peter Buckman (ed.), *Education Without Schools*.

Newsam, Peter, 'The Good Old Days', *Education*, no. 3, March 1978.

Nyberg, David, 'Ambiguity and Constraint in the "Freedom" of Free Schools' in Kenneth A. Strike and Kieran Egan (eds), *Ethics and Educational Policy*.

Ollendorf, Robert, 'The Rights of Adolescents' in Paul Adams, *et al.*, *Children's Rights*.

Ollendorf, Robert, 'Sex and the Teenager', in *Children's Rights*, no. 1, pp. 19–20.

Palfreman, Judy, 'Black Paper 2 — and its Liberal Critics', *Rank & File*, no. 8, December 1969, pp. 13–16.

Peacey, Nick 'Could It Happen Here?' *Times Educational Supplement*, 2 October 1981.

Peters, R.S., 'The Philosophy of Education', in Paul H. Hirst (ed.), *Educational Theory and Its Foundation Disciplines*.

Pinn, D.M., 'What Kind of Primary School', in C.B. Cox and A.E. Dyson (eds), *Black Paper Two: The Crisis in Education*.

Punch, Maurice, 'Tyrannies of the free school', *Guardian*, 8 May 1973, p. 19.

Ree, Harry, 'The Lost Generation', *Times Educational Supplement*, 10 October 1980.

Rogers, Carl, 'Personal Thoughts on Teaching and Learning', *Libertarian Teacher*, no. 3, July 1967, pp. 11–12.

Rosenberg, Chanie, 'School Self-Government: The Russian Experiment', *Rank & File*, no. 17, Winter 1971, pp. 13–15.

Sadiev, Roger, 'The Free Schools Campaign', *Libertarian Teacher*, no. 5, April 1969, p. 11.

Samuel, Raphael, 'Breaking Up is Very Hard to Do', *Guardian*, 2 December 1985.

Simon, Brian, 'Streaming and Unstreaming in the Secondary School', in David Rubinstein and Colin Stoneman (eds), *Education for Democracy*.

Stevenson, Mike *see* Cosgrove, Jim.

Summerfield, Geoffrey, 'Brainwashed Replicators', *Times Educational Supplement*, 31 October 1975.

Tassinari, Gastone, 'The "Scuola and Quartiere" Movement: A Case Study' in Ian Lister (ed.), *Deschooling*.

Townsend, Jules, 'A.S. Neill: A Critical Appreciation', *Rank & File*, no. 28, p. 7.

Truefitt, Alison *see* Newell, Peter.

Vulliamy, Graham, 'What Counts as School Music?' in Geoff Whitty and Michael Young (eds), *Explorations in the Politics of School Knowledge* (Nafferton Books 1976).

Waks, Leonard J., 'Freedom and Desire in the Summerhill Philosophy of Education', in David Nyberg (ed.), *The Philosophy of Open Education*.

Walter, Nicholas, 'Tool of Conviviality', in *Libertarian Education*, no. 16, p. 10–11.

Ward, Colin, 'A Modest Proposal for the Repeal of the Education Act', *Anarchy*, no. 53, July 1965.

Watt, I. *see* Goody, J.

White Lion Street Free School, 'Community School on the Way', in David Head (ed.), *Free Way to Learning*.

White Lion Street Free School, 'A Free School "Curriculum" ' in Geoff Whitty and Michael Young (eds), *Explorations in the Politics of School Knowledge*.

White, Lynn, 'The Changing Canons of our Culture', in Lynn White (ed.), *Frontiers of Knowledge in the Study of Man*, pp. 301–16.

Wilcox, Preston R., 'The Community Centred School', in Ronald Gross and Beatrice Gross, *Radical School Reform*, pp. 119–31.

Williams, Raymond, 'The Teaching Relationship: Both Sides of the Wall' in David Rubinstein and Colin Stoneman (eds), *Education for Democracy*, 2nd edn. pp. 214–21.

Williams, Wyn and Rennie, John, 'Social Education', in David Rubinstein and Colin Stoneman (eds), *Education for Democracy*, 2nd edn, pp. 157–63.

Worpole, Ken, 'The School and the Community', in Douglas Holly (ed.), *Education or Domination*.

Worpole, Ken 'Towards a Socialist Critique of Secondary Education', *Rank & File*, no. 14, Spring 1971, pp. 16–18.

Wright, Ian, 'And Now for a Bit of Theory', *Libertarian Education*, no. 21, Spring 1977, pp. 8–9.

Wright, Nigel, 'A Black and Red Herring', *Rank & File*, no. 19, Spring 1972.

Wright, Nigel, 'In Need of Theory', *Lib Ed*, vol. 2, no. 7, Spring 1988.

Wright, Nigel, 'Lesson for the People', *Undercurrents*, no. 36, October–November 1979, pp. 31–2.

Wright, Nigel, 'One Disaster After Another', *Libertarian Education*, no. 22, Summer 1977, pp. 10–11.

Wright, Nigel, 'Standards and the Black Papers', in Henry Pluckrose and Peter Wilby (eds), *The Condition of English Schooling*.

Wright, Nigel, 'Teacher Politics and Educational Change' in Geoff Whitty and Michael Young (eds), *Explorations in the Politics of School Knowledge*.

Young, Michael, 'Hackney Survey: Support for Alternatives', *Where*, no. 150, July–August 1979.

Zander, Ernst, 'The Great Utopia', *Contemporary Issues*, vol. 2, no. 5, Winter 1950, pp. 3–22.

Periodicals

American Journal of Sociology
Anarchy
Arse
ASS
Black Voice
British Journal of Teacher Education
Camerawork
Case-Con
CASE (Confederation for the Advancement of State Education) *Newsletter*
Catonsville Roadrunner
The Children's Book Bulletin
Comparative Studies in History and Society
Contemporary Issues
Copeman
Critique of Anthropology
Cultural Studies
Education
Education for Teaching
Education Today and Tomorrow
Feminist Review
Forest School Camps Magazine
Forum
Freedom
Gay News
Gen
Guardian
Harvard Educational Review
Heavy Daze
History Workshop Journal
Humpty Dumpty
Issues in Multi-Racial Education

Issues in Radical Therapy
IT (International Times)
Liberal Education
Needle
New Era
New Left Review
Open Secret
Oz
Partisans (Paris)
Peace News
Race Today
Radical Alternatives to Prison
Radical Philosophy
Radical Science
Radical Statistics
Real Time
Red Rag
Red Rat
Red Scientist
Resurgence
Schooling and Culture
Science for People
Screen Education
Self and Society
Shrew
Socialism and Education
Social Problems
The Spectator
The Teacher
Times Educational Supplement
Undercurrents
Where

Index